Dealing with People You Can't Stand

How to Bring Out the Best in People at Their Worst

Dr. Rick Brinkman
Dr. Rick Kirschner

Third Edition

D0012766

New York   Chicago   San Francisco   Lisbon   London
Madrid   Mexico City   Milan   New Delhi   San Juan
Seoul   Singapore   Sydney   Toronto

1 2 3 4 5 6 7 8 9 0   QFR/QFR   1 9 8 7 6 5 4 3 2

ISBN   978-0-07-178572-3
MHID   0-07-178572-8

e-ISBN   978-0-07-178573-0
e-MHID   0-07-178573-6

Library of Congress Cataloging-in-Publication Data

Brinkman, Rick.
   Dealing with people you can't stand : how to bring out the best in people at their worst / by Rick Brinkman and Rick Kirschner.—Rev. and expanded 3rd ed.
     p. cm.
   ISBN 978-0-07-178572-3 (alk. paper)—ISBN 0-07-178572-8 (alk. paper)
   1. Interpersonal relations.   2. Interpersonal communication.   3. Psychology, Industrial.   I. Kirschner, Rick.   II. Title.
   HM1106.B75 2012
   302.3—dc23   2012016233

McGraw-Hill books are available at special quantity discounts to use as premiums and sales promotions or for use in corporate training programs. To contact a representative, please e-mail us at bulksales@mcgraw-hill.com.

This book is printed on acid-free paper.

*We dedicate this book to global peace
and a world that works for everyone,
which will happen when people make peace
with the people they can't stand.*

Contents

Part 1. Getting to Know the People You Can't Stand

We reveal the 10 (+3) Most Unwanted and provide you with the Lens of Understanding and show you how the road to hell is paved with good intentions!

Here are 10 (+ 3) specific behaviors that represent people at their worst!
The Tank ... The Sniper ... The Grenade ... The Know-It-All ... The Think-They-Know-It-All ... The Yes Person ... The Maybe Person ... The Nothing Person ... The No Person ... The Whiner ... The Judge ... The Meddler ... The Martyr

A magnifying glass on behaviors reveals the motives behind them.
What Determines Focus and Assertiveness? ... It's a Question of Balance ... As Intent Changes, So Does Behavior ... You Can Hear Where People Are Coming From ... Shared Priorities, No Problem ... What Happens When the Intent Isn't Fulfilled?

Part 2. Surviving Through
Skillful Communication

You find out why united we stand, but divided we can't stand each other, as well as how to listen to understand, reach a deeper meaning, get what you project and expect, and change your attitude.

Part 3. Bringing Out the Best in People at Their Worst

You learn specific skills and strategies to deal with Tanks, Snipers, Know-It-Alls, Think-They-Know-It-Alls, Grenades, Yes People, Maybe People, Nothing People, No People, Whiners, Judges, Meddlers, Martyrs, and Your Difficult Self.

Part 4. Communication in a Digital Age

*We reveal the limitations and pitfalls of phone communication and
e-mail and show you how to turn the limitations into advantages
with a pound of prevention.*

Acknowledgments

We wish to thank the following people for their help and support on this project: our wives, Lindea K. and Lisa B., and our daughters, Aden K. and Carle B., for their encouragement, inspiration, intuition, and advice; our parents, Lois and Alan K. and Simone and Felix B., for their examples, unconditional support, and faith in us; the cats for staying up late with us when no one else would; Robert Doughton, M.D., for showing us the way; our editor, Betsy Brown, for her pleasant confidence, helpful suggestions, and timely responses; Jimmy and Jeff for giving us the opportunity to get the word out; Fred H. and Alan S. for their guidance and counsel; the many people who sharpened our understanding of and insight into people problems and problem people through their words and/or actions: Leslie Cameron Bandler; David Gordon; John Grinder; Milton Erickson, M.D.; Robert Dilts; and Virginia Satir; also Ken Keyes, Jr.; Lenny Katz; Max and Moshe Goldman; Fidel Ramirez; Juarez Shapiro; Robert Bolton, Ph.D.; Robert M. Bramson, Ph.D.; Burt Miller; and Roland and Theodore Clover; all the people whose names we forgot to mention; and the hundreds of thousands of people who have attended our seminars, watched our taped programs, and shared their stories with us; and lastly, K & S, for teaching us to boldly go.

Introduction

People you can't stand: they're those difficult people who are either not doing things you want them to do or doing things you do not want them to do—and you don't know what to do about them. Well, you don't have to be their victim anymore! While you can't change difficult people, you can communicate with them in such a way that they change themselves. It's a matter of knowing how to get through to them when they're behaving badly.

This book will help you to identify and assemble elements of effective communication. In that sense, communication with problem people is similar to making a phone call. You have to dial all the numbers in the correct order if you want to get through. Leave out just one digit (only 10 percent of the whole number if you include the area code), and your call will not go through. Dial the area code as an afterthought, and your call will get through to the wrong party. But it is possible to learn the number, dial it correctly, and completely transform your interactions with the people you can't stand!

Unfortunately, there will always be a few difficult people who, no matter what you do, refuse to answer the phone and take your call. In those rare instances, you can switch metaphors and think of dealing with people you can't stand as making a trip to the communication gym. Difficult people will help you work out your communication muscles and develop your communication stamina. In turn, this may be the very strength you'll need, at some later time and place, to preserve a more valuable relationship.

We will direct your attention to five key areas for solving your people problems:

1. First, we'll examine the forces that compel people to be difficult in such a variety of ways. Where one person starts yelling, another shuts down and says nothing, while yet another starts sniping. These fascinating differences are indicators of differing behavioral intentions that have been thwarted. Once you understand these differences, you'll be less inclined to personalize difficult behavior.

2. Then we'll examine essential communication skills that turn conflict into cooperation, emotion into reason, and hidden agendas into honest dialogue. The good news is that you use these essential skills already in your dealings with people that you get along with. The bad news is that, when dealing with problem people, the failure to use these skills is a big part of the problem. We're going to make the process of communication explicit, so you can begin to use these skills when you most need them with people at their worst.

3. Next, we'll focus on specific strategies for dealing with the 10 (+ 3) most difficult behaviors of the people you can't stand. You'll learn exactly what you can do to get people to stop whining, attacking, blowing up, and breaking promises.

4. Increasingly, we define our relationships with others using the phone and e-mail. We hope you make the most out of these tools to avoid conflict and build cooperation instead.

5. Toward the end of the book, we will address the subject of what to do when you can't stand yourself. By that time, you will probably have recognized yourself in some of the descriptions of problem people. Chapter 23 will help you identify and alter your own difficult behavior, which will help you because the less difficult you are, the fewer the number of difficult people you'll have to deal with.

We recommend that you read Chapters 1 through 9, then turn directly to the chapter that deals with your difficult person.

Before you read on, allow us to introduce ourselves and tell you how we came to write this book.

We're Rick and Rick, best friends, business partners, and Naturopathic physicians. (Although our profession was born in the United States over a hundred years ago, you may have never heard of it until now.°) We became friends while med students, but our friendship blossomed when a physician and surgeon from an area hospital

---

° Following conventional premedical education, a Naturopathic doctor (N.D.) is trained as a holistic primary care physician in a four-year medical school. Naturopathic physicians learn the same scientific research, diagnostic, and clinical skills as conventional doctors (M.D.s), but the education emphasizes health restoration, wellness, and disease prevention rather than symptom management through drug treatments and removal of troublesome body parts. Students are required to take four years of clinical nutrition (compared with a few weeks for conventional doctors), and they receive training in counseling skills, so that they can guide patients in making lifestyle changes, and training in natural therapies that enhance and utilize innate healing forces for the treatment of the disease. To learn more, go to the website for the American Association of Naturopathic Physicians (AANP) at www.naturopathic.org.

became our mentor. With his guidance and encouragement, we studied health from an attitudinal point of view. We hoped to determine the principles of mental and emotional health and to find out how these principles might be used to prevent or heal physical illness. Time and again, we found that when people clarify their values, work to fulfill their goals, and learn effective communication and relaxation skills, they feel better. And as their mental and emotional health improves, many of their specific physical symptoms disappear. Since the word *physician* means "teacher," we began sharing these ideas through seminars and workshops.

In 1982, a mental health organization asked us to create a program on how to deal with difficult people. That marked the official beginning of the research project that has culminated in this book, and in the process, we changed the way we define what we do. We now view all our work as a kind of continuing education in people.

For over two decades, we've been learning about people's hopes and fears, how people build their lives or destroy them, how people communicate, what makes people difficult, and how best to deal with people at their worst. We've written this book to pass that information along to you. We've presented these ideas to enthusiastic response in seminars, on tape, and in print to over a million people. It is our hope and belief that the ideas in this book will make a meaningful and lasting difference in the quality of your life.

Dr. Rick Brinkman and Dr. Rick Kirschner

PART 1

Getting to Know the People You Can't Stand

We Reveal the 10 (+3) Most Unwanted and Provide You with the Lens of Understanding and Show You How the Road to Hell Is Paved with Good Intentions!

1

The 10 (+3) Most Unwanted List

In your repertoire of communication skills, there exist varying degrees of knowledge and ignorance, with their consequent interpersonal strengths and weaknesses. As a result, you may have no trouble at all dealing with that overly or unemotional person whom no one else can stand. You may have more difficulty with people who whine and are negative, or you may find dealing with aggressive people to be the most challenging. Passive people may frustrate you, or you may have a low tolerance for braggarts and blowhards. Likewise, you probably frustrate several people yourself because everybody is somebody's difficult person at least some of the time.

You may agree or disagree with this or that person about who is the difficult person and who is not. Nevertheless, there is a certain consensus in polite society about who difficult people are and what it is they do that others find difficult. We've identified 10 specific behavior patterns that sane people resort to when they feel threatened or thwarted, which represent their struggle with or withdrawal from undesired circumstances, followed by three patterns of bad behavior more likely to be problematic in families. Here are 10 (+ 3) difficult behaviors that represent normal people at their worst!

The Tank

It was a beautiful day. The sky was clear, and Jim could hear birds singing outside his window. He was moving forward on the project, and the office was humming with activity and teamwork.

Suddenly, there was a familiar and inescapable sound!

It reminded Jim of the sound of tank treads rumbling down the hallway. It seemed as though the ground actually began to tremble, and Jim could almost hear the distant ping of radar being activated. As Jim listened, Joe "The Tank" Bintner rounded the corner and came into view. Raising his arm like a turret-mounted cannon, he pointed in Jim's direction. Somehow, Jim could sense the cross hairs locking on to a target ... himself! In desperation, he mentally waved a white flag, but the Tank continued moving in his direction. As he stared in shock at the cannon-like finger now pointed at his face, Bintner unleashed a verbal blasting of accusation and scorn.

"... You're an idiot, a moron. You're completely incompetent and an embarrassment to the human race! You must be a genetic mistake. You've been working on this for two weeks, and you're already three weeks behind. I won't listen to any more of your excuses. Pay attention, because this is what you are going to do ..."

Out of the corner of his eye, Jim could see that everyone else in the office had either run for cover or was standing frozen, paralyzed with fear. Like the sound of distant thunder, Bintner barked out his orders. Then, as suddenly as it began, the determined assault ended. Bintner was moving off in a new direction, and Jim was left sitting amid the rubble of his best efforts and good intentions.

The Tank is confrontational, pointed, and angry, the ultimate in pushy and aggressive behavior.

The Sniper

Sue had never worked harder to prepare a report. This was the big day, and if she could deliver it in a professional and polished manner, there was a good chance she would be rewarded with a promotion. All eyes were on her as she began her presentation. She knew all her numbers would fit into place, and she could sense that victory was just around the corner.

Then, as she made her move to the bottom line, there was a stirring like the rustling of leaves, and she saw a slight movement off to the side of the room. That's when she heard the shot:

"Hey," said an insistent, scoffing voice. "That idea of yours reminds me of something I saw in a book. I think it was in Chapter 11!"

First a solitary, diabolical laugh filled the room, but then one uneasy chuckle after another joined it. Sue's mind wandered, her concentration broken, the point she was about to make lost. "Huh?" she mumbled awkwardly, as she looked around for the source of the disruption. And there, grinning like a Cheshire cat was the Sniper, preparing to take another shot.

"Maybe it was Chapter 13? Ha ha. Don't mind me. Please go on. I'm just beginning to understand how little you actually know about this subject."

Whether through rude comments, biting sarcasm, or a well-timed roll of the eyes, making you look foolish is the Sniper's specialty.

The Grenade

It had been a good day for getting work done. A pleasant breeze drifted lazily through the window as Ralph double-checked the numbers before him. That's when Bob walked into the room, his face a rigid mask, hands balled into fists. Ralph could sense that something was wrong, but a second glance at Bob's close-lipped expression prompted him to mind his own business. Bob passed Ralph's desk, and as he did, he brushed against a stack of papers perched precariously on the desktop. The papers tumbled to the ground like so many autumn leaves drifting in the breeze. Ralph didn't mean to say anything, but in spite of himself, a tiny voice escaped his throat, "Careful, there, Bob!"

In a timeless moment, Bob whirled about, eyes widening, facial muscles twitching, hair standing on end, arms trembling, as his voice exploded:

"Why don't you watch where you put that %#@*& stuff, anyway #@!&?*!!@! How the *&!? was I supposed to know that was there!? I don't know why I even bother to show up here! Nobody cares what I'm going through! That's the *&^!@ problem with the world today! Nobody gives a &%* ..."

As the volume of Bob's voice escalated, the breeze seemed to became a violent wind with scraps of ideas whipping about in a flurry of epithets and emotional shrapnel. It seemed like forever, but at long last Bob's anger began to subside. He stopped yelling, looked around at everyone staring at him, and stormed out the door without another word, slamming the door behind him. A lone sheet of paper drifted lazily to the floor.

After a brief period of calm, the grenade explodes into unfocused ranting and raving about things that have nothing to do with the present circumstances.

The Know-It-All

"Hello. This is XYZ Tech Support. My name is Frank. How may I help you?" Frank answered.

The customer began to explain. "My name is Thadeus Davis. I am the MIS director at my company, and I have worked with hundreds of hard drives." Davis went on to describe the problem, concluding, "There is clearly something wrong with your product."

"Well, Mr. Davis, I am very familiar with this product. What you have described does not sound to me like it's mechanical, but it does sound like a software conflict. Could you tell me which extensions you have loaded?"

"It is not a software conflict."

"Sir, that's what I am trying to determine. How do you know it isn't a software conflict?"

"Aren't you listening? It is not a software conflict. The problem is with your product!"

Frank tried another question. "Did it generate a sense key condition? Do you recall what it said?" Davis didn't remember, and he impatiently repeated that the product was at fault. Frank tried again. "Sir, have you tried the drive with another computer?"

Davis retorted, "We know it is not a problem with the computer because we can put any other drive on the computer. Let me speak to your supervisor!"

Seldom in doubt, the Know-It-All has a low tolerance for correction and contradiction. If something goes wrong, however, the Know-It-All will speak with the same authority about who's to blame—you!

The Think-They-Know-It-All

Dena didn't plan on it happening this way. She had the most expertise on the investment committee, and she had poured her heart and soul into the research. She really believed she was finally going to show what she was capable of doing. She forgot to consider the possibility that Leo might interfere. Like a bad dream come true, Leo was dominating the meeting. He was making claims about the performance of various funds that were pure hokum. No one else seemed to realize what he was doing! He had completely taken the group's attention away with the conviction of his communication. And once Leo had the floor, there was no stopping him.

"Leo," she pleaded. "Those funds are …, well, when you look at their track record …" She struggled with the information, not knowing how to stop this before it was too late.

"You got a question about that, or anything else, just ask!" Leo proclaimed without missing a beat, then turned back to his spellbound audience. "I know exactly what we need. Of course, for me, picking the right investments is a piece of cake! Yeah, no sweat! In fact, I kind of enjoy it! That's an ability I have, you know. Plus, I have followed these funds for years. Great track record! Trust me!"

Great track record? From what he was saying, it was obvious to Dena that he knew nothing about those funds. It was equally obvious to her that she had no idea how to stop him. Her heart sank as she looked around the room and watched helplessly, as one by one, people were swayed by Leo's sureness and enthusiasm. How could they know that he didn't know what he was talking about, when Dena was the one who had done the research?

Think-They-Know-It-Alls can't fool all of the people all of the time, but they can fool some of the people enough of the time, and enough of the people all of the time—all for the sake of getting some attention.

The Yes Person

Alice was just about the nicest person you could ever meet. So nice that she just couldn't say no. So she didn't. Instead, she said yes to everyone and everything, and she sincerely hoped that this would make everybody happy.

"Would you do me a favor?" asked Tom.

"Sure!" Alice would say.

"Drop this off for me, would you?" requested Mark.

"No problem!" was Alice's reply.

"Could you remind me to return this call?" begged Ellen.

"All right!" Alice answered cheerfully.

"Finish this up before you leave, okay?" said the boss.

"My pleasure!" was Alice's immediate response.

But more often than not, Alice didn't remind Ellen, didn't do Tom the favor, didn't drop off Mark's package, and didn't finish the work her boss requested. She could always offer excuses and explanations for failing to do what she'd said she'd do, and yet, to her surprise, that just wasn't good enough.

When promises aren't kept, people get upset, and upset people become confrontational. Mark, Tom, Ellen, and the boss all confronted Alice, each in his or her own way. They assessed her problem and offered solutions, to which Alice always agreed because she wanted to avoid confrontation at any cost . Still pleasant on the outside, she was soon seething with silent hostility on the inside, and she decided that she had no intention of ever doing what she promised for these nasty people.

In an effort to please people and avoid confrontation, Yes People say yes without thinking things through. They react to the latest demands on their time by forgetting prior commitments, and they overcommit until they have no time for themselves. Then they become resentful.

The Maybe Person

Marv found himself up against a deadline that required a decision from Sue. Sue knew that the moment of decision was at hand, yet strangely, she was nowhere to be found. After a prolonged search of every hall and stairwell, he caught up with her at last. "I don't have time to talk, Marv. I'm really sorry." She tried to rush off, but Marv hustled to keep up with her and pressed his case.

"So, have you decided who we will be sending to the convention in Hawaii?" asked Marv urgently.

"Well ..., I'm still thinking about it," was Sue's tentative reply.

"Still thinking about it!?" Marv had to accelerate, as Sue was pulling away rapidly.

"Sue, the convention is in just three weeks. I asked you to choose somebody six months ago. This is the biggest event of the year, and we always send our best sales rep."

"Well …, I know, but …, I guess I'll decide …"

Marv, breathing rapidly, hustled to keep up. "You guess? When?"

Sue stopped walking. "I don't know. Soon." She looked down at the floor absently for a moment, then spun around and headed back the way they'd come. Marv stood there, looking after her, astonished and breathing rapidly. There was no doubt in his mind that this decision would be put off until it was too late to act.

In a moment of decision, the Maybe Person procrastinates in the hope that a better choice will present itself. Sadly, with most decisions, there comes a point when it is too little, too late, and the decision makes itself.

The Nothing Person

If Nat had anything to say for himself, Sally would never know. His ability to sit and stare was unnerving, to say the least. The longer they were married, the less he would say. These days, it seemed to Sally that she did all the talking. There could be worse problems, of course. At least Nat wasn't a bully, and he never talked unkindly about people. But then again, he hardly ever talked. Maybe a bit of gossip would be an improvement over the sound of silence. Sally thought she'd give it try. "So, uh, Nat, what do you think about the president's work?" Nat didn't seem to hear her. He just shrugged and kept reading the paper. Sally tried again. "Nat? So, uh, do you like him?"

The movement of his eyes upward to meet hers was almost imperceptible. Looking into his eyes was like looking into a vacant room. It appeared that nobody was home. "I … don't … know." That's all he said, and then he lowered his eyes in that same nondescript manner, and he began reading again.

Sally couldn't stop herself from pursuing this, now that she had begun it. After all, they had been married for over 17 years. She felt as if the distance between them was miles instead of meters and that it was her responsibility to build a bridge between them. So she tried again. "Nat, uh, it seems like we never talk. You never tell me you love me anymore. Do you still love me?"

Nat gave her that same look, then slowly turned his head until he was facing the window. He put the paper down and simply said, "Nothing is going on. I told you 17 years ago I love you. If something changes, I will let you know." And that was that. He picked up his paper and went back to reading, and Sally's hopes drifted off into the void.

No verbal feedback, no nonverbal feedback. Nothing. What else could you expect from … the Nothing Person.

The No Person

Jack had just completed the third quarter of his seminar presentation when a woman in the back raised her hand. "Yes ma'am? You in the back. Do you have a question?"

She gazed at him through narrowed eyes. "That won't work," she said finally.

"Have you ever tried it?" He asked, unsure what they were talking about.

"What would be the point of trying it if it doesn't work?" Whatever it was, it seemed obvious to her.

"How do you know it doesn't work?" he tried again.

"It's obvious."

"Obvious to whom?" Jack asked. Desperation seized him and wouldn't let go.

"To any intelligent person capable of thinking it through." Her determination was remarkable.

"Well, it's not obvious to me!" said Jack, believing he had gained the upper hand.

"Well now, what does that say about you?" She replied triumphantly.

More deadly to morale than a speeding bullet, more powerful than hope, able to defeat big ideas with a single syllable. Disguised as a mild mannered normal person, the No Person fights a never ending battle for futility, hopelessness, and despair.

The Whiner

Just as Joann was regaining her concentration, Cynthia began whining again. This was the 112th time she had been interrupted by Cynthia, and it wasn't even noon.

To make matters worse, Cynthia's voice dragged on and on, and it had the resonance of a chain saw. "Did I tell you that I just brought my new charcoal grill home after saving up for it for the last year and a half? It was very heavy, and I had a great deal of trouble getting it out of the car. My husband offered to help me, but he has a bad back, and I didn't think that it was a good idea, so I wouldn't let him. But the box was an awkward size. Not only that, but it's very difficult to move a box when it doesn't fit your arms. But I tried. Finally, after I'd bruised myself in several places, I got out a wheelbarrow …"

"Cynthia," Joann implored. "If you didn't have any other way to get it out of your car, why didn't you wait until a time when you had help before picking it up at the store?"

"But I couldn't ask anyone else to help with it. And anyway, two people couldn't have done it more easily than one. And I cut my finger on a staple on the box when I opened it! If people had been helping me, they would have cut themselves and blamed me. And besides, I didn't know how long the sale would last, and I really wanted it. And my husband would have been very disappointed if I had waited because he was anxious to try it—as anxious as I was. And anyway, it didn't work right, and I had to take it back, but it was too heavy to get it back in the box, and I …"

As Cynthia's voice drilled deeper into Joann's unconscious, Joann thought to herself, "What's wrong with her? All she ever does is complain!"

Whiners feel helpless and overwhelmed by an unfair world. Their standard is perfection, and no one and nothing measures up to it. But misery loves company, so they bring their problems to you. Offering solutions makes you bad company, so their whining escalates.

BONUS PEOPLE: RELATIVES

The Judge

The Giant dreaded his mother's visits because she criticized or complained about everything. On her last visit, he gave her in a room in the tower because it had the best view. But she whined about having to walk up all the stairs. The time before that, he gave her a ground floor room, and she said, "What? I'm not special enough for a tower room?" So far, this visit was proving to be no different.

"Look at the way you're dressed! A sloppy schlump! How can you expect people to fear you?"

"But, Ma, it's not easy to find size extra-extra-extra-extra-large shirts."

"Are you so lazy that you can't do what it takes to look scary anymore? Yes, you are! And look at this place. You certainly haven't done any yard work since I was last here. How can you let that unsightly giant bean stalk grow in your front yard? And you can't clean up once in a while? Why, fee fi fo fum, it smells like the blood of an Englishman around here! Well, at least I hope you have taken good care of my dear goose."

As his mom went into the castle to find her goose, the Giant rolled his big eyes, then plopped down onto the stone steps. He slumped sadly, feeling so incredibly small.

The Judge sets a standard that no one can meet, then pronounces judgment along with a running commentary of criticism.

The Meddler

Daphne stood up, surprised to see her future mother-in-law. "Hera, how nice of you to drop by! To what do I owe this honor?"

"Daphne, my future daughter-in-law." Hera took hold of both Daphne's shoulders, leaned back, and eyed her up and down. "I have come to help you dress. Let us begin, because much work will be required."

Before Daphne could utter a word, Hera breezed by her and walked through the columned entrance into her apartment. Daphne chased after her. "Sorry, Hera, this isn't exactly a good time. I haven't had a chance to pick up." But as she arrived in the main living space, Hera was nowhere to be seen. "Hera?" she called out.

"In here," came Hera's voice from Daphne's bedroom.

From my bedroom! How dare she! Daphne thought. She walked into the bedroom and was about to say something when again she was stunned into silence. Hera was going through her closet like a whirlwind. Some outfits were thrown on the floor, others on the bed, and Hera had something to say about each in turn.

"Trash. Trash. This one you can wear on your honeymoon. This one, forget it, you'll never fit into it. This one, it's a rag ..."

Caught between her outrage and her desire to not offend her future mother-in-law, Daphne silently simmered. And as Hera went through her closet, Zeus's head appeared out of nowhere and hovered in the center of the room, surrounded by roiling clouds. Oh, my god! Daphne thought. He's as invasive as she is!

Meddlers think they know what's best for you, decide you're incapable, and seek to manage your life for you.

The Martyr

"Ho ho ho," Santa laughed. "Well, Pinky, it's one week before the big night, and we seem to be ahead of schedule! I am delighted."

Pinky, the head elf, was always cautious about getting overly optimistic. But even he had to admit things were in great shape. He replied,

"Yes, this is the first year in a century that I can remember having elves standing around at this time of the season."

Santa smiled, leaned back in his chair, and prepared to light a celebratory pipe. At just that moment Mrs. Claus appeared at the door, with the phone in her hand. "Dear, I have my mother on the line. She is inviting us to come down to the South Pole for Christmas Eve dinner."

Santa put his pipe down, took a deep breath, and said, "You well know, my dear, that I have to work on Christmas Eve."

Mrs. Claus pulled the phone away from her ear, and Santa could hear his mother-in-law starting to complain: "Don't tell me he can't stop by for a dinner! He has to eat, doesn't he? He certainly looks like he eats. And who told him to do everything in one night anyway? Not to mention that it was I who gave him the down payment on that magic sled and those reindeer in the first place. That's why he's able to be such a big shot! If not for my sacrifices on his behalf, he would still be a fat old man delivering presents in a small village in Sweden."

Santa put his head in his hands and muttered, "That was 800 years ago! Do I still have to hear about it after all this time?"

Martyrs are needy givers, giving gifts whether you want them or not. Each gift comes with an obligation.

These are the difficult people whom most people can't stand working with, talking with, and dealing with. But if you're fed up with laziness, frustrated by bullies, disappointed in human nature, and tired of losing, don't despair. Instead, remember that when dealing with difficult people, you always have a choice. In fact, you have four choices:

1. *You can stay and do nothing.* That includes suffering through it and complaining to someone who can do nothing about it. Doing nothing is dangerous because frustration with difficult people tends to build up and get worse over time. And complaining to people who can do nothing tends to lower morale and productivity, while postponing effective action.

2. *You can vote with your feet.* Sometimes, your best option is to walk away. Not all situations are resolvable, and some are just not worth resolving. Voting with your feet makes sense when it no longer makes any sense to continue to deal with the person. If the situation is deteriorating, if everything you say or do makes matters worse, and if you find yourself losing control, remember that discretion is the better part of valor, and walk away. As Eleanor Roosevelt said, "You're nobody's victim without your permission." However, before you decide to walk, you may want to consider your other two choices:

3. *You can change your attitude about your difficult people.* Even if the difficult people continue to engage in the difficult behaviors, you can learn to see them differently, listen to them differently, and feel differently around them. There are attitudinal changes that you can make in yourself that will set you free from your reactions to problem people. And a change in attitude is absolutely necessary if you hope to find the willpower and flexibility to make the fourth choice:

4. *You can change your behavior.* When you change the way you deal with difficult people, then they have to learn new ways to deal with you. Just as certainly as some people bring out the best in you and some people bring out the worst in you, you have this same ability with others. There are effective, learnable strategies for dealing with most problem behaviors. Once you know what needs to be done and how to do it, you will be well on your way to taking charge over unpleasant situations and redirecting them to worthwhile results.

2

The Lens of Understanding

This chapter is about understanding ... the kind of understanding that will help you communicate effectively, prevent future conflict, and resolve current conflict before it gets out of hand ... the kind of understanding that results when you place your difficult person's behavior under a magnifying glass, look through the lens, and closely examine the difficult behavior until you can see the motive behind it.

Did you ever wonder why some people are cautious and others carefree, some quiet and some loud, some timid and some overwhelming? Did you ever notice how one minute people might be trying to intimidate you, and the next minute they're nice, and even friendly? Have you ever been astonished at how quickly people's behavior can change from one moment to the next?

As you focus your Lens of Understanding on human behavior, first observe the level of assertiveness. Notice that there is a wide range from passive to aggressive, and most people find their own comfort zone within that range. Then observe the extremes. Passive, or nonassertive, reactions to a given situation can be submissive or yielding, and even complete withdrawal. Aggressive reactions to situations can range from bold determination to domination, belligerence, and attacks.

LESS   ASSERTIVE   MORE

Passive ◄────────────────────────────► Aggressive

Everybody responds to different situations with different levels of assertiveness. During times of challenge, difficulty, or stress, people tend to move out of their comfort zone, and they become either more passive or more aggressive than their normal mode of operation. When challenged, a highly assertive individual might make his or her presence known by speaking louder or taking action faster. An individual of low assertiveness might be increasingly reticent about the same activities. You can recognize how assertive people are by how they look (directing their energy outward or inward), how they sound (from shouting to mumbling to being silent), and what they say (from making demands to offering awkward suggestions).

When you look through your Lens of Understanding, you can also observe that there are patterns to what people focus their attention on in any given situation. For example, have you ever become so absorbed in what you were doing that you forgot there were any people around?

When attention is focused almost exclusively on the task at hand, we call that a *task focus.* Have you ever been so caught up in what people were doing around you that you found it impossible to concentrate on anything else? When attention is focused almost exclusively on relationships, we call that a *people focus.*

Within this range and depending on the situation, behavior can quickly go from one extreme to another, from friendly and down-home, to getting down to the business at hand, or vice versa. During times of challenge, difficulty, or stress, most people tend to focus with greater exclusiveness on either the what (i.e., the task) or the who (i.e., the people) of the situation, rather than on their normal mode of operation. To discern people's focus of attention, listen closely. When people are task focused, their word choices reflect where their attention is. "Did you bring the report?" "Did you finish your homework and chores?" "Do you have those figures?" "How close is that project to completion?" When people are people focused, their word choices reflect that. "Hey, how was your weekend?" "How's the family?" "How are you feeling today?" "Did you see what I did?"

Now put it all together. People can focus on other people aggressively (e.g., belligerently), assertively (e.g., with involvement), or passively (e.g., with submission). People can focus on a task aggressively (e.g., with bold determination), assertively (e.g., with involvement), or passively (e.g., by withdrawing). These behavioral characteristics can be observed through your Lens of Understanding, in others and in yourself. All people have the ability to engage in a wide range of behaviors observable through this lens, sometimes dynamically, sometimes with a lot of static. Yet for each of us, there is a zone of normal—or best— behavior, and exaggerated—or worst—behavior.

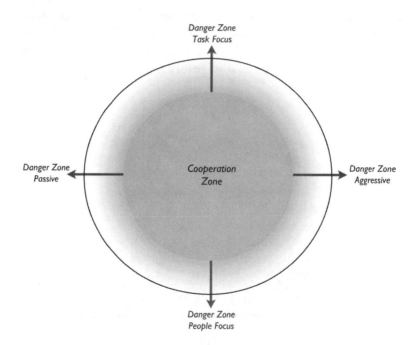

What Determines Focus and Assertiveness?

Every behavior has a purpose, or an intent, that the behavior is trying to fulfill. People engage in behaviors based on their intent, and they do what they do based on what seems to be most important in any given moment. For our purposes, we have identified *four general intents* that determine how people will behave in any given situation. While these are obviously not the only intentions motivating behavior, we believe that they represent a general frame of reference in which practically all other intents can be located. As an organizational framework for understanding and dealing with difficult behaviors, these are the four intents:

Get the task done
Get the task right
Get along with people
Get appreciation from people

Just as people choose what to wear from a variety of clothing styles (e.g., formal-wear, office-wear, or weekend-wear), so people choose from a variety of behaviors that are situationally dependent. You may have a favorite shirt or pair of pants, and you may also have a behavioral style that you prefer. But rather than having one behavioral style all the time, your behavior changes as your priorities change.

You may find it helpful to identify these four intents in yourself and recognize their connection to your own behavior in various types of situations. This will make them easier to observe and understand in others.

Get the Task Done

Have you ever needed to get something done, finished, and behind you? If you need to *get it done*, you focus on the task at hand. Any awareness of people is peripheral, unless they are necessary to accomplishing the task. When you really need to get something done, you tend to speed up rather than slow down, to act rather than deliberate, to assert rather than withdraw. And when finishing a task is an urgent need, you may even become careless and aggressive, leaping before you look, and speaking without thinking first.

But it's not only important to *get it done*. Sometimes it is more important to avoid making mistakes—to be certain every detail is accurate and in place.

Get the Task Right

Have you ever sought to avoid a mistake by doing everything possible to prevent it from happening? *Getting it right* is another task-focused intent that influences behavior. When *getting it right* is your highest priority, you will likely slow things down enough to see the details, thus becoming increasingly focused on and absorbed in the task at hand. You will probably take a good, long look before leaping, if you ever leap at all. You may even refuse to take action because of a particular doubt about the consequences.

Sometimes It's a Matter of Time. Of course, it is important to find a balance between these two intents. We call that *getting it done right* because if it's not done right, then it's really not done, is it? But any number of variables can shift this balance. For example, if you were given two weeks to complete a task, initially you might lean more toward *getting it right*, and go slowly and carefully. As the deadline approached— and especially the night before—the balance could shift dramatically toward *getting it done*! You might suddenly be willing to make sacrifices in detail that before seemed unthinkable.

Get Along with People

Another intent behind behavior is to *get along with people*. This is necessary if you want to create and develop relationships. When there are people with whom you want to *get along*, you may be less assertive as you put their needs above your own. If *getting along* is your top priority and people ask where you would like to go for lunch, you might respond, "Where would you like to go?" They may want to *get along* too and say, "Wherever you like. Are you hungry?" To which you might respond, "Are you hungry?" In this situation, personal desires are of lesser importance than the intent to *get along* with other people.

Sometimes, however, standing out from the crowd becomes a higher people priority.

Get Appreciation from People

The fourth general intent, *get appreciation from people*, requires a higher level of assertiveness and a people focus, in order to be seen, heard, and recognized. The desire to contribute to others and be appreciated for it is one of the most powerful motivational forces known. Studies show that people who love their jobs, as well as husbands and wives who are happily married, feel appreciated for what they do and who they are. If *getting appreciation* is your intent when you go to lunch with friends, you might say, "There's this fantastic restaurant I want to take you to! You're going to love it. People thank me all the time for bringing them to this place."

Sometimes You Get What You Give.   It is important to find a balance between these two intents. We believe that you *get appreciation* by giving it. Giving appreciation and *getting along* with others go hand-in-hand. But any number of variables can shift this balance. For example, if you were the new employee in the office, initially you might lean more toward *getting along*, taking care to be considerate, concerned, and helpful. As the time approached for promotions, the balance could shift dramatically toward *getting appreciation*! If you were afraid your efforts would be overlooked, you might care less about the feelings of others than before. Similarly, in the courtship that precedes marriage, people tend to show great concern for each other's needs and interests. Years later, it is not uncommon to hear marriage partners demanding that their own needs be met.

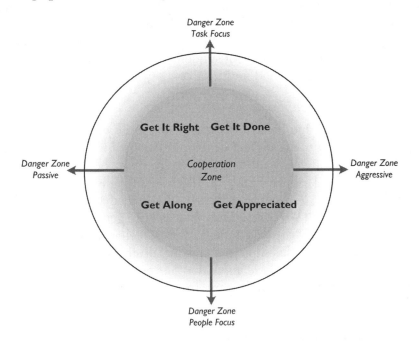

It's a Question of Balance

All of these intents, *getting it done, getting it right, getting along,* and *getting appreciation,* have their time and place in our lives. Often, keeping them in balance leads to less stress and more success. To *get it done,* take care to *get it done right.* If you want it done right, avoid complications by making sure everyone is *getting along.* For a team effort to succeed, each party must feel valued and appreciated. Though the priority of these intents can shift from moment to moment, the shaded inner circle represents the normal balance of these intents in us all. We call it the *Cooperation Zone.* When people are in the *Cooperation Zone,* though their intents may differ, they are not in conflict or threatened by each other.

As Intent Changes, So Does Behavior

Consider the following situations to observe how behavior changes with intent.

Jack has been given a project to do at work. He has three weeks to do it, and since it could lead to a promotion, he really wants to make sure it is done right. He needs some figures from his coworker Ralph. Ralph hands him the paper and says, "The bottom line came to about 1050." Jack says, "What do you mean 'about 1050.' What specifically is it?" Ralph says, "1050." Jack says, "Are you sure?" Ralph replies, "Yeah, pretty sure." Jack calls his wife and tells her he will be coming home late. That night he locks himself in his office to slowly and methodically check Ralph's figures. Where do you think he is in the lens?

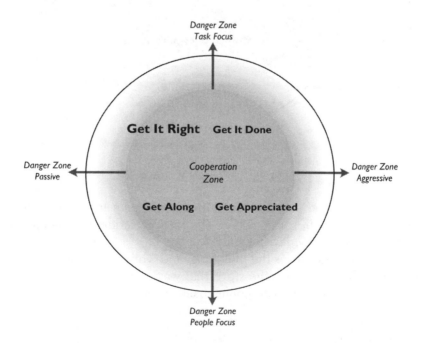

Obviously his priority is to *get it right*. He slows down and withdraws into the task to make sure it is done correctly.

It is the weekend now, and Jack is working away in his home office. His seven-year-old daughter comes in and says, "Daddy, Daddy, come look at the painting I did in my room." Jack pushes his work aside and spends the rest of the afternoon playing with his daughter. That night his wife says she got a sitter, and she suggests that they go out for a nice dinner alone. When she asks where he would like to go, he replies, "Wherever you want." At dinner she asks if he will have time tomorrow to fix that leaky faucet in the kitchen. Jack thinks of his project and knows he doesn't really have time but says, "Okay. Sure thing." Where is he now?

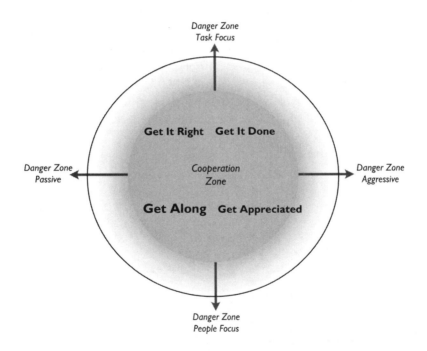

Obviously, to *get along* is Jack's intent. He puts his needs aside to please the people he cares about. The project suddenly becomes secondary to *getting along* with family.

The next day Jack fixes the plumbing, and while he is in a fix-it mode, he repairs the burner on the stove that wasn't working and replaces a torn screen. When his wife comes back from shopping, she wants to show him what she bought, but he first insists on showing her what he did. Where is Jack now?

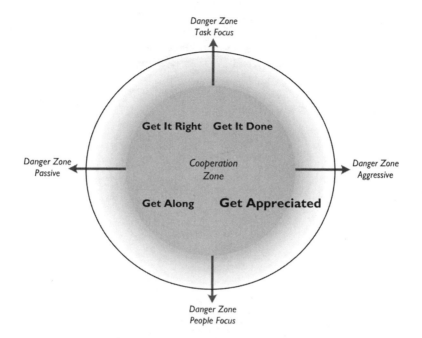

If you said *"getting appreciated,"* very good. Take note that when his wife comes home, if he were in a *getting along* mode, he probably would first look at what she had bought. Since *getting appreciated* is primary, he can't wait to show her what he did.

Jack doesn't get as much done over the weekend as he had hoped, and the next week gets eaten up in crisis. Suddenly the deadline is upon him. He is working at home when his youngest daughter comes to him and asks if he will sit in her room while she goes to sleep and protect her from monsters. He says, "There are no monsters in your room. Now go to bed." A little later his wife asks if he wants to have some tea with her. Without looking up, he just flatly says, "No." Then she inquires about what they might do this upcoming weekend and offers some options. "Look, I don't have time for this right now!" he testily responds. "Just pick one." He turns back to his work. "Darn!" he thinks. "I am going to have to guess at some of these figures."

Now where is Jack?

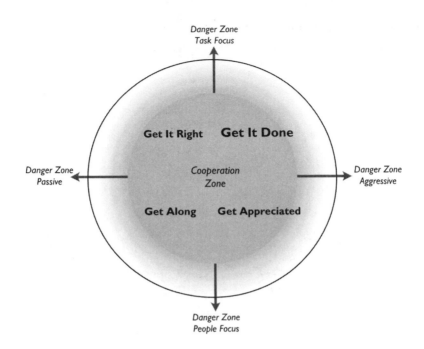

"*Get it done*" is the answer. Under the pressure of a deadline, Jack becomes more task focused and is not willing to take time for family. His communications are more direct and to the point. He is now willing to guess at some of the figures. That would have been unthinkable a few weeks earlier, when he had the luxury of time to *get it right*.

Notice in these examples how Jack's behavior changes according to what is most important to him in a particular situation and time. The point here is that behavior changes according to intent, based on the top priority in any moment of time. We all have the ability to operate out of all four intents. To communicate effectively with other people, you must have some understanding of what matters most to them.

You Can Hear Where People Are Coming From

So how can you identify the intent of other people? One rapid indicator is their communication style. Let's go to a meeting where four people with different primary intents each have something to say. Your mission is to attend to each one's communication style and determine that person's primary intent.

The first person says, "Just do it! What's next on the agenda?"

Which intent would most likely be represented by such a brief and to-the-point communication style? If it sounds to you like *"getting it done"* is the priority here, then you're ready to move on to the next example. When people want to *get it done,* they keep their communications short and to the point.

The next person at the meeting says, "Uh … given the figures from the past two years, and taking into account inflation, fractionation of markets, foreign competition, and of course extrapolating that into the future … I … uh … think it would be to our benefit to take more time to explore the problem fully, but if a decision is required now, then … do it."

Which intent would most likely be represented by such an indirect and detailed communication style? If you're thinking *"get it right,"* you just got it right. Notice that both people said "Do it." But the *get it right* person would never think to say that without backing it up with details.

Now a third person at the meeting speaks up: "I feel … and tell me if you disagree because I really value your opinions—in fact I have learned so much working with you all—but I was just thinking … if everybody agrees, then maybe we really should do it? Is that what everyone wants to do?"

Which intent would most likely be represented by such an indirect and considerate communication style? If you feel comfortable with this as an example of *"getting along with people,"* then you'll fit right in. A person in the *get along* mode will be considerate of the opinions and feelings of others.

Suddenly, the fourth person at the meeting stands up (though everyone else has been sitting) and loudly proclaims, "I think we should do it, and I'll tell you why. My granddaddy used to tell me 'Son … if ya snooze, ya lose.' I never knew what he meant, but I never let that stop me. Y'know, that reminds me of a joke I heard. You're going to love this one …"

While that person keeps on going, we'd like you to stop and consider which intent would most likely be represented by such an elaborate communication style. If you're thinking *"get appreciation from people,"* you've done a fine job so far of learning to recognize intent from a person's style of communication. The person in the *get appreciated* mode is more likely to be flamboyant.

Can you understand how people with different primary intents can drive each other crazy?

Now think of the problem people in your life. In the situations in which you find them difficult, can you recall how they communicate? How about your communication? Who was more direct and to the point? Who was more detailed? Who deferred to others? Who was more elaborate? Who focused more on the task, and who focused more on the people? Who was aggressive, and who was passive? By observing behavior and listening to communication patterns with your problem people, you can recognize primary intent.

Shared Priorities, No Problem

When people have the same priorities, a misunderstanding or conflict is highly unlikely. For example:

The person you are working with on a project wants to get it done. You're focused on the task, you're getting it done, and your communications with them are brief and to the point.

The person you are working with wants to get it right. You're focused on the task, you're paying great attention to the details, and your reports to them are well documented.

The person you know wants to get along *with you*. With your friendly chitchat and considerate communications, you let him know that you care about him and like him.

The person you know wants to get appreciation *for what they're doing*. With your enthusiasm and gratitude, you let her know that you recognize her contributions.

What Happens When the Intent Isn't Fulfilled?

When people's intents are not met, their behavior begins to change. When people want to *get it done* and fear it is not getting done, their behavior naturally becomes more *controlling*, as they try to take over and push ahead. When people want to *get it right* and fear it will be done wrong, their behavior becomes more *perfectionistic*, finding every flaw and potential error. When people want to *get along* and they fear they will be left out, their behavior becomes more *approval seeking*, sacrificing their personal needs to please others. When people want to *get appreciation* and fear they are not, their behavior becomes more *attention getting*, forcing others to notice them. And so it begins. These four changes are only the beginning of a metamorphosis into people you can't stand. Using our lens, these changes are represented by the area just outside the Cooperation Zone called the *Caution Zone*.

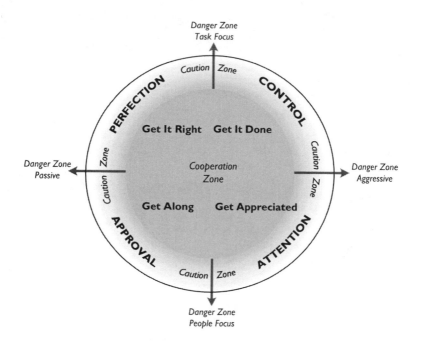

If you notice these changes in behavior, then you should immediately focus on *blending* (Chapter 4) with those people. But what if they aren't willing to be flexible? *Well, do you want to see something really scary? Their behavior will continue to change until they become your worst problem-people nightmare.*

3

The Road to Hell Is Paved with Good Intentions

Once people determine that what they want is not happening or that what they don't want is happening, their behavior becomes more extreme and goes into the *Danger Zone*. Let's observe how threatened or thwarted positive intentions lead to the behaviors of difficult people.

Threatened Intent to *Get It Done*

Through the distorted lens of the thwarted intent to get it done, others appear to be wasting time, going off on tangents, or just plain taking too long. The intent increases in intensity, and the subsequent behavior becomes more controlling. The three most difficult controlling behaviors are the Tank, Sniper, and Know-It-All.

The Tank. On a mission, unable to slow down, pushing you around, or running right over you, the Tank has no inhibitions about ripping you apart personally. Yet the irony is … it's not personal. You just happened to get in the way. In an effort to control the process and accomplish the mission, Tank behavior ranges from mild pushiness to outright aggression.

The Sniper. Strategists when things aren't getting done to their satisfaction, Snipers attempt to control you through embarrassment and humiliation. Most people live in fear of public embarrassment—a fact that Snipers use to their advantage, by making loaded statements and sarcastic comments at times when you are most vulnerable.

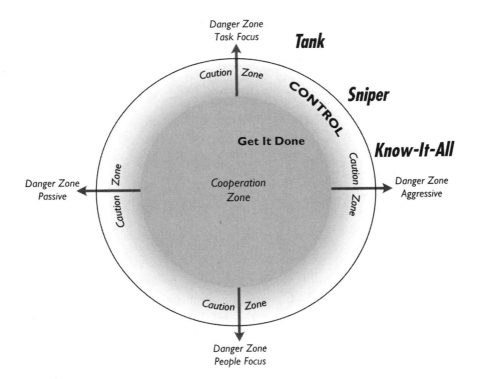

The Know-It-All. Know-It-Alls control people and events by dominating the conversation with lengthy, imperious arguments, and they eliminate opposition by finding flaws and weaknesses to discredit other points of view. Because Know-It-Alls are actually knowledgeable and competent, most people are quickly worn down by their strategy and finally just give up.

Threatened Intent to *Get It Right*

Through the distorted lens of the thwarted intent to get it right, everything around these people begins to seem haphazard and careless. To add insult to injury, people seem to address these concerns with horrifyingly fuzzy words, like *pretty much*, and *roughly*, and *probably*. When sufficient intensity is reached, the behavior becomes increasingly pessimistic and perfectionistic. The Whiner, the No Person, the Judge, and the Nothing Person, all exemplify this kind of behavior.

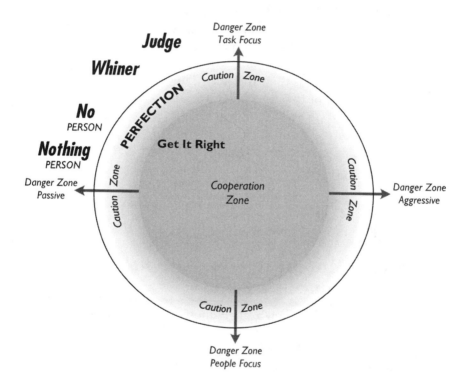

The Whiner. In our imperfect world, Whiners believe that they are powerless to create change. Burdened and overwhelmed by all the uncertainty around what can go wrong, they abandon all thought of solutions. Instead, as the feeling of helplessness increases, they focus on any problems they can use as evidence for their massive generalization. They begin to whine: "Oh, ... nothing is right. Everything is wrong." This, of course, serves only to drive everybody else crazy, and the deteriorating situation provokes further whining.

The No Person.   Unlike Whiners, No People do not feel helpless in the face of things going wrong. Instead, the No People become hopeless. Certain that what is wrong will never be set right, they have no inhibition about letting others know how they feel: "Forget it, we tried that. It didn't work then, it won't work now, and you're kidding yourself if anyone tells you something different. Give up and save yourself from wasted effort on a lost cause." This gravity well pulls others into the No People's personal pits of despair.

The Judge.   Unlike Whiners and No People, Judges are not caught up in generalizations that nothing is right. Instead, their attention is on specific areas where they have decided that you are not measuring up. Judges can range in behavior from nitpicking (focused on details of no real consequence) to condemning you and then writing you off. Unconstructive criticism is their specialty. They may express their judgments directly to you or to others behind your back.

The Nothing Person.   When events fail to measure up to their standard of perfection, some people get so totally frustrated that they withdraw completely. There may be one last shout at the powers-that-be for failing to get it right: "Fine! Do it your way. Don't come crying to me if it doesn't work out!" From that point on, they do and say ... nothing.

Threatened Intent to *Get It Right* and *Get It Done*

Not all behaviors are based on a single motivation. When people straddle the line between *get it right* and *get it done*, they can view you through a critical eye, judge you of being incapable of doing what needs to be done, and then take over.

The Meddler.   When you combine the critical perfectionist eye of the Judge with the *get it done* controlling nature of a Tank, you get a Meddler. These people know what's best for you and insert themselves into your life and try to get you to do what they are sure you need to be doing. They can range from nosy to interfering to manipulative. From what you wear, to whom you spend time with, to how you talk, to what you do, the Meddler is keeping an eye on you.

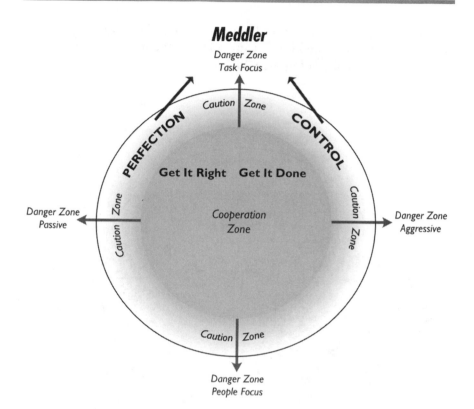

Threatened Intent to *Get Along* with Others

Through the distorted lens of the thwarted intent to get along with people, uncertainty about how others feel about them leads them to take other people's reactions, comments, and facial expressions personally. Behavior becomes increasingly geared toward gaining approval and avoiding disapproval. The three most difficult approval-seeking behaviors are the passive Nothing Person, the wishy-washy Yes Person, and the Maybe Person.

The Nothing Person.   Timid, uncomfortable, and uncertain, get along Nothing People excel at tongue biting. Since they don't have anything nice to say, they don't say anything at all. At their worst, they say nothing almost all the time. This, in many ways, is the perfect strategy to avoid conflict, to avoid hurting someone else's feelings, and to keep from angering anyone. It's almost a perfect plan, but there is a fly in the ointment. Since Nothing People can't relate authentically or speak honestly, they don't really get along with anyone.

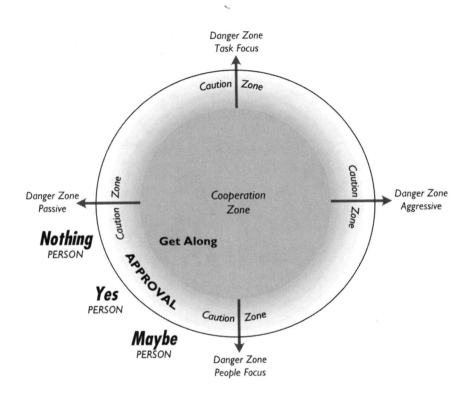

The Yes Person.   Yes People seek approval and avoid disapproval by trying to please everyone else. The Yes People answer yes to every request, without actually thinking about what is being promised or the consequences of failing to follow through. "Sure," say the Yes People. And to the next request, "Okay," and "Of course," to the next request. Before long, the Yes People have overpromised and under-delivered to such an extent that the very people they wanted to get along with are furious. In the rare instance where the promises are kept, Yes People's lives are no longer their own because all their choices are made around everyone else's needs and demands. This produces a deep-seated anxiety and much resentment in the Yes People, which can even lead to unconscious acts of sabotage.

The Maybe Person.   Maybe People avoid disapproval by avoiding decisions. After all, the wrong choice might upset someone, or something could go wrong and who would be blamed? The solution is to put the decision off, waffle, and hedge until someone else makes the decision or the decision makes itself. Like all the other difficult behaviors, this behavior perpetuates the problem it is intended to solve by causing so much frustration and annoyance that the Maybe People are locked out of meaningful relationships with others.

Threatened Intent to *Get Appreciated* by People

Through the distorted lens of a thwarted intent to get appreciation from people, the lack of positive feedback combines in their mind with the reactions, comments, and facial expressions of others, and it all tends to be taken personally. The intent to get appreciation intensifies in direct proportion to the lack of appreciative feedback, and the behavior becomes increasingly aimed at getting attention. The three most difficult attention-getting behaviors that result from the thwarted desires to *get appreciation* are the Grenades, the Snipers, and the Think-They-Know-It-Alls.

The Grenade.   They say they don't get any appreciation and they're not getting any respect. When the silence and lack of appreciation become deafening, look out for the Grenade: the adult temper tantrum. "Kaboom! @#$° Nobody around here cares! That's the problem with the world today. Kapow! °%^&@# I don't know why I even bother! No one appreciates just how hard it is for me! Katung! &%$#°." Ranting and raving are difficult to ignore. But since this desperate behavior produces negative attention and disgust, the Grenade is ever more likely to blow up at the next provocation.

The difference between the Tank, described earlier, and the Grenade is that the Tank uses focused fire in a single direction, while the Grenade produces an out-of-control explosion in 360 degrees. The Tank takes aim with specific charges but leave other useful people and office equipment standing. The Grenade introduces elements that have little or nothing to do with the present circumstances. A Tank attack is a demand for action. A Grenade tantrum is a demand for attention.

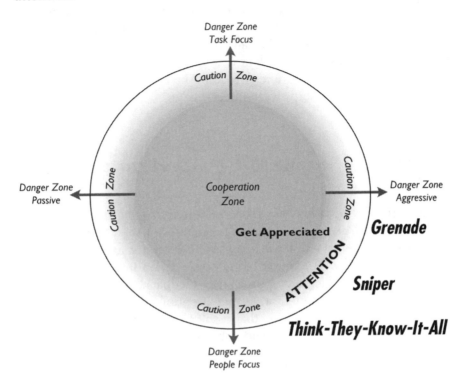

The Friendly Sniper.   These Snipers actually like you, and their sniping is a "fun way" of gaining attention. "I never forget a face …, but in your case I will make an exception." Many people have relationships that include playful sniping. Normally, the best defense is a good offense because instead of offending, a return snipe is a sign of appreciation. But if people on the receiving end don't give or receive appreciation in this manner, they may be laughing on the outside while bleeding from an emotional wound on the inside.

The Think-They-Know-It-All.   Think-They-Know-It-Alls are specialists in exaggerations, half truths, jargon, useless advice, and unsolicited opinions. Charismatic and enthusiastic, these desperate-for-attention people can persuade and mislead an entire group of naive people into serious difficulties. If you argue with them, they turn up the volume and dig in their heels, then refuse to back down until you look as foolish as they do.

Threatened Intent to *Get Appreciated* and *Get Along*

Straddling the line between the intent to *get appreciated* and the intent to *get along* creates a tension that causes people to go out of their way to please and help others, while also desperately wanting the appreciation for doing so in return.

The Martyr.　　Martyrs can be pleasant on the surface, as they go about doing everything for everybody. But what they really seek is appreciation and significance in the lives of others. Unfortunately the things they do are not necessarily what others want done, and so they often don't get the appreciation they desire. This finally leads to a Martyr meltdown, when they complain that they do everything for everybody and question why no one cares about them.

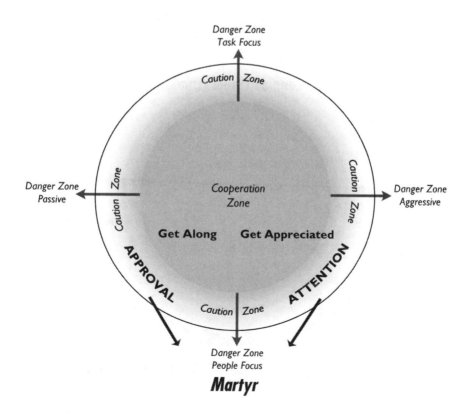

To Summarize

- Behavior becomes more controlling when the intent to get it done is thwarted, leading people to become Tanks, Snipers, and Know-It-Alls.

- Behavior becomes more perfectionistic when the intent to get it right is thwarted, leading people to become Whiners, No People, Judges, and Nothing People.

- Behavior becomes more perfectionistic and more controlling when the intent to *get it right* and *get it done* is thwarted, leading people to become Meddlers.

- Behavior becomes more approval seeking when the intent to get along is thwarted, leading people to become Yes People, Maybe People, and Nothing People.

- Behavior becomes more attention getting when the intent to get appreciation is thwarted, leading people to become Grenades, Think-They-Know-It-Alls, and Snipers.

- Behavior becomes more attention-getting and more approval-seeking when the intent to *get appreciated* and *get along* is thwarted, leading people to become Martyrs.

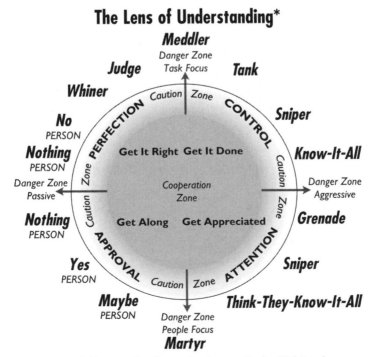

°Find a color printout of the Lens of Understanding at www.DealingWithPeople.com.

As you read these descriptions of the 10 (+ 3) difficult behaviors that people can't stand, perhaps you noticed that when your intentions are thwarted, you occasionally become some of these people too—we wouldn't be surprised since everybody is somebody's difficult person some of the time. Who hasn't whined; complained; become hopeless; exaggerated a story; withheld their true feelings; felt ignored, put upon, or dismissed; procrastinated in making a decision; lost their temper; loudly accused; or withdrawn completely? The difference between you and your difficult people in this regard may be a matter of degree and frequency, or recognition and responsibility. But the essential point here is that these behaviors are observable and changeable.

The behavior of the people you can't stand is determined by their perception of what they think is going on as it relates to what they think is important. Their behavior interacts with your behavior, which is based on your own perception of these same variables. This produces an outcome, either randomly or intentionally. The results of your dealings with people at their worst is, in large measure, up to you.

Part 2

Surviving Through Skillful Communication

You Find Out Why United We Stand, but Divided We Can't Stand Each Other, as well as How to Listen to Understand, Reach a Deeper Understanding, Speak to Be Understood, Get What You Project and Expect, and Change Your Attitude.

4

From Conflict to Cooperation

An ounce of prevention is worth a pound of difficult people.

You already communicate successfully with most people, and you have difficulties with only a few people. Our purpose in the following chapters is to bring into your awareness communication skills that you unconsciously use already to build trust in relationships with people you care about. Once you recognize these skills, you can begin to use them on purpose, with problem people to turn conflict into cooperation.

Two Essential Skills: Blending and Redirecting

What is it about people that makes some so easy to relate to and others so difficult to deal with? How is it possible that you can get along with one and get into conflict with the other? The answer to these questions is that United We Stand, but Divided We Can't Stand Each Other. Conflict occurs when the emphasis in a relationship is on the differences between people. The more divided you seem to be, the sooner you fall.

You get along better with people when the emphasis is on similarities between you. The difference between conflict with a friend and conflict with a difficult person is that with a friend the conflict is tempered by the common ground you share. Success in communication depends on finding common ground before attempting to redirect the interaction toward a new outcome. Obviously, reducing differences is essential to your success in dealing with people you can't stand.

That's where blending and redirecting come in. *Blending* is any behavior by which you reduce the differences between you and other people in order to meet them where they are and move to common ground. The result of blending is an increase in rapport. *Redirecting* is any behavior by which you use that rapport to change the trajectory of that interaction.

Blending is an essential communication skill. It's something people do automatically and naturally when they share a common vision, care about each other, or want to deepen a relationship. You may be amazed at how much a part of your life blending already is.

For example, have you ever been in a conversation with someone when, unexpectedly, you found that you both grew up in the same place? In that moment of discovery, differences were reduced, and you felt closer. That's the experience of blending.

Have you ever gone to a restaurant with friends, looked at the menu, and asked, "What are you having?" Your question may have had little to do with what they wanted to eat and a lot to do with sending a signal of friendship. If, before the meal, they ordered a drink and so you ordered one too, that was another example of blending.

When your child comes home from the playground teary-eyed from an injury on that little knee, what do you do? If your love for your child is strong, you will either pick the child up so that you are eye to eye or you will bend down to the child's level. You may even put your hand over your own knee, crinkle up your face, and in the same tone of voice say, "Does it hurt?" That's blending, and it shows your child that you care.

Have you ever been in a conversation with people who have a strong regional accent, and you found yourself talking with a little bit of that accent yourself? If so, that was your natural urge to blend with people you like.

If you have ever gone somewhere all dressed up, only to find everyone else in shorts and T-shirts, then you know the feeling of not blending!

You blend with people in many ways. You blend visually with your facial expression, degree of animation, and body posture. You blend verbally with your voice volume and speed. And you blend conceptually with your words. But as natural as it is to blend with people that you like or with people that you share an objective with, it is equally natural *not* to blend with people whom you perceive as difficult. And the failure to blend has serious consequences because without blending, the differences between you become the basis for conflict.

Key Point.   *No one cooperates with any one who seems to be against them.* The fact is, in human relations there is no middle ground. Unconsciously or consciously, people want to know, "Are you with me or not?" You come across as either hot or cold to the relationship, perceived as being on common ground or worlds apart. Believe it or not, that's one of the things you have in common with your difficult people.

Key Point.   *Blending always precedes redirecting, whether you're listening to understand or speaking to be understood.* Only after establishing some rapport with your difficult people through blending will you be able to redirect the interaction and change the trajectory toward a worthwhile outcome. In the following strategies, you will find specific blending and redirecting skills for effective communication with problem people. As you read, try to recall instances when you have successfully used these strategies, and imagine future times when you might use them again. In the second half of the book, we will draw on these skills and strategies to deal effectively with the 10 (+ 3) most difficult unwanted behaviors.

Blending Nonverbally with Body and Facial Expressions

Some people talk with their hands; others talk only with their mouths. Some people smile politely with just about everybody; others scowl at anybody, while still others are inscrutable. Some stand to speak; some sit down to speak. Some slouch, some stand straight, and some lean against the furniture. These differences in style can be the sources of misinterpretation, hallucination, and misunderstanding. The people who talk with their hands see the people who talk only with their mouth as real sticks in the mud. The people who talk only with their mouth see the people who talk with their hands as out of control. The people who smile see the people who scowl as hateful, while the people who scowl see the people who smile as phony or goofy.

When people get along with each other, they naturally blend by mirroring each other's body posture, facial expressions, and degree of animation. If you're enjoying a conversation with people who are sitting with their legs crossed, after a time you cross your legs in the same manner. If they uncross their legs and lean forward, within moments you respond by doing the same. If they're smiling, you smile back. If they're telling you about something that is upsetting to them, you show your concern. If they're talking with their hands, you respond in kind. It can get to the point where, if they scratch their head, you may suddenly get an itch on your head in the same place. In fact, if you could watch a video of yourself with people you communicate well with, and you could put that video on fast forward, you would see what appears to be an unconscious and automatic game of Simon Says.

For the rest of this day, pay attention to the way people mirror each others' nonverbal behavior. Watch how you blend with others and how others blend with you. Watch two people from a distance, and see how they blend nonverbally. If you see a couple having an argument, watch how there is very little blending and an exaggeration of differences.

Most of the time, nonverbal blending happens automatically and usually goes unnoticed by both parties. Blending or the lack of it can create an atmosphere of trust or distrust, cooperation or noncooperation, between you and other people. One way to take charge with difficult people in a poisoned atmosphere is to purposely blend with their body posture, facial expressions, and degree of animation. Blending sends the signal that "I'm with you! I'm not the enemy! I'm interested in what you say and do!"

Important: It is not necessary to do so much nonverbal blending that the other people notice; you don't want them to think that you are mocking them. It is unnecessary to mirror what other people are doing from head to toe. You want only to simulate behavior that would normally occur if all of you were getting along. In a normal situation, there are time delays before mirroring changes in posture. Sometimes, nonverbal blending is similar but different. Ever meet a foot wiggler? You may not start wiggling your foot, but before you know it, you are wiggling your pencil to the same rhythm.

One thing you should never blend with is a hostile gesture directed at you. If someone shakes his or her fist at you and yells, "I think you're a jerk!" please don't shake your fist back and start yelling, "Well, I think you're a jerk too!" That is not blending. We do not recommend meeting aggression with aggression. The key to blending with aggression is to underplay it assertively, and we'll talk about that when we talk about the Tanks and Grenades.

When we examine the 10 (+ 3) types of difficult behaviors, you'll discover how useful nonverbal blending can be. Using your body, you can help Yes People, Maybe People, and Nothing People feel comfortable with you, and you'll be able to nonverbally demonstrate to Tanks that you can stand up for yourself without having to be aggressive.

Blending Vocally with Volume and Speed

Whenever you successfully communicate with people, you naturally blend with their voice volume and speed. If they talk louder, you talk louder. If they talk faster, then you speed up. Faster-talking people enjoy the race; slower-talking people enjoy an easy pace. Quiet people like quiet. Loud people like volume. If you fail to blend with other people's voice volume and speed, you will probably end up talking to yourself or dealing with serious misunderstanding.

A mother and teenage daughter sought counseling in a last ditch attempt to resolve seemingly irreconcilable differences. We observed that when the mother was angry with her daughter, her communications would speed up. However, her communications also sped up for other reasons besides anger. But no matter what the reason for the mother's acceleration of speech, the daughter withdrew from it. She stopped listening to whatever her mother said, not because of what she said but because of how she said it. The mother found this to be incredibly frustrating, and she inevitably lost her temper. The daughter withdrew further. Through time, they grew so far apart that they had to shout at each other.

Unfortunately, this pattern is typical of many parent-child relationships. It's not that there isn't enough love. The problem is, there's not enough blending. We pointed this out to the mother and daughter, and we helped them to become aware of their communication differences. They both changed their behavior. Once the mother realized that she wanted her daughter's attention while speaking to her, she began to purposely slow her communication down, blending with what worked for her daughter.

The daughter was equally eager to have good communication with her mom, instead of the constant sound of harassment. So she began making the effort to pay attention to what her mom had to say independent of the speed, knowing that it didn't just mean anger. Using their love for each other to keep them on track, they both did their part to improve their communication. Here, as is often the case, it was the process rather than the content of the communication that was causing the difficulty.

5

Listen to Understand

People Want to Be Heard and Understood

When people express themselves verbally, they want feedback that they've been heard, and they also want to be understood. This is true even when they don't understand themselves, as is the case when people who are upset try to describe their feelings and thoughts. But when two or more people want to be heard and understood at the same time and no one is willing to listen and understand, an argument or exit is almost inevitable. For this reason, masterful communicators make it their goal to listen and understand first, before attempting to be heard and understood.

Here's the bad news: our strategy for listening requires you to temporarily set aside your own need to be heard and understood, at a time when you least want to. Now the good news: by helping your problem people express themselves completely, you increase the likelihood of their being able and even willing to hear you in turn. In fact, there can be no doubt that when people have the experience that they've been listened to and understood, they let go of their preoccupation with their own thoughts and feelings. The door to their mind swings open, and that makes it much easier for them to hear you.

Understanding occurs on two levels: *emotionally*—people feel that you understand what they are feeling—and *intellectually*—people believe that you understand what they are saying. When people become difficult people (i.e., their positive intentions are threatened or thwarted), listening to understand their feelings and thoughts is a useful objective. A simple, yet effective, strategy for accomplishing this requires that you listen actively rather than passively. If you make a habit of listening in the manner we are about to describe, you will actually prevent some people from ever becoming people you can't stand.

Step 1. Blend.   How do people know that you are listening and understanding? In essence, it's through the way you look and sound while they're talking. While they vent their emotions, blow off steam, whine, complain, unload their problems, talk about things that are irrelevant or misleading, and provide you with detailed information that you have no known use for, your task is to give visual and auditory evidence that what they're saying makes sense to you (even when it doesn't!).

Rather than distracting your difficult people with puzzled looks, interruptions, or statements of disagreement, we suggest that you help them to completely express themselves. Simply put, you do this by nodding your head in agreement, while making occasional and appropriate sounds of understanding like "Uh-huh," "Oh," and "Hmm," and then repeating back what they've said so they know they've been heard. Everything about you, from your body posture to your voice volume, must give the impression that you hear and understand.

At some point you will need to become more actively involved. You'll know for certain that you have reached that point when your problem people begin to repeat what's already been said. When this occurs, consider it a signal that the people need some feedback from you.

Step 2. Backtrack.   One form of giving feedback is *backtracking*, or repeating back some of the actual words that other people are using. This sends a clear signal that you are listening and that you consider what the other people are saying to be important.

Backtracking is not the same as translating or rephrasing. Words are symbols for experience, and the word-symbols that people choose to express their experience have unique meanings to them. Changing their words into your words with well-intended statements like "In other words ..." or "So, what you're really trying to say is ..." may prolong the communication process with difficult people. They might hear these different symbols as evidence that you don't understand.

Nor does backtracking require you to become a parrot and repeat everything back to your problem people. How much backtracking you do is relative to the situation you're in. When dealing with an attacking Tank, a minimal amount of backtracking is required because the Tank has a two-sentence attention span. When dealing with a Know-It-All, copious backtracking is required, or you'll have to hear the lecture again. With wishy-washy Yes and Maybe people, it becomes more important to backtrack their feeling statements. You will find yourself using a version of this skill with all of the 10 (+ 3) people you can't stand.

Backtracking is particularly important when dealing with problem people over the phone because the only visual information they have about you is what they extrapolate from the sound of your voice and the words that you use.

Step 3. Clarify.   Having heard what they have to say, begin to gather information about the meaning of their communication. It's alright to look confused at this point, as you become genuinely curious and ask some questions. *Clarification questions* are open-ended questions that ask for more than a grunt in response. They begin with words like *what, who, where, when,* and *how.* "Whom are you talking about? What are you referring to? Where did it happen? When did it happen? How did it happen?" After gathering this information, you may begin to explore why they are saying it and what criteria they are hoping to satisfy by their behavior.

It is essential that you develop your ability to switch into an information gathering mode rather than a reactionary one. When you deal with difficult people, being able to ask the right questions may turn out to be worth far more than having all the right answers. "All of us are smarter than any of us" is a useful principle. The people asking the questions stand to gain the most by putting this greater intelligence to work.

When dealing with people who are upset, however, putting the greater intelligence to work isn't always possible. Emotions so cloud the reasoning capabilities of people that it seems as if their brains are no longer connected to their mouths. How many times can you recall when you were upset and said something you didn't actually mean? And while it is virtually impossible to reason with emotional people, it is possible to look and sound like you understand, backtrack what you've heard, and then become curious enough to ask questions.

Benefits of Asking Clarification Questions

- *You can gather higher-quality information than what is offered.* Questions allow both of you to clarify the details and understand the specifics of a problem, rather than coping with, and reacting to, vague generalizations.

- *You can help the other people become more rational in the process.* Asking the right questions helps people who are upset to fill in the blanks in their thinking until they become reasonable again.

- *You can patiently and supportively demonstrate that you* care *about what they are saying.* In this way, problem people are more likely to become calm and cooperative people.

- *Asking questions can slow a situation down long enough to see where it's heading.* This allows you to take corrective action sooner instead of later.

- *You can surface hidden agendas and reveal lies without being adversarial.* That's what Peter Falk's detective character did in the hit TV show *Columbo*.

As a general principle, it is probably better to do more clarifying than less, even when you think you do understand what people are saying. All too often, people think they understand what other people are saying when, in fact, they do not. Also, asking a specific question doesn't mean you automatically get a specific answer. Both the Whiner and the No Person tend to speak in sweeping generalizations.

Step 4. Summarize What You've Heard. To make certain that both you and your problem people have the experience that you really do understand, summarize back to them what you've heard. "So then, if I understand you correctly, this is the problem, this is who it involved, and this is when it happened, where it happened, and how it happened?"

When you do this, at least two things happen: (1) If you've missed something, they can fill in the details. And (2), you've demonstrated, yet again, that you are making a serious effort to fully understand. This increases the likelihood of gaining their cooperation in changing direction down the line.

Step 5. Confirm. Having listened carefully, you've now arrived at a crucial juncture. Rather than assuming anything, be certain that the difficult people are satisfied that the problem has been fully voiced. Ask, "Do you feel understood? Is there anything else?"

When enough sincere questioning, listening, caring, and remembering are brought together, understanding is achieved, and difficult people become less difficult and more cooperative.

Quick Summary

When Your Problem Person Is Talking
   Your Goal: Listen to Understand
   ACTION PLAN
   1. Blend visibly and audibly.
   2. Backtrack some of the person's own words.
   3. Clarify the meaning, intent, and criteria.
   4. Summarize what you've heard.
   5. Confirm to find out if you got it right.

6
Reach a Deeper Understanding

So far, we've discussed listening as a method for increasing trust, cooperation, and understanding. Yet sometimes the most important and useful aspects of communication are hidden not just from the listener but from the speaker as well. When you identify these elements, you simultaneously blend and redirect the interaction.

Identify Positive Intent

We define *positive intent* as the good purpose meant to be served by a given communication or behavior. We assume that all behavior originates from a positive intent, and that includes negative behavior. The failure to recognize and appreciate positive intent can have lasting consequences.

Frank owned a sporting goods shop. It was a seasonal business, and the store had just finished a very unprofitable season. The cash flow was low, and for that reason many of the lights in the shop were burned out, and they remained unreplaced. A new employee, noticing this problem, took it upon himself to order bulbs and replace them all. He also filled the stockroom with two more years' worth of new bulbs, so the store wouldn't be in the dark again.

Frank was furious that the store's limited financial resources had been used in this way, and he gave the new employee a dressing down in front of his other employees. Two years later, Frank wondered why this employee had demonstrated no initiative and instead had to be told everything.

Isn't it obvious what had happened? The owner failed to acknowledge positive intent in his employee!

What was the good intent? Perhaps he cared how shoddy the place looked and wondered what the customers would think of the quality of goods if the store were kept in such a manner. Perhaps he just wanted to be liked by everyone, and he tried to do something nice for his fellow workers. Or perhaps he was looking for a way to stand out of the crowd and be noticed. It could have been for any one of these reasons. What matters is not which positive intent motivated the act of initiative. What matters is that failure to acknowledge positive intent destroyed initiative.

If Frank had blended with the employee by identifying and acknowledging his positive intent, he might have said something like this:

"Thank you for taking the initiative to change the lightbulbs around here. I appreciate that you care about the way this place looks. I bet you figured that if customers see a shoddy looking store, they may think the same about our equipment. And your coworkers no doubt appreciated a little more light shed on the subject. You must not know that we have a serious cash flow problem. We'll have to send the extra bulbs back. But thank you for taking the initiative. I definitely want to see more of that. And I'll do my best to keep everyone informed around here from now on."

Do you think the employee would have risked future initiatives? You bet. A powerful key to bringing out the best in people at their worst is to give them the benefit of the doubt. Assume a positive intent behind their problem behavior, and then deal with them accordingly.

Ask yourself what positive purpose might be behind people's communications or behaviors, and acknowledge it. If you are not sure about the positive intent, just make something up. Even if the intent you try to blend with isn't true, you can still get a good response and create rapport.

Applying the Blending Strategy to the Four Intents Seen Through the Lens of Understanding

- If you're dealing with people who you perceive want to *get it done* as their top priority, and if in your conversations with them, you acknowledge this and your communications with them are brief and to the point so as not to obstruct them, you will increase cooperation and decrease misunderstanding.

- If you're dealing with people who you perceive want to *get it right* as their top priority, and if in your conversations with them, you acknowledge this and you pay great attention to the details in your communications with them, you will increase cooperation and decrease misunderstanding.

- If you're dealing with people who you perceive want to *get along* with you as their top priority, and if in your interactions with them you show you care with friendly chitchat and considerate communications, you will increase cooperation and decrease misunderstanding.

- If you're dealing with people who want to *get appreciation* as their top priority, and if in your interactions with them you recognize their contribution with words of enthusiastic appreciation, you will increase cooperation and decrease misunderstanding.

Practice asking yourself what positive intent might be behind people's actions or communications. What else could they mean? What positive purpose might they be trying to accomplish with their behavior or their communication? The next time a spouse or friend says something in an attacking manner, rather than defend against the attack, blend with the intent by saying, "I appreciate that you care about me, and I want to clear the air between us." There's a real possibility that the person will stop in his or her tracks and calm down and that real communication will ensue.

Identify Highly Valued Criteria

Criteria are the filters on our point of view, the standards by which we measure ideas and experiences to determine if they are good or bad. They are the means for determining what a thing should be, the benchmarks by which people gauge whether they are "for" or "against" an idea, or "why" people think that a point of view is worth defending. Criteria become especially important when differing ideas or points of view are being discussed. Anytime you identify criteria in a discussion, you generate more flexibility and cooperation.

We facilitated a meeting for a company that was trying to decide the best location for a seminar. One person suggested the company training room. Another person reacted negatively to that, and someone else then suggested a hotel. Another faction started pushing for a resort on the coast. As sides were taken and lines were drawn, the tug-of-war began.

We innocently inquired of the first person, "Why do you think the training room is best?" She replied, "Because it won't cost us anything." *Money* was high on the list of her criteria for a successful seminar.

Then we asked the next person, "Why do you prefer the hotel?" The answer we got was, "If we do the seminar in our own facility, people will be distracted by their responsibilities, and they will keep running back and forth getting and answering their messages. I've seen it happen before. We need a neutral place where everyone can focus on the topic." This person's highly valued criteria included *ability to focus* for a successful seminar.

Then we asked, "Why the resort?" and got this reply: "Well, if we get everyone away to a nice place, we'll be able to relax and bond together as more of a team." *Bonding* and *teamwork* were high on this person's list.

Apparently, these people were not talking just about the seminar. They were also talking about money, focus, relaxation, and teamwork. Once these criteria were exposed, the next step was prioritizing them. Everyone agreed that focus was primary and that there was enough money for a hotel but not for a resort. The group got into a brainstorm about how they could get people to relax and bond as a team within their budget. They finally came up with the idea of having a party the night of the seminar that included loved ones. By identifying and prioritizing criteria, the group was able to satisfy all parties and throw a party at the same time.

Once you've asked questions about criteria and you are reasonably certain that you know what those criteria are, sum it all up for them. "So then, if I understand you correctly, this is why this is important to you. ..." Once again, you will have demonstrated that you listened, cared, and remembered, which blends with the desire to be understood. Make sure the difficult people are satisfied that their criteria have been fully voiced, by asking: "Do you feel understood? Anything else?"

Whenever a discussion starts to degenerate into conflict, try to ascertain the reasons why people are for or against something. Then look for an idea or solution to the problem that blends those criteria together. That's another way to turn conflict into cooperation.

Quick Summary

When Discussions Degenerate into Conflict
   Your Goal: Reach a Deeper Understanding
   ACTION PLAN
   1. Identify positive intent.
   2. Identify highly valued criteria.

7

Speak to Be Understood

So far, we've discussed blending and listening as methods for increasing trust, cooperation, and understanding. Yet, what we say to people can also produce positive effects. The signals, symbols, and suggestions that constitute our communication output provide a profound opportunity to influence relationships for the better. The following keys should help you in this regard.

Monitor Your Tone of Voice

Your tone of voice sends people either a positive or a negative message about your opinion of them as human beings. At the tone, many people think it's time to take something personally, even if it has nothing to do with them at all. Have you ever had a really rotten day at the office, and then you got a call from home? Have you ever had a rotten day at home, and then you got a call from the office? Even when your words are well chosen, if your tone of voice is hurried, defensive, or hostile, people may imagine something very different from what you had intended.

Mixed messages, caused by voice tones that don't match spoken words, can cause big problems in relationships of all kinds. When receiving a mixed message, people will respond to the tone and ignore the words. The irony is that people often try to suppress their emotions to avoid conflict. Their words give voice to the direction they would like things to move, but their emotions leak out through tone of voice. The receiver ignores the words and responds to the tone, and then the sender feels misunderstood, and conflict ensues. If you ever hear yourself giving someone a mixed message, call attention to it and explain what your voice tone is saying: "Sorry if I sound a bit rushed. That's because I am." Or: "I know I sound angry, but that is because this issue is so important to me."

When you acknowledge your tone and clarify what it is saying, you decrease the likelihood that the other person will take offense.

State Your Positive Intent

If effective communication can be likened to the correct dialing of a phone number, then "intent" is the equivalent of the area code. It works best up front. When you assume that someone understands your positive intent, or you imply your intent rather than state it clearly, misunderstanding can result. Maybe that is what the saying "The road to hell is paved with good intentions" is trying to warn us about. To prevent such misunderstandings, learn to begin communication with your positive intent.

Tim and Rosie were seeing a marriage and family counselor on a regular basis, hoping to bring more happiness into their relationship. It was the end of a successful session, and Rosie turned to Tim and said, "Honey, let's go to the Rose Gardens."

But Tim didn't seem at all interested and said, "Nah."

Rosie seemed very disappointed in his answer. The counselor asked her what her intent was in bringing the Rose Gardens up in the first place. She said, "Well, we seemed to be feeling closer than we have in a long time, and we have an hour before we have to pick up the kids. I just thought it would be nice to have some quiet time together."

Suddenly Tim brightened and said, "That's a great idea! But I don't want to be outside. It's too hot and buggy. I know a great little café that just opened up down the road from here! Would that work?"

And Rosie said, "Oh Tim! That's a great idea!"

Notice that going to the Rose Gardens was not really important to Rosie. Rather, spending time together was what really mattered to her, and that was her real intent. Out of an infinite number of possibilities, going to the Rose Gardens was only one way to fulfill her intent.

If you're at all typical, you probably don't tell people your intent when speaking to them. And the irony is that it's probably the most important part of your communication. After all, that's the purpose you are trying to achieve. The trick to communicating intent first is to ask yourself before you speak, "What is my real purpose in saying what I'm about to say? What result am I really aiming for?"

Suppose that you are angry with a loved one, and you have the intent to clear the air so that life together can be fun again. If you begin to talk about how upset you are, you run the risk of your loved one feeling attacked and reacting accordingly. Once you react to this reaction, and your loved one reacts to your reaction, the conversation could turn into a declaration of war! Instead, you might begin by saying, "I care about you and hate to waste time being upset around you. I would like to clear the air, so we can enjoy our time together." Now your loved one knows where you are coming from. In such a receptive environment, communication is far more likely to occur.

Have you ever been in a conversation in which someone is telling you something and you find yourself wondering, "Why is he or she telling me this?" Telling people why you are telling them something before you actually tell them is a simple method for directing attention where you want it to go. If you give people a good reason to listen to you by stating your positive intent, you will communicate more clearly and have less conflict.

We knew a secretary named Doris who had an overly sensitive boss who was mismanaging her time. After keeping a time log to determine if the problem was real or imagined, Doris found she was spending two hours each week making and delivering coffee and an hour and a half each week turning the sprinklers on and off. Meanwhile, her boss would get mad at her for not getting enough done, even though he was the one giving her the other tasks. The first time Doris tried to communicate to him about this, she said:

"Sir, I think you have to take a look at how you are mismanaging my time. You keep giving me low-priority work, and it's keeping me from getting my work done."

To which he replied, "Oh, I am, am I? Well, listen, and listen well because I don't intend to repeat myself. If you find it so difficult to work here, perhaps you ought to start looking for more meaningful employment! Now, get out of my office, stop wasting time, and get back to work!"

Undaunted, Doris studied communication and mastered the art of redirection, and a few weeks later:

"Excuse me, sir. I know you're busy. I'll only take a minute." [Blending: She acknowledges the fact that he's busy and the importance of time]

"I want to be the most productive secretary that you have ever had. [She is now stating her intent. She states the intent of the time log.] To accomplish this goal, I have kept a log of how my time gets spent. The reason I am here is to show you this log, so that you can help me improve my productivity." [Intent behind this meeting]

He decided it was important enough to look at it immediately. He was stunned when he saw how her time was being spent. He apologized to her, and together they worked out the details of a new relationship that made better use of her abilities and freed her from mundane, time-wasting activities.

Speaking your intent first lets people know where you are coming from and prevents many misunderstandings.

Tactfully Interrupt Interruptions

You may find it challenging to believe that the words *tactful* and *interruption* can coexist in the same sentence when talking about difficult people. That's because most intentional interruptions are rude aggressions aimed at overwhelming the voice of another. Yet there are occasions when it is necessary to interrupt a difficult person. If someone is yelling at you or dominating a meeting and not letting anyone else get a word in edgewise, or complaining in endless cycles of increasing negativity, an interruption may be an elegant solution.

A tactful interruption is made without anger, without blame, and without fear. Just say the difficult person's name over, and over, and over again, in a matter-of-fact sort of way, until you get his or her attention: "Mr. Jackson. Mr. Jackson. Excuse me, Mr. Jackson." If you don't know the person's name, use the gender: "Sir. Sir. Sir. Pardon me, sir. Uh, sir? Sir." If you attempt to interrupt aggressive people, they may try to override you by raising the volume of their voice. In such a case, you must persist anyway. These repetitions of name or gender create an irresistible force that so distracts the Tanks, Know-It-Alls, Grenades, or Whiners that they must stop talking to find out what it is you want! Once you have their attention, you can move forward by stating your intent, by clarifying something they were saying, or by using any of the other choices suggested in this chapter.

Tell Your Truth

Honesty can be effective no matter what difficult behavior people engage in *if you tell your truth in a way that builds them up rather than tearing them down.* The more trust you have with people, the more likely it is that you will be heard. So you may want to spend a few weeks, or even months, building up the trust level with blending behaviors before you attempt open and honest conversations with your difficult people. And remember to tell the people *why* you are telling them your truth before you actually *tell* them your truth. State your positive intent and why you think it is in their interest to know. Here are other important keys to open and honest discussions:

- *Use "I" language.* "From my point of view" and "The way I see it" are softening phrases that take the fight out of your words. They tell your difficult people that what you're expressing is *your* truth, rather than claiming to be *the* truth. This makes listening to you more comfortable and less oppressive.

- *Be specific about the problem behavior.* Talk about the problem behaviors rather than about the problem people. Generalizations like "Every time we are at a meeting, you always exaggerate" will not help. Give specific examples instead.

- *Show them how their behavior is self-defeating.* To create self-motivation for change, you have to show them how something important to them is lost because of their behavior.

- *Suggest new behaviors or options.* Make some specific suggestions as to what they can do differently in those situations and what the likely results will be. Perhaps the biggest obstacle to being honest with people is concern about hurting their feelings. But you do not do them a favor by withholding information and allowing them to continue behaviors that don't work for them either.

- *Reinforce behavioral change.* When people make the effort to change their behavior it is critical that you catch them in the act of doing it right. When you see or hear them act in desired or desirable ways, immediately (or as soon as possible) acknowledge and appreciate them. Building on success is one of the best ways to bring out the best in people.

For example, a counselor we know told us this story:

In my first year of practice, I had a patient named Joe whose problem was that, at age 23, he had never been on a date. He was desperate. Joe seemed like a decent guy, lanky in frame, about 5 foot 10, and not bad looking although unkempt in his appearance. I asked him if this was a confidence issue. He said no, he had no problem talking to women or walking up to a stranger to ask her out. When asked to demonstrate, he seemed overly aggressive, awkward, inexperienced, and anxious. The way he dressed also left a lot of room for improvement. The thought crossed my mind to be blunt with him about what he could change in his behavior and appearance, but not wanting to hurt his feelings, I used his first visit just to gather information. He made another appointment.

At the next visit, I again procrastinated being blunt with him, and instead I worked with him on his self-esteem. It soon became apparent that his self-esteem was fine, and I knew that the help he needed required me to give him honest feedback about his appearance and courting behavior. On his third visit to my office, I said, "Joe, I really want to help you with your problem [my intent], and I would like to be honest with you. I am just not sure how to tell you this." He said, "Well, just tell me." I said, "Okay, let's go stand in front of this mirror."

As we looked at him in the mirror, I pointed to his head and said, "Your hair needs to be cut to fit your bone structure, but the way your hair is cut, or not cut, everything is leaning to the left." I said, "Regarding your clothes: Different colors work or don't work for different people depending on complexion. The colors you seem to consistently choose make you look like you have a chronic liver disease. I also bet you dress for comfort." He agreed. "Well," I continued, as I pointed first to the pattern in his shirt, then the pattern in his pants: "I think ['I' language] they need to be a bit less, um, complicated and a bit more stylish. And one last thing about clothing. I believe there are two kinds of pants for men: long and short. You need to make a decision because ankle length just doesn't work." [Being specific about the problem]

"Let me give you Teresa's number. [Suggest new options] Call her. She will cut your hair to fit the shape of your face. She will tell you what colors work best for you, and if you want, you can hire her to take you shopping. She will help you find clothes that are comfortable and in style. Now regarding the way you approach women, …" And I continued to be specific about what probably didn't work and what might work better.

Finally, the visit was over. I had no idea how useful this visit had been for him until it was time to pay. I was charging $40 at that time. He handed me a $100 bill, and as I started to look for change, he said, "Keep the change. Thank you." Oh, and he called me two weeks later with good news: He got a date!

Be Ready to Listen

Whenever you speak to be understood, your communications will inevitably have an influence on your problem people. If they become defensive, be willing to temporarily drop what you are saying and totally focus on their reaction to it. Do your best to fully understand by back-tracking, clarifying, summarizing, and confirming. While this may seem like a long process, it will probably take less time and produce less wear and tear on your thoughts and emotions than an action/reaction type of conversation that produces no worthwhile outcome at all.

Remember, you get what you reward in relationships. When people make an effort to change, acknowledgment of their progress is a reward to them. People turn to appreciation like leaves turn to the sun. So when you see or hear people engaging in different behaviors, make sure you acknowledge them for it. And if they fall back into the old behaviors over time, take the time to offer a gentle reminder of who they are and what they're capable of, based on the better behavior you have observed.

Honesty is almost always the best policy. We're often amazed at how many strategies people employ to deal with each other without first attempting to talk it out. We highly recommend engaging in an honest dialogue with problem people as one of the most effective strategies for bringing out the best in people at their worst.

Quick Summary

When You Communicate with Problem People
   Your Goal: Speak to Be Understood
   ### ACTION PLAN
   1. Monitor your tone of voice.
   2. State your positive intent.
   3. Tactfully interrupt interruptions.
   4. Tell your truth.
   5. Be ready to listen.

8

Get What You Project
and Expect

When people become problem people, the thoughtless negative reactions of people around them tend to provoke and then reinforce more of the same. If you want to have a positive influence, thoughtful responses are required. It is in your interest to assume the best by giving them the benefit of the doubt. It is also in your interest to help them break their associations to negative behaviors and limiting self-concepts and to reinforce their associations to the behaviors you want them to engage in. If you do this habitually, difficult people may come to see you as a valued ally rather than an enemy, and surprisingly they may fulfill your positive expectations.

Pygmalion Power

We heard of an interesting study many years ago in the Chicago school system that shed light on the power of expectations. The researchers conducting the experiment asked a few teachers for their assistance. The teachers were told that they were picked because of their teaching abilities and that gifted children were to be placed in their classes. The experiment was designed, the researchers explained, to find out how gifted children would perform in school if they did not know they were gifted. Neither the children nor the parents would be told of the experiment.

The result: The scholastic performance of the children, as the teachers expected, was exceptional. The teachers told the researchers that working with the children had been a delight, and they expressed the wish that they could work with gifted children *all* the time. Robert Rosenthal and Lenore Jacobson then informed the teachers that the children were not necessarily gifted since they had been chosen at random from all the students in the Chicago school system! Before the teachers could get swelled heads about their own gifts, the researchers informed them that they too were chosen at random.

The researchers called this remarkable performance outcome the *Pygmalion effect* in the classroom. The teachers' high expectations for the students, though never officially expressed, helped the students to believe in themselves and act accordingly. Other studies have similarly revealed that to some degree, people rise or fall to the level of others' expectations.

Perhaps you have experienced the difficulty in overcoming someone's negative opinion of you, where in spite of your best efforts, anything you said or did was distorted into something else. Parents use *Pygmalion Power* whenever they tell their children, "If I've told you once, I've told you a thousand times! You're messy / clumsy / a liar / a slob. You don't care about anyone but yourself!" This mechanism can be utilized, instead, to bring out the best even in people at their worst. Wise parents will find it far more valuable to tell their children, "That's not like you! You care about your appearance. / You know how to take care of your things. / You're a loving and honest person. / You know we love you. / You are capable of doing anything you put your mind to!"

When your difficult people are engaging in their problem behavior, you may be tempted to think or say, "That's the problem with you. You always ..." or "You never ..." To use Pygmalion Power effectively, learn to say, "That's not like you! You're capable of ...," and describe how you want them to be as if they truly are capable of living up to your description. And whenever your difficult people behave in a manner that you would like to see repeated, learn to say, "That's one of the things I like about you. You ...," and describe their positive behavior as a way of reinforcing their identification with it.

Betsy had been married to Sullie for several years. Sullie had a terrible temper. Sullie was one of those people to whom home is where you go when you're tired of being nice to people. As soon as he walked in the door, he would unload all his frustration about work on Betsy.

Betsy honestly asked herself if she wanted to leave the relationship, and she decided she didn't. She resolved then and there to change her own behavior in order to change the situation. That evening, when her husband walked in the door and began his habitual outpouring of anguish, she raised her voice loud enough for him to hear and said, "Sullie, that's not like you!"—even though it was! She continued, "You know we don't deserve this. You're the kind of man who cares about his family, and I know you would never want to upset us intentionally." Her remark caught Sullie by surprise. Not knowing how to respond, he spun around and left the house, coming back home a little later and keeping to himself.

Betsy continued to greet his temper tantrums with these kinds of statements, and after about three weeks, a remarkable thing happened. Sullie walked in the house upset about a day at the office, but before she could say a word to him, he held up his hand to silence her, and he nodded his head: "I know, I know. That's not like me!" He laughed, she laughed, and that was the end of the negative behavior pattern. Her use of Pygmalion Power changed their lives.

We realize that Pygmalion Power is not the easiest thing to use when people are acting like jerks. You may have to spend some time mentally rehearsing it before you're able to talk this way with ease. You may have to force yourself to hope that they have it in them to change, when no evidence of such an ability is apparent. Yet, we have no doubt that you can surprise yourself delightfully with your power to bring out the best in people at their worst.

Assume the Best and Give the Benefit of the Doubt

Joe was an engineer facing a crushing deadline. He had retreated to his office in the hopes of getting some quiet time to concentrate on getting the work done. Yet here was Carl, a fellow engineer, sitting in his guest chair giving him advice about the project. The advice was nothing Joe needed. He just needed to be left alone. If Joe had said, "Look, Carl, I don't have time for this right now," Carl might have left thinking, "Fine! Last time I try to help him out." But instead, Joe said, "Carl, I really appreciate your willingness to help me out on this project, with your time and your ideas." To which Carl proudly replied, "Anything for a pal." Then Joe continued, "What would *really* help me out, at this point, is if I could be alone for a while, so I can focus my attention. Would you do *that* for me?" And of course Carl said, "Sure. No problem."

Assuming the best can have a positive effect on problem people, whether it's true or not. In the last example Carl may not have been trying to help. Maybe he was sitting in Joe's office avoiding something he didn't feel like working on. But when Joe acknowledged the positive intent of Carl trying to help him, Carl was not going to say, "Help you? Nah, you got me all wrong, Joe. I am just sitting here wasting your time while I procrastinate on what I don't feel like doing."

Whenever you tell people they are doing something wrong, they will get defensive. You minimize defensiveness in other people by giving them the benefit of the doubt and assuming the best.

For example: Let's say you have gotten negative feedback from some customers about a particular service rep's behavior. If you just come out and tell the rep about the complaints, your behavior may be perceived as a daily dose of abuse, and the rep may argue with you or try to prove his or her innocence. Or the rep may begin an internal dialogue of self-justification and not hear another word that you say.

On the other hand, if you begin by assuming the best, you can say, "I know you really care about giving great customer service because you care about our customers." It is highly unlikely that the rep will respond, "No, I like to annoy our customers because I could care less." Instead, given the opportunity to identify with a positive intent, the rep is more likely to say, "Of course I do." Then you can state your intent. "And I would like to see you succeed in doing the best job you can do." You have now made it clear that your goal is to help. "To that effect, I have some feedback for you from a few customers that I'd like you to take into consideration in your service efforts."

Appreciate Criticism

If you're one of those people who have a knee-jerk reaction to criticism, particularly when it seems unfair, perhaps you've noticed that defending yourself tends to make things worse. "Methinks thou dost protest too much!" said the Bard. The implication is that your defenses are an admission of guilt, and anything you say may be used against you. So the more you try to explain, the more the criticism seems to stick. Here's a simple short circuit to rapidly bring criticism to a close without internalizing it or fighting against it: Verbally appreciate the criticism as a way of ending it. No defense, no explanation, no justification. A simple "thanks" is all that it takes, and it's over.

At a conference we attended a few years ago, a participant named Marge took offense at a joke told by the speaker, Leo. On a break, Marge charged up to Leo and angrily accused him of being a horrible and vicious human being for telling that joke. Leo tried patiently to explain that he had been asked to tell that joke by the woman who organized the conference. He didn't even know what it meant! Marge refused to listen, characterizing his efforts at explaining himself as an attempt to weasel out of responsibility for his behavior and as proof of his lower-than-a-slug character. Then Leo got a little angry, and he took a stand, demanding that Marge stop name-calling and try listening to him for a change. That didn't work either, and soon they were both shouting at each other. With a finality that didn't ring true, he declared, "Ma'am, I don't really care what you think!" With that, he spun himself around and stormed off, stewing in his own anger about being misunderstood.

Later, after most of the conference attendees had left the room, Leo approached Rick, complaining about Marge's wild accusations and calling her names. With some degree of amusement and dispassion, Rick said, "That was an interesting way of dealing with it."

"Oh really!? And how would you have handled the situation?" demanded Leo. Rick replied, "I would have just said, 'Thanks for being honest with me about how you feel,' and I would have let it go at that." Leo slapped himself on the forehead, then said, "Unbelievable. Now, why didn't I think of that?" Then he walked off muttering about the subtlety of simplicity.

When you verbally appreciate people who are criticizing you, you're letting go of the need to defend, explain, or justify your behavior. You simply hear the other people out, and you thank them for communicating. You don't have to ask any questions about what you're hearing unless you think it might be valuable and want to find out more. If you don't resist it, once critical people have had their say, they're done with it. Say "Thanks for being honest" or "Thanks for taking the time to let me know how you feel" or "Thanks for caring so much." Simple, subtle, and sweet.

We know a young man who, after moving out of his mother's home, didn't speak to her for almost a year. He was furious with her for her bossy attitude and Know-It-All behavior, and he likened the sound of her voice to a chain saw that started up anytime he failed to meet her expectations. But there came a time when he was traveling, and he came down with a respiratory infection while staying in a hotel. Surrounded by strangers, almost delirious with a cough and fever, he found himself thinking of his mother and the excellent care she had provided him whenever he got sick in his childhood. Oh, how he longed for her chicken soup! Without thinking it through, he picked up the phone at his bedside, and he dialed her phone number. She answered the phone.

"Hello?"

After a moment's hesitation, he said, "Mom? [cough, cough]"

"Son, is that you?"

"Yeah, it is. Mom, I miss you. [cough, cough]"

She started up the chain saw. "You do not! If you really missed me, you would have called, or written, or something, instead of leaving me to worry about …," and on she went, pouring out her anguish and despair.

But in his fevered condition, he had no energy to argue with her. All he could do was lay there, coughing and listening. And as he listened, a strange thing happened. For the first time in his life, he could hear what was fueling that chain saw. He could hear that she was willing to drive herself crazy for his sake. All those years of lectures, sermons, and tirades, he realized, were the result of her efforts to be a good mother, and she had done the best she could with what she knew. Love had been her sole motivating force, and he'd never even thanked her for it.

She stopped, as if running out of things to say. In that moment of quiet, he weakly told her, "Mom [cough, cough, sniffle], thanks for loving me. You really do love me, don't you?"

"Why of course I do! Honey, are you okay?"

And for the next 25 minutes, all they had to say to each other was "I love you," and they said it a thousand different ways. Instead of arguing over differences of opinion, defending their points of view, or any of the other futile and frustrating behaviors that had marred their relationship over the years, all that really wanted to be said was "I love you."

The next time someone criticizes you, try this strategy. You may initially find it hard to keep that knee down, but in exchange for some critical appreciation, you'll receive a big peace dividend in the long run.

Quick Summary

When People Are at Their Worst

   Your Goal: Project and Expect the Best

   ACTION PLAN

   1. Use Pygmalion Power.

   2. Give the benefit of the doubt.

   3. Appreciate criticism.

9

How to Change Your Attitude

To be effective with people you can't stand, it is essential that you gain control over your attitude toward the problem people in your life. But how do you find the courage to stand your ground when you want to cry or to step forward in the face of determined opposition? How do you restrain yourself when you want to attack? How can you get an attitude adjustment when you need one, so that your reactions to difficult people are effective and, excuse the term, semiautomatic?

Your ability to be effective with the strategies in the rest of the book is directly proportional to your ability to master your attitude. In each subsequent chapter we will point out what attitudes to take to be successful with that particular difficult behavior. This chapter is about the process of how you change your reactions.

The answer is found in the mechanism that produced your attitude toward your problem people in the first place. Consider for a moment how quickly and automatically you react when the difficult behavior you can't stand begins again. That type of stimulus-response mechanism is triggered in you over and over again each day, and most of the time its effects are benign. You know how a certain song, or picture, or fragrance can transport you to another time earlier in your life. Likewise, negative past events can produce fearful associations and phobic reactions to objects and experiences in the present. There are at least two factors that strengthen these stimulus-response mechanisms, *repetition* and *intensity*. And you can use these factors consciously to change your reactions to people you can't stand!

Changing Your Reactions

The first step is to decide what you want. What attitude will help you get along with your difficult people? Do you want to be calm? Confident? Assertive? Relaxed? Caring? Patient? Determined? A combination of these? Give the resource a description name. If you name it, you can have it.

Now, try to find a time or place in your life where using that attitude comes naturally to you. If you think you lack the needed resource, get it from someone else. Modeling others is a skill you were born with. Remember all those things that your parents said or did that you vowed you would never say or do? Don't you do some of those things anyway? What happened? You modeled those behaviors.

If you know some people who deal well with your problem people, seek them out and ask how they do it: what do they think, how do they view the problem people, and what kinds of things do they say to themselves. Become a resource detective, and find out what the internal state is that allows them to deal with your difficult people so differently from the way you do. Keep asking questions until it makes enough sense to you that you can mentally rehearse what you've found out. Walk through the situation with your difficult people using this new internal state until you've made it your own.

It doesn't matter if the models you choose are people you know, or people you don't know, whether they are movie stars or political figures. Your models don't have to be any more real than characters from books or movies. All that matters is that you think the models have the attitudes or behaviors that you want to learn and use as resources.

Finally, you should make it a habit to positively replay the past and preplay the future in the safety of your mind's eye. The more realistically you imagine responding in a different way and the more times you repeat the internal fantasy, the stronger the association gets.

An elderly patient, Marge, was having problems dealing with her overly aggressive boss. She frequently felt that he was being unfair to her, but she couldn't find it within herself to take any action. So day after day, she listened to his tirades, swallowed her pride, and sometimes cried. As her frustration increased, Marge's health deteriorated. She told us she needed to "be more assertive with her boss."

We asked if there was anywhere in her life she was assertive. She couldn't think of one. So we asked if she knew of anyone who could handle her boss. She said, "Katharine Hepburn! She wouldn't take any guff from my boss!" We then asked Marge to imagine Katharine Hepburn sitting at her desk at the office, as the boss walks in. Not surprisingly, Katharine Hepburn had the right stuff. Marge watched, listened, and learned, and then she walked herself through the same scene as if she were Katharine Hepburn. *She deepened her association by repeatedly imagining herself as Katharine Hepburn dealing with her boss.*

The next week she reported what she termed "a 20 percent improvement." She said she was a little more assertive with her boss, but what really shocked her was that at a restaurant where her meal was not cooked right, she sent it back. She said she had never done that before in her whole life, and then suddenly without even thinking, she had just done it.

Marge made a habit of replaying annoying past events. Anytime she was dissatisfied with an interaction with her boss, she would go back and imagine doing it with the attitude she would have liked to have. One month later she was absolutely delighted. Her boss began to throw one of his tantrums, and with only a moment's hesitation, she told him that she wanted to be treated with respect, that she knew he was capable of it, and she expected it in the future. Then she turned around and walked out. Imagine her boss's surprise!

She told us that what had helped her the most from this little stretch of the imagination was the self-esteem Katharine Hepburn seemed to have. Hepburn had the self-respect to elegantly stand up to Marge's boss! Marge said that after watching this mental movie, her boss looked smaller, somehow. That shift in perception helped her see his ranting and raving in a new light. She realized for the first time how insecure he must be to treat her like that and that it had next to nothing to do with her personally.

Changing Your Perspective

The way you look at a situation will dramatically affect your attitude. Have you ever had a dream in which something is chasing you, and then at some moment in the dream, your perspective shifts and you are no longer running, but instead you are watching yourself running? There are two different perspectives here. One is the experience of watching, of seeing through your own eyes, and that's called *association*. The other, in which you experience yourself from a third-party perspective, is called *dissociation*. You remember memories and experiences this way too. You can be inside the memory, reliving it by seeing through your own eyes and feeling the experience from the inside as if you are there again. Or you can dissociate from the memory, watching it from a distance, while having thoughts and feelings about it.

We recommend that you dissociate yourself from unpleasant memories and start learning from them. There are a number of dissociation techniques that you can use to step away from unpleasant events or difficult people and adjust your point of view:

- You can compare your difficult people problems to more difficult times in your life or imaginary worst-case scenarios. How does dealing with these people compare to losing a leg, a loved one, or your mind completely?

- You can mentally go beyond the problem and project yourself to a future time, when the problem could not possibly matter anymore. We call this the *Alan Kirschner technique*, named after Rick Kirschner's dad, because Alan used this technique repeatedly in order to keep his perspective while Rick was growing up. In challenging times, and even in a crisis, Alan would say to himself, "100 years from now, what difference will it make?"

- You can mentally edit the memory as if you were editing a film. Try this with a memory. Recall your last unpleasant encounter with your most difficult person, and watch it on a movie screen in your mind, from the last row in the theater. Make the memory smaller or further away. Remove the color from the image, and make it black and white and see if that reduces its intensity! Play it backward. Cut and reedit the memory into a new sequence. Trade it with your friends.

- Through rigorous self-discipline, you can develop a part of you that serves as an impartial and dispassionate observer, regardless of circumstance. Right now, see yourself reading this book, noting your feelings and thoughts.

- You can reframe the problem and change the meaning of the experience. Teresa was waiting for a bus in front of a hospital. Suddenly a drunken man staggered up to her, and with beer bottle in hand, he began telling her his story. His daughter had been in a motorcycle accident and had lost her legs. He blamed himself for the accident because he was the one who bought the bike for her. Now, he declared, he was going to drink himself to death. Teresa yelled at him: "Hey! You just be glad your daughter has a head on her shoulders, that she can think and speak, and her two arms still work. And right now she is going to need a father who can be there for her and be strong, not some drunk lying face down in the gutter." Tears came to his eyes. Without saying another word, he kissed her hand, dropped his beer bottle, and ran into the hospital.

- You can compare dealing with your difficult person to something worse. Rick Brinkman's mother, Simone, always kept the book *Mengele* on her bookshelf. This was a book about the infamous Nazi doctor who experimented on twins at Auschwitz. Simone was a twin at Auschwitz and just missed meeting Mengele personally, a chilling thought that helped her keep her perspective in trying times and difficult situations. All she had to do was pull out the book and read a page or two and, just like that, the present circumstances wouldn't seem so bad.

The picture remains the same, but the frame changes. With a new frame, the picture takes on new meaning. Teresa showed the drunken father another way of interpreting the same situation. Realizing his daughter's best interests and recognizing a better way to express his love, the father acted consistently with this new point of view.

Let's try reinterpreting the behavior of difficult people. Every difficult person that crosses your path, when placed in a positive frame of reference, presents you with the golden opportunity to develop your communication skills. The skills you practice with one person who isn't that important to you may be just the skills you need to save a marriage or a relationship that is more dear to you. In this way your difficult person has helped you save it. If you look at it that way, you will immediately feel better.

Changing the Way You Talk to Yourself

Have you ever stopped to listen to the way you talk to yourself with that voice inside your head? Ever said to yourself, "What a jerk! I can't believe this is happening to me!" or "I don't get paid for this kind of abuse!"? How do those thoughts affect your attitude and your behavior? Do those thoughts help or hinder you?

Just as what you think has an effect on what you say, so does what you say to yourself influence what you think. When you change the way you talk to yourself about a problem, you change the way you think about it at the same time. We recommend that you take charge over the things you say to yourself. Become conscious of the things you tell yourself, and substitute positive, supportive thoughts for negative ones. As you listen to your internal dialogue, make sure that your language helps you to get where you want to go.

You must learn to speak purposefully to yourself to change your attitude for the better. You can develop a few quick-draw mental comments that help you to keep your sense of humor and perspective around difficulties. For example, here are some great things to say to yourself, with brief explanations of how they are true:

- *"I go for what I want, and I want what I get."* The branch that bends with the snow lives to see another winter, but the branch that resists the snow breaks. When you resist (struggle with, try to change, limit, inhibit, withdraw from) your difficult people, it's usually you that breaks.

  Don't get us wrong. We are not saying that you shouldn't do something about the situation. But as soon as you accept the situation for what it is, you can begin to access your resources and act constructively to influence difficult people's behavior. It is what it is, it ain't what it ain't, and that's the way it is. Only by accepting the situation can you begin to take aim at a worthwhile outcome.

- *"Somewhere in this experience is an opportunity."* Perhaps every dark cloud has a silver lining. But everyone knows that gold, silver, and diamonds are found in muddy water, dirt, and rocks. You just have to look for them, or at least be willing to see them when they present themselves. Opportunities work the same way.

- *"Any experience I can learn from is a good one."* What you learn from dealing with difficult people will develop your character, make you stronger, and help you in many other areas of your life.

Learning means getting feedback instead of failure out of an experience. When you look at the cause-and-effect relationship between what you did and what you got, you can learn what is working and what is not.

- *"I can be flexible."* If what you are doing isn't working, your behavior comes with an ironclad guarantee: it doesn't work! Anything else you try that doesn't have that guarantee will have a greater chance of succeeding than something that is guaranteed not to work. Experiment! Try novel approaches. Be outrageous. Do the last thing you would ever think to do first!

- *"I know that anything is possible."* They told Tom Edison that electric light wasn't possible, and a lightbulb switched on in his head. They said that if human beings were meant to fly, they would have wings, and now the flight attendant pins them on our kids' jackets. The people who believe that anything is possible are the ones who get the breakthroughs. So think about it: if people can fly and you can turn on a light, then it must be possible to deal with your difficult people. Someone may be doing it successfully right now! If you haven't gotten the result that you want, remember that it's better to hit the light switch than to curse the darkness.

- *"Oh well."* Whether you like the situation or dislike it, your opinion of it won't really change much of anything, except the way that you feel. So instead of making a big deal out of facts that you don't like, you might as well take a deep breath and say "Oh well" and drop your opinion. Let it go, and then go on from there.

- *"All things must pass."* When you are struggling to deal with difficult people, you may sometimes feel like it will never end. But the feeling that this situation will go on forever is naught but an illusion. Just think for a moment about how old you are and about all you've been through. Can you believe how fast all that time went by? This time with your difficult people will also pass. If you look into the future with that knowledge, you may gain perspective and make the whole process easier on yourself.

- *"This used to bother me. That's all behind me now."* Speaking of the past, why not start talking about your reaction to the difficult people as if the situation is already behind you? Whether you're talking to yourself or talking to others, use the past tense, so you can stop being tense in the present.

- *"In God we trust."* According to the ancient proverb, all things work together for good. It is possible that something wonderful is emerging from your present situation and that you haven't seen it yet. Just as the stars hang in the sky and the seasons have their cycle, there is a big picture at work in your life also, and in time all will be revealed. The pain you've been experiencing may be only the breaking of the shell that encloses your understanding. Hang in there. Or let go. In due season, everything will be revealed and resolved.

All the tools we've described in this chapter are available to you whenever you have need of them. You can adjust your reactions and your interpretation of events at any time. Remember, an occasional attitude adjustment frees you from the stress and leads to success as you bring out the best in people at their worst.

Quick Summary

To be more effective with all kinds of difficult behaviors, to prevent yourself from winding up in the danger zone, and to change your attitude when all else fails.

Your Goal: Master Your Attitude and Reactions

ACTION PLAN

1. Change your reactions.

2. Change your perspective.

3. Change the way you talk to yourself.

PART 3

Bringing Out the Best in People at Their Worst

You Learn Specific Skills and Strategies to Deal with Tanks, Snipers, Know-It-Alls, Think-They-Know-It-Alls, Grenades, Yes People, Maybe People, Nothing People, No People, Whiners, Judges, Meddlers, Martyrs, and Your Difficult Self.

10
The Tank

Martin, born and raised in New York City, was in his late thirties. He had a cutting sense of humor and a good dose of street wisdom, which you could see in his clear blue eyes. He had just moved to the West Coast to take a managerial position with a construction company. At work, he was the new guy with no clue. Yes, Martin had heard a few of the stories about his new bosses, Joe Sherman and Larry Panzer, and he had found most of them to be *slightly* unbelievable. But on his second day at work, Martin suddenly felt like he was staring at the business end of a loaded cannon, as his new boss, in no uncertain terms, informed Martin that there was no room for goof-offs and slackers in *his* outfit. Eyes bulging, voice blustering, Joe Sherman warned Martin not to even *think* about wasting time on this job because there were *plenty* of people desperate for work, and there were some who would even *pay* for the chance to work for this company. Martin could feel the eyes of his coworkers taking in the scene, as the Tank blasted away at him. "Who does this guy think he is?" Martin thought to himself, trying to decide whether he was more amused or ticked off about these threats and intimidations.

It wasn't that his new boss had anything personal against Martin. Rather, in classic Tank fashion, Sherman's aggressive verbal attack was motivated by an intense drive to *get things done*. In his view, what had to happen wasn't happening, so he was asserting his control through aggression and a single-minded focus. Martin just happened to be in the line of fire.

When you're under attack by the Tank, you've been targeted as part of the problem. The aggressive behavior is meant to either shove you back on course or eliminate the obstacle that you represent. Since all is fair in love and war, virtually any situation can turn into a battlefield. Whether it's the boss who needs to keep a project on track, an angry customer who needs help from a low-key customer service rep, or even a spouse who is trying to concentrate during interruptions in his or her home office, the Tank is focused on an end result and impatiently pushes ahead.

There is nothing subtle about the direct approach of the Tank. The attack can be a full, frontal assault, loud and forceful, or it can have the quiet intensity and surgical precision of a laser. And while the Tank can rip you apart personally, the irony is that it's nothing personal. The attack is simply a means to an end result. And to the Tank, the end justifies the means.

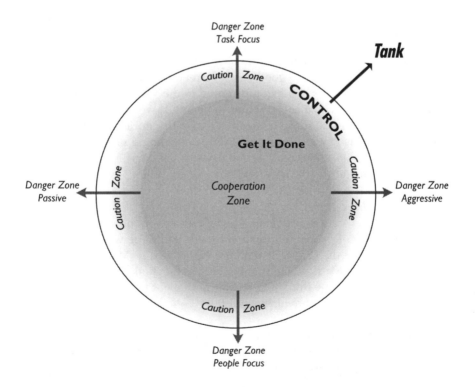

You'd Better Adjust Your Attitude

Watch your emotions because they can be your greatest point of vulnerability. There are three typical emotional responses to an attacking Tank. They're natural, and quite futile:

- *In a burst of anger, you may be tempted to counterattack!* If you are an assertive person, you'd still be well advised to avoid engaging in Patton-versus-Rommel, Tank-to-Tank warfare. While it is true that superior armament and ordnance could win you the battle, you could still lose the war because the Tank might choose to escalate by building an alliance against you.

- *You might attempt to defend, explain, or justify your position.* Unfortunately, the Tank has no interest in hearing your explanations because they change nothing. If anything, your defensive behavior is likely to further antagonize the Tank, who will engage in ever more offensive behavior in response. If you have ever had to listen to someone making excuses when you wanted results or you've had to listen to a customer service rep explain a problem instead of solving it, this should come as no surprise, as you know how infuriating this can be. So if the Tank says you're a genetic mistake, it's futile to offer your mother's prenatal records.

- *You could shut down and become a Nothing Person.* In a wave of fear, you may want to withdraw from the battle, slink off and lick your wounds, or lose yourself in private thoughts of hateful vengeance. Yet you must avoid wimpy, weak, and fearful reactions at all costs. Fear is a sure-fire signal to the Tank that the attack is justified and you are somehow deserving of the pounding the Tank is giving you. Fear may even inspire the Tank to give no quarter and show no mercy.

Any attempt to attack, defend, or withdraw will work against you. Instead, you must restrain these reactive tendencies, find the *courage* to stand your ground, and then step forward in the face of this determined opposition. Assuming that you either have a Tank in your life at this time or you have dealt with one sometime in your past, here are a few suggestions on how you might adjust your attitude.

As you look at the Tank in your mind's eye, try to imagine this character as a wind-up toy that needs to wind down. Or recall a time in your own past when you stood up to a bully. If you know people who know how to handle your Tank, imagine being those people and thinking or feeling whatever it is they feel or think that allows them to be more effective. Identify models of people who have the self-confidence, self-esteem, and self-control to deal calmly and professionally with pushy people. For example, imagine what it would feel like to be Clint Eastwood, saying, "Go ahead. Make my day." Whichever of these methods you use, make it a mental habit to rehearse dealing with your Tank at least a few times, until you feel comfortable with the prospect of using it.

As the final part of your attitude adjustment, consider the part you may have played in the attack. Perhaps you went into too much detail, when a shorter explanation would have sufficed. Maybe your people-oriented conversation seemed off task to the Tank, even distracting and disruptive. You may want to put yourself in the Tank's shoes and look at the situation through his or her eyes. This may give you the best clues for handling and preventing your Tank's attacks once and for all.

Your Goal: Command Respect

Whenever you're being verbally assaulted, attacked, and accused, your goal must be to *command respect* because Tanks simply don't attack people they respect. Aggressive people require assertive responses. Your behavior must send a clear signal that you are strong and capable because anything less is an invitation for further attacks. However, you must send this signal without becoming a Tank yourself. When you stand accused, your character is being tested. The strength of character that you reveal will ultimately determine the Tanks' perception of you and future behavior toward you.

Action Plan

Step 1. Hold Your Ground.   The first step is to stay put and hold your ground, neither running away nor gearing for battle. Do not change your position, whether you happen to be standing, sitting, leaning, or making up your mind. You don't have to go on the offensive or the defensive. Instead, silently look the Tank in the eyes, and shift your attention to your breathing. Breathe slowly and deeply. Intentional breathing is a terrific way to regain your self-control. And while you compose yourself, the Tank has the opportunity to fire off a round unimpeded.

When Martin found himself under attack, he restrained his impulse to counterattack. Instead, he held his ground. He looked into his boss's eyes, kept breathing, and waited for the blasting to stop. When it did, Martin asked, "Is that everything?"

Apparently, that wasn't all. The Tank loaded up another round a of abuse and fired it off. Martin held his temper in check, took a slow breath, and asked evenly, "Anything else?"

"Why, you ..." Sherman loaded up his last round and fired it off. He was now completely out of ammunition, having said every rotten thing he knew how to say. At that point, he just stood there silently glaring at Martin, as if waiting for an answer.

Martin calmly said, "Well, then, I'm going to get back to work now." And he did. He turned around and calmly walked away.

What's the nonverbal message in Martin's communication? I am *focused* on my job, I am *getting* it done, and *you* are a distraction! Now, that isn't something you can say directly to most Tanks on your second day at work, but you can show them because *action speaks louder than words.*

In some situations, drawing the line at Step 1, going no further than self-control, is the best possible course of action. For example, if you're in the armed forces and your commanding officer is blasting away at you, maintaining your self-control can gain hisrespect. As Jim, a captain in the U.S. Navy told us, "Frankly, fellas, if the admiral tells me I am a genetic mistake, the only thing I can say is, 'Yes, sir!'" We agree. In the military power structure, being all that he can be in this type of situation may mean nothing more than making eye contact and breathing through the attack.

The situation you find yourself in when the attack begins can help you determine the most appropriate response. If the Tank is your customer, then the customer is always right. If the Tank is your spouse, you must follow through. If the Tank is an unpredictable stranger, then take no chances, especially if you suspect the Tank is crazy—voting with your feet may be your best bet. If the Tank is your boss, well, do you plan to continue in this line of work? Are there other people present? Timing can be everything. Maybe you will address your boss's attack later in private. Remember, discretion is the better part of valor. Holding your ground, in and of itself, is often enough to command the respect of some Tanks.

However, there may be times when you will want to cross the line, and take the next step in our strategy for dealing with an attacking Tank.

Step 2. Interrupt the Attack. The best way to interrupt people, whether they are yelling or not, is to evenly say their name over and over again until you have their full attention—first name, last name, title, whatever name you use for them in the normal course of your relationship.

In the case of attacking Tanks, it works best to say their name firmly, clearly, and repeatedly, until they stop attacking. Five or six repetitions should be enough to bring the most determined Tank to a halt. Although some Tanks may attempt to override your voice by raising the volume of theirs. Nevertheless, persevere, and continue to repeat their name until they come to a complete stop:

> "Joe, Joe, Joe."
> "Don't you interrupt me! I'm telling you ..."
> "Joe, Joe."
> "I said, don't you ..."
> "Joe, Joe."

Once you've begun this course of action, backing off may be worse than never having done anything at all. There is no need to try overpowering the Tank. Your intent is to speak assertively, not aggressively, and to calmly persevere. Aggressive people actually like assertive people who stand up for themselves, as long as the assertiveness isn't perceived as an attack.

Step 3. Quickly Backtrack Their Main Point. Once you have a Tank's attention, backtrack the main accusation. Backtracking sets a good example of listening with respect, and it conveys that you have heard the Tank. This also saves the Tank from having to repeat anything, and it sets the stage for the next step. But be quick about it. In the words of *Dragnet*'s Sgt. Friday, "Just the facts." Tanks are geared up for action, and they want these situations to be over with as badly as you do. Since Tanks are speaking and thinking at a rapid pace, you can blend by speeding things up.

"You know, I understand that there's no room in this outfit for goofing off or wasting time!"

Step 4. Aim for the Bottom Line and Fire! The bottom line varies according to your situation, but it usually is about two sentences long. The attention span of a Tank is extremely short, so you have to cut to the chase as fast as you can. Preface your bottom line with your ownership of it, by saying, "From my point of view," or "The way I see it." This prevents your shot at the bottom line from restarting the war. What you say after that depends on your situation. For example:

The boss confronts you at the office, demanding to know, "Why isn't that project finished yet? You've worked on it for two weeks, and you're already a month behind!"

You reply: "Boss, I understand that you think the project ought to be finished already. [Blending by backtracking] From my point of view, the time I'm investing in it now will save time and money in the future." [Bottom line]

Or in a completely different case, when under attack, your bottom line may be:

"Mary, Mary, Mary. [Interrupt] I hear that you are having a problem with the way this is being done. [Backtrack] But I am not willing to discuss it, if this is how you are going to talk to me. [Bottom line] When you are ready to speak to me with respect, I will take all the time you want to discuss this." [Redirecting to the future]

In customer service situations, you'll want to clearly establish that you and the customer are actually on the same side:

"I understand that our service hasn't satisfied you. [Backtracking] Your satisfaction is our goal. So that I may help you quickly, I'll need some information, and you can help me to help you by answering a few questions." [Bottom line]

Note that stating "So I may help you quickly" points out that you and the customer are on the same side. Then when you say "by answering a few questions," you are offering the Tank some control over the interaction. Getting results is all that matters to Tank customers. By backtracking, you show you understand they want help, and by redirecting with intent, you show that you are on the same side. In this case, you can also redirect with a question: "Do you mind if I ask you some questions?"

Step 5. Peace with Honor.   Never close the door in the Tank's face. If you do, that action may be taken as a challenge and the Tank will crash through it. When you leave the door open, a Tank has room to back off. When the accusations of Tanks are untrue, their perceptions unrealistic, or their demands unfair, you must redirect to a peaceful solution by offering them the last word, but you decide where and when.

Begin with an assumption and speak with determination in your voice: "When I am through making my presentation" asserts the assumption that you will get through with your presentation. "When you are ready to talk to me with respect" assumes that they will be ready to speak to you with respect.

Now you assign the time and conditions for their last word. For example: "When I am through making my presentation, I will be more than happy to hear your feedback." Or "When you are ready to speak to me with respect, I'll be ready to discuss this matter."

If you're someone operating in a *get along* mode, being so blunt and assertive may look, sound, and feel as threatening to you as a nuclear war. But to Tanks, these behaviors amount to no more than a little give-and-take between people. It gives them a chance to see what you're made of as they take their measure of your character and commitment. Assertive people like assertive people. But don't expect to see them waving a white flag of surrender. More likely, they will fire off a parting shot and move on. You may not win every battle, but you can win more respect. In fact, don't be surprised if your assertiveness wins them over as your ally in some future skirmish with another Tank!

What If the Tank's Accusations Are True and You Are in the Wrong?

All of the preceding suggestions assume that the Tank is wrong about you. But what if the Tank is right on target? What if you were wasting time, money, or energy on unfocused and inappropriate activities? If ever a Tank's accusations about you are true, then a simple three-step strategy will suffice to solve your problem. The fastest way to end the shooting is to take these steps:

Step 1. Admit to your mistake.

Step 2. State briefly what you've learned from your experience.

Step 3. State what you will do differently in the future to prevent it from happening again.

Step 3 is crucial. Many people have successfully done Steps 1 and 2, only to be frustrated by a continued attack. But consider this from a Tank's point of view. If the Tank is concerned that the unfocused activity may happen again in the future, the attack may resume based on the fear of a repeat performance. Your assurance that the lesson is learned is essential to bringing the attack to a halt. But once you've given your assurance, then stop talking about it. Tanks don't require and cannot tolerate sniveling and groveling. It takes courage to admit a mistake and to learn from it. So stand tall, soldier.

Great Moments in Difficult People History

Sherman & Panzer, Inc.
It had been only one year since Martin first took the managerial job with Sherman & Panzer, Inc., and he had already been promoted to second in command. His rapid rise through the ranks could be attributed to two factors: Martin had exceptional people skills, and the company had an unusually high rate of attrition in the ranks of management. The latter could be attributed to the two owners of the company, who were firm believers in management by harassment, or the "seagull system" of management (if something went wrong, the owners would fly in, make a lot of noise, and dump all over everyone!).

In the brief time Martin had been with the company, he had received more than his share of abuse, though of a lesser intensity than in the beginning, but he had noticed there was still enough to go around, and then some. One day, Martin decided he'd had enough and that something had to change, or that he'd change the situation by leaving it. He resolved to cross the mental Maginot Line, defy the bunker mentality, and confront the owners.

He called a meeting with his bosses, Joe Sherman and Larry Panzer. He began by saying, "Productivity is my goal in this job. [Blending with what he believed to be their intent] But we've got a serious morale problem that's affecting productivity." By aiming his remarks at productivity, Martin got their attention.

Larry sneered, "Oh yeah, and what morale problem is that?"

To which Martin replied, "From my point of view, it's you guys! You come on to job sites, fly off the handle without just cause at whoever crosses your path, and demoralize the crew. You hire me to manage these people, but then you curse at me in front of them and circumvent my authority. You fire people at random, and you don't know what you are doing because you fire the good ones and keep the bad ones. It demoralizes the crews. I can't get anybody to do quality work because of it. People are engaging in sabotage and theft to get even with you guys. Now, I know this is your company [Blending by acknowledging their point of view], and you can run it anyway you want. [Blending] You can fire me right now if you don't like what I'm saying. [Blending with what they were then thinking] You want profits [Blending], but you're not getting them.

[Here was the redirect.] "Now if you want to see what is *really* possible around here, I will show you. But you need to back off for a while. Give me two months. You don't show up at job sites unless you are willing to be cordial. If you have a problem with anyone or anything, you come to me first and let me handle it. And when you come to me, you treat me with respect. If you call me up and start cursing, I will hang up on you. Or else I leave today. It's your decision. What do you want to do?" [He gave them the choice, blending with their need for control.]

The two owners looked at each other for a moment, their faces showing shock and surprise, then stood up, waved Martin off, and said, "Okay, okay, two months!" They walked out of the room, and when they were just out of earshot, Joe said to Larry, "Whew, I didn't know that S.O.B. had it in him."

A few weeks later, Joe and Larry called Martin into a meeting and gestured for him to have a seat. He did so, and they stood there looking down at him for several seconds. Then they pulled up chairs of their own, and Joe said confidentially, "Martin, we didn't tell you this when we hired you, but we were thinking about selling this business so we could move to Florida. Now we are thinking about staying in it if, well, how would you like to buy in, become a partner, and run New York when we go to Florida?"

What happened? More often than not, Tanks respect people who speak up for themselves. Martin had shown guts and determination. Joe and Larry knew they could rest easy in Florida if Martin was in charge of New York because he wouldn't take any nonsense from anyone. And without skipping a beat, Martin happily took the deal.

The Gentle Confrontation

It was one of those days in the life of frequent flyers where anything that can go wrong does go wrong. Planes didn't work, replacement parts that were to arrive in 10 minutes came hours later, and the planes had to take a number just to take off. Upon arrival, many of the passengers could not locate their

luggage among the living. A long line formed at the lost-baggage counter—
that place people love to hate.

One guy in the line kept muttering as he waited, with an occasional antag-
onistic comment to the weary passengers in front of and behind him. When it
was finally his turn to go through the lost-luggage claim ticket ritual, he
decided to make the woman at the baggage claim pay personally for the injus-
tice being perpetrated on him by "her" airline.

Maybe she was trained in exceptional customer service, or maybe she was
a natural. But considering the circumstances, she was incredible. She let him
vent, she backtracked, she reassured, she even agreed! But no matter what
she did or how many times she did it, he continued to treat her as if she had
personally and purposely mislabeled his bags.

Finally, with incredible grace and patience, she set her pen down and
looked him right in the eye. He glared back. Then after a long pause she
calmly and sincerely said, "Sir, there are only two people standing at this
counter who could possibly care about the future of your luggage." She
paused, to let that sink in. "And frankly, sir, one of them is rapidly losing
interest." Another long moment of silence followed, and confusion flickered
across the once fiery face. Then, almost magically, the madness melted away
from his countenance.

This suddenly mild mannered gentleman meekly apologized, "Look, uh,
I don't mean to cause any trouble here. Uh, I'm just very disappointed, and
uh well, you understand. Heh-heh, I, uh, I'm sorry I lost my temper. What
do I, what do *we* have to do to get the bags back?" And just like that, he
became her ally instead of making her his enemy.

Let's examine what happened here. When she said, "Sir, there are only two
people standing at this counter who could possibly care about the future of
your luggage," she was blending with the Tank's intent. She lets him know
that she knows what is important to him and at the same time tells him that
this is her intent too. The subtext of her entire communication is that they are
potentially on the same side. Then when she says, "And frankly, sir, one of
them is rapidly losing interest," she aims at the bottom line, showing him that
his behavior is defeating their common purpose. But what really made it work
was the *sincerity* in her tone and in her facial expression. Had there been any
sarcasm, it wouldn't have worked. She was firm but not aggressive, and it
snapped him out of it.

Even though it makes good business sense to remember that the customer
is always right, sometimes you have to have the customer's help if you're
going to be of any help to the customer. Realistically, her job was to gather
information, help the customer, and then help the next customer as well.
After trying other appropriate strategies, she opted for a gentle confrontation,
by reflecting the Tank's inappropriate behavior back in an appropriate way.
Obviously, this lost-luggage lady had found a good internal strategy for letting
go while going forward.

Quick Summary

When Someone Becomes a Tank
   Your Goal: Command Respect
   ACTION PLAN
   1. Hold your ground.
   2. Interrupt the attack.
   3. Quickly backtrack the main point.
   4. Aim for the bottom line and fire!
   5. Peace with honor.

11

The Sniper

Darren and Jay were engineers in a high-tech firm. Darren was five years older than Jay, and he had been with the company three years longer. For that reason, everyone figured that the promotion would go to Darren. But Jay was easy to get along with, he was a hard worker, and he had demonstrated a lot of initiative and creativity. His efforts had finally been noticed by the powers that be and rewarded: Jay was promoted to regional sales manager.

One week after his promotion, Jay parked his car and entered the building. As he headed for his new office, he could see his entire staff gathered around Darren in the hallway. They appeared to be hanging on Darren's every word and laughing excitedly. As Jay drew nearer to the group, their laughter quieted down, until Darren's voice could be heard clearly. "Yeah, that Jay!" Darren was saying. "You ask him what time it is, he tells you how to make a watch! He's got nothing to say, but you have to wait so long to find out!! Ha ha ha ha!" Noticing that his audience was no longer laughing, Darren turned his head in the direction of everyone else's gaze, only to find himself looking at Jay's flustered expression. "Oh, uh, here's the big man himself!"

"What did I do to deserve this?" thought Jay to himself, as he tried to figure out how to respond to being targeted by a Sniper.

There are several motivations for sniping behavior. Some people snipe when they're angry about the way events have turned out, and they are carrying a grudge against the person or people who interfered with their plans. Some people snipe as a way of undermining anyone who might interfere with their plans. And some people snipe just to get some attention from people they like.

Unfriendly Fire

When events don't go as planned or they are obstructed by others, a *get it done* person may try to eliminate the opposition through sniping. To avoid retaliation, a covert operation is called for, so the Sniper hides behind such devious techniques as rude comments, sarcastic humor, biting tones of voice, and the classic roll of the eyes. Snipers can use confusion as a weapon, by making irrelevant remarks that throw people off track and leave them looking foolish. A few well-placed shots and in time, the Sniper is the only one left standing and in control.

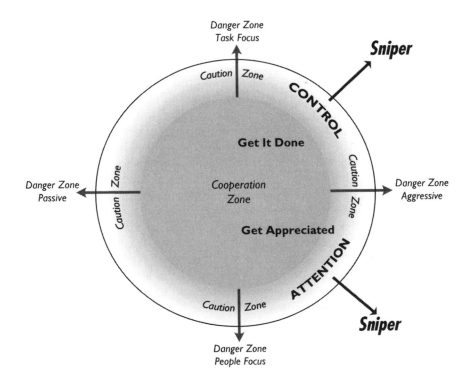

When there is a grudge associated with sniping, "Don't get mad, get even!" becomes the Sniper's modus operandi. Here are a few of the grudges that have inspired Sniper attacks, as reported by people in our seminar audiences:

The chauvinist who didn't like working for a woman supervisor

The elder who didn't want to answer to a young upstart who lacked his experience

The functionary who believed she'd been bypassed on an important project

The girlfriend who was in love with the guy her best friend married

The mother whose advice about whom to marry was ignored

The father whose daughter married someone who wasn't good enough for her

The classmate who was jealous of the new student's successes

In the case of Darren and Jay, Darren was angry about being bypassed for the promotion, and he wrongly blamed Jay.

Friendly Fire

Not all sniping is meant to kill or even wound. There *is* such a thing as the relatively innocent, attention-getting, playful snipe. Sometimes, teasing is an attention-getting strategy motivated by the desire to make people laugh and thus gain appreciation. Good friendships sometimes thrive on the playful rivalry of "put-down humor." In the artificial and ever present world of television, they call this a "situation comedy." Everyone teases everyone else mercilessly, then the studio audience laughs loudly, and it's on to the next scene. But in the real world, not everyone likes sarcasm or has the ability to laugh at a well-aimed put-down. Instead of merely grazing the intended target, a playful snipe can cause a mortal wound. And the playful Sniper might never know that any damage was done because the target of the jibe was smiling on the outside while bleeding on the inside.

You'd Better Adjust Your Attitude

If you don't like to be teased and sniping wounds you, it may become common knowledge that you're an easy target. Once word gets out, a time may come when someone will try to take advantage of your weakness. (Witness the way grade school kids torment each other, and you'll see that the most vulnerable ones take the brunt of the teasing!) And every time you react to the sniping, you'll be setting yourself up, as they gain encouragement to dish out more of the same.

Provoked in this way, you may want to lash out blindly or run away, but in either case the Sniper will extract a victory from your defeat. Or you may tease back, but be warned: if you've never learned how to say obnoxious things in a humorous way to difficult people, your half-hearted attempts at revenge will surely backfire on you. So you might as well face up to it: to get sniping to stop, you're going to have to learn how to live with it because if the Sniper can't get you to react, the behavior loses its value.

The attitude to develop with Snipers is one of *amused curiosity*, so you can put the behavior in perspective. When the Sniper snipes, instead of taking it personally, get curious enough to focus on the Sniper instead of yourself. Since sniping may be a symptom of insecurity, you may find the humor in the behavior by seeing your problem person as an insecure grade schooler. Perhaps you recall the single best response to sarcasm: "I know you are, but what am I?" Or the second best response: "I am rubber, and you are glue, and anything you say bounces off me and sticks to you." Thinking these thoughts can be a great help. Difficult as it may be to believe, saying them can too!

Mary used to have to deal with a coworker named Ron sniping at her in meetings. One day after a snipe she said in a childlike voice: "I know you are, but what am I?" Everyone in the meeting laughed at the exchange except Ron. Mary had lightened things up with honor, discharged her discomfort, and revealed the Sniper's childish behavior for what it was in one easy line. Ron, clearly *not* amused, never sniped at her again.

If sniping really gets to you, learn to become an invincible master of your own responses. Find someone to serve as a model of *cool, calm,* and *collected.* Or mentally change history by reviewing the memory of a time when someone sniped at you, only this time you calmly take out your Sniper with a simple flick of the verbal wrist.

If you are dealing with the innocent Sniper who really doesn't mean anything by it, some reframing is in order. See the remark as a sign of affection or a behavioral quirk. If you can't laugh at it, at least you can learn to laugh it off.

Your Goal: Bring the Sniper Out of Hiding

Your goal when dealing with Snipers is to *bring them out of hiding*. Whatever type of Sniper you face, whether the playful snipe, the controlling snipe, or the grudge snipe, you need to remember only this: Snipers can't snipe if there's nowhere to hide. Since Snipers' limited power is derived from covert, not overt, activity, once you have exposed their position, that position becomes useless. By dealing directly and assertively with Sniper behavior, you take the fun out of it for them, and you even the odds by forcing them out of their hiding place and onto common ground.

Action Plan

Step 1. Stop, Look, Backtrack. Since your goal is to bring Snipers out of hiding, you must first zero in on their hiding place. If, because of something that's said or the way something is said, it seems to you that someone is taking shots at you, *stop!*—even in the middle of a sentence or a word. Interrupt yourself, and bring all your activity to a complete standstill. Scan for the Sniper, and then backtrack whatever they said, all in one smooth move.

There is a great deal of power in interrupting yourself. Whether you're one-on-one or there are witnesses present, self-interruption brings all attention to bear on the Sniper, including the attention of the Sniper. If the snipe is a facial expression that others have seen, you may not be able to backtrack it verbally, but you can do a quick imitation of the facial expression you saw. Chances are, it will get a laugh and relieve some tension on everyone's part. Whenever you follow a Sniper's interruption with a quick backtrack of the offensive remark, that's equivalent to catching a bullet in midair and letting it fall harmlessly to the ground. The nonverbal message is "You missed me."

Jay stopped walking, and he stood there facing Darren in the silence. He scanned the faces of the hallway assembly, then locked eyes with Darren. In a level tone and curious manner, Jay said, "So, I heard you say that I have 'nothing to say, but you have to wait a long time to hear it.'" [Backtracking]

Step 2. Use Searchlight Questions.   Now it's time to turn on the search-light, by asking a question to draw the Sniper out on a limb to expose the behavior. There are two types of searchlight questions that you can ask the Sniper:

- *The intent question:* "When you say that, what are you really trying to say?" You can ask for the true meaning of the communication, and you can possibly expose grievances the Sniper is holding against you.
- *The relevancy question:* "What does that have to do with this?" You can ask for the relevance of the communication to the present situation.

Whichever searchlight you use, the keys to using it well are to keep your tone neutral and to have an innocent look on your face. Don't let any sarcasm creep in. The more calm and professional you are, the more powerful the effect.

Let's examine these two searchlight questions, using the situation in the hallway between Darren and Jay.

If Jay were to ask Darren the intent question, it might go like this:

"When you say that it takes a long time to find out what I have to say, what are you really trying to say, Darren?" [Searchlight question, probing for the grievance]

"Nothing! Just a joke, that's all. What's the matter?" Darren says, trying to get in a second shot. "Can't take a joke?" Darren's face is now strictly business.

"Darren, when you say 'Can't take a joke?,' I'm still wondering, what are you really trying to say?" [Searchlight question, probing for the grievance]

Or Jay could use the other searchlight question, which asks for the relevance of the Sniper's remark. To search for relevance, first state the purpose of the present situation or activity, as you understand it. Then ask for the relevancy of the Sniper's comment to the stated purpose, as in "What does that [what the Sniper said] have to do with this [what you stated as the purpose of the activity]?"

If Jay were to ask Darren the relevancy question, it might go like this:

"Darren, we all have to work together in this division. [Stating purpose] My purpose in this job is to encourage teamwork. [Aligning himself with that purpose] What do your remarks about me have to do with our ability to work together as a team?" [Searchlight question, asking for relevancy]

By using searchlight questions to inquire about the relevancy of a confusing or sarcastic remark, you refocus attention on a worthwhile purpose so that you can get back on track. In fact, you may find out what the relevancy is and in turn be able to resolve the problem.

Whichever searchlight question you choose to use, the Sniper has three response options:

- *Back off.* In that case, get on with what you were doing before the interruption.
- *Keep sniping until the limb the Sniper is out on breaks.* In that case, keep backtracking and questioning. After a couple more failed attempts, the sniping behavior will stop.
- *Drop out of the tree and launch a full-scale frontal Tank attack.*

Step 3. Use the Tank Strategy If Needed. If the Sniper becomes a Tank and starts accusing you of being the cause of this or that problem, no problem. In a sense, you'll have actually improved the situation because now you've found out what the problem is to some degree. But it is important to use the Tank strategy to command respect not only from the Sniper but also from those who witnessed the attack.

Remember to hold your ground, interrupt their interruption, backtrack the main accusation, and in this case aim at your own bottom line before offering them the olive branch at a time and place of your own choosing.

Step 4. Go on a Grievance Patrol. If you suspect that someone is holding a grudge against you, but you're not certain, go on patrol and see what you can scout out. If you find evidence of a grudge, you may want to clear the air. The best place to do this is in private. It sometimes helps to have a neutral third party present but not for the first meeting. To begin the conversation, remind your Sniper of any past negative statements that were made that you are aware of, and find out what the Sniper was really trying to say by asking the intent question.

If the Sniper denies any hidden agenda, try to put yourself in the Sniper's shoes. Mentally review the course of events as you understand them. Once you've come up with an idea, suggest it, and watch for a reaction. If you think of several possibilities, rattle them all off. Preface your guesses by saying, "I don't know what is going on for you" or "I am guessing here, but ..." Once you've guessed correctly, the Sniper is likely to acknowledge what you've said and fill in any details you've overlooked.

If you are successful in bringing the grudge to the surface, it is imperative that you listen carefully to *all* your Sniper has to say. Your goal is to have the Sniper express his or her point of view completely until you understand it. Understanding doesn't mean you agree or disagree or that you have to do anything about it. There is, therefore, no need to defend, explain, justify, or make excuses. Instead, backtrack, clarify, and help the Sniper express the grievance fully, with no resistance on your part, doing your best to see events as the Sniper sees them. Once you fully understand the nature of the grievance, let the Sniper know that you understand, and express your appreciation for the candid description of the problem.

If the grievance is just, acknowledge the validity of the grievance or admit to a mistake. Doing this will enhance your credibility and earn respect. If you have information that you believe would shed light on the situation, this is the point to let it be known. "May I tell you how this happened?" If the answer is no, simply reply, "Fair enough." This is true even with a grievance expressed in a public setting, where anyone curious to hear your side of the story will ask for it, either at the time or later on.

For example, you are at a meeting. The Sniper makes a sarcastic comment. You backtrack and ask the intent question, searching for the grievance. The Sniper tells you, "You are taking too long to tell us too much. We don't need all these details right now, and you've already gone over the time allotted to you. Other people need to speak too, you know." If you determine that the accusation is true, simply say, "You're right. I'll finish this up, and I'll yield the floor to someone else."

If you get into this private meeting and the Sniper won't talk, then the Sniper qualifies as a Nothing Person. You'll find more information on dealing with this difficult person in Chapter 17.

Step 5. Suggest a Civil Future.   Whether in private or in public, finish the interaction by suggesting an alternative behavior for the future. It can be helpful to first unite with the Sniper on a higher intent, that is, the good of the company, the team, and so on. Then say "In the future, if you have a problem with me, come talk to me about it one-on-one. I promise to hear you out."

Until you've made it explicit, the Sniper may not have known that talking with you was even an option. At the end of any encounter or discussion with Snipers, it's important to let them know that your preference in the future is open and honest communication.

Special Situation: Friendly Fire

So what about the Snipers who actually like you and are just playfully teasing you? How do you get them to stop making jokes at your expense? Remember that it is best to call attention to the behavior in private because embarrassing them or humiliating them in public serves no one's long-term interest. Use the honesty strategy to let them know that you don't enjoy or appreciate the put-down humor. Tell them that it isn't fun for you and that whenever it happens, you want to avoid them. Let them know that you would prefer to feel great about them, and then ask for what you want. Though they may not understand how anyone could take offense at something clearly so benign and playful, they probably will change their behavior around you, at least for a couple of weeks. Your goal in that two-week period is to appreciate them every time they make a joke that is *not* a snipe. Since their intent is to *get appreciation*, they just might find that they can get it through your positive reinforcement.

Special Situation: Third-Party Sniping

Occasionally, you hear a report that "so-and-so" said "such-and-such" about you. The question is, who's the Sniper in this scenario? Is it the "so-and-so," or is it the person who's telling you this is so? Sometimes informants are really Snipers in disguise. They frame other people with a comment taken out of context, sharpen it to a point, and then plunge it into your chest with an innocent, "Did you hear what 'so-and-so' said about you?"

If the reason that you're being told about the supposed snipe by this particular informant somehow escapes you, turn on the searchlight. Ask, "Does 'so-and-so' know that you are telling me this?" If the answer is no, then tell the informant that you'll discuss this further only with all parties involved: you, the accused, and the informant. "Let's go talk to 'so-and-so.'" That will end it right then and there, as the informant seeks to get away from the bright searchlight of your questions.

Suppose, however, that your informant is a trusted confidant whom you can count on for reliable information. In that case, drop what you're doing and go directly to the possible Snipers. Tell them what you've heard, and *ask if it's true* because even a reliable source can get it wrong. If the supposed Sniper asks "Who told you that?" remember to protect the identity of your source, and answer the question by restating the original question. "Actually, that's not the question. I'm asking you, did you say this about me?" The strategy with Snipers, whether the snipe is done to you, around you, or behind your back, is to bring them out of hiding by making the behavior of sniping uncomfortable. If the supposed Sniper denies having said anything, let it go because the Sniper's discomfort, rather than a confession, is your goal. Should you hear about it again, repeat the process because Snipers can't snipe if you don't let them hide.

Great Moments in Difficult People History

Let's rejoin Jay and Darren and see how Jay handled his Sniper.

Jay and Darren

"Yeah, that Jay!" said Darren to Jay's coworkers. "You ask him what time it is, he tells you how to make a watch! He's got nothing to say, but you have to wait so long to find out!! Ha ha ha ha!" And then, turning his head in the direction of everyone else's gaze, "Uh oh.†Here's the big man himself!'"

"Hi everyone," said Jay. "Darren, I need your help with something. Can I talk to you in my office for a moment?" Once they got there, Jay didn't mince words. "Darren, it must be very tough for you to have been here as long as you have and to have someone younger and more junior in the organization come in and snatch a promotion from you that you deserved." [Go on a grievance patrol] Then he stopped and looked at Darren, waiting for a response.

Darren sat there tight lipped, brow furrowed, staring at Jay with a smoldering fury in his eyes. Jay continued, "I know it doesn't matter that I didn't ask for or want this promotion. If I were in your position, I guess I'd feel a bit unappreciated by this company." Darren sighed.

Jay went on. "I think you are very capable, and I have learned a lot from you in the time we've worked together. We are here to make a quality product that will in turn make people's lives with computers easier and more productive. To do that successfully we need to be a team. [Uniting on higher intent] I want you on that team, Darren. I think you have a lot to offer. What are we going to do?"

Finally Darren spoke: "Well, you're right about one thing. It's not fair. I have been here so much longer than you. I have put in the effort." Jay just listened silently, nodding and occasionally backtracking as Darren continued. Once Darren has vented his grudge, he seemed to transform back into the rational person Jay had originally known him to be. "But I guess it isn't your fault."

Then Jay spoke: "If there is a problem between us in the future, can I count on you to come to me rather than talk about me?" [Suggest a civil future]

Jay moved the relationship into the future himself when he asked, "Then I can depend on you to be the constructive team member I know you to be?"

"Yeah." Darren said somewhat shyly and then added, "*Mr.* Manager."

Then they both laughed.

The Great Relevancy Challenge

Sue worked for a small manufacturing company in Indiana. She was the only woman in her department, and she was the only woman at the weekly staff meetings. One of the men attending these meetings was a sexist Sniper, who seemed to find great pleasure in irritating and undermining Sue with his provocations. Whenever she tried to call attention to his sometimes cruel, consistently crude remarks, his response was typically, "Hey, don't get all emotional. Can't you take a joke?" The other men would snicker and chuckle, and Sue would become despondent.

One day, Sue decided she needed an attitude adjustment. She came to us with her story, telling us how "They're all against me," and we offered her another point of view. We pointed out to her that the other men in the group might not be laughing at her after all. They might be laughing out of their discomfort because that's what a lot of people do when they don't know what else to do to get beyond an uncomfortable moment. We asked if she had ever laughed nervously. "Yeah," she laughed nervously. "I guess I have."

Next we suggested that she should focus her attention on the Sniper, instead of on the rest of the men in the group. We gave her the Sniper strategy, asked her to mentally rehearse it a few times before trying it out, and sent her on her way. A couple of weeks later, she called in great spirits, and she reported on her progress.

She said that she had neutralized the Sniper with the searchlight for relevancy, and it worked like a charm. After the snipe, she had turned to the Sniper and with calm curiosity said,

"It is my understanding that the purpose of this meeting is to come up with innovations for our quality improvement program. [Stating the purpose of the meeting] My proposal is intended to improve quality. [Aligning herself with that purpose] I am just wondering how your comment [Here she backtracked the sexist remark] contributes to that purpose of improving quality?" [Searchlight relevancy question]

She followed this with her most innocent look. He responded in his typical way: "Hey babe. Don't get all emotional. Can't you take a joke?" But she was ready. With growing curiosity, she backtracked this remark, then asked:

"What does my emotional state and sense of humor have to do with innovations to improve quality?" [Searchlight relevancy question]

No matter what he said, she backtracked and asked for relevancy. In the glare of her searchlight questions, his former allies suddenly started looking at him as if to say, "Who let that jerk in here? We don't know him." His last words? "Forget it." And that was the end of that. Except for later, we suspect, when his former allies teased him mercilessly for the way *she* got the better of *him*!

Quick Summary

When Someone Becomes a Sniper

    Your Goal: Bring the Sniper Out of Hiding

    ACTION PLAN

1. Stop, look, backtrack.

2. Use searchlight questions.

3. Use the Tank strategy if needed.

4. Go on a grievance patrol.

5. Suggest a civil future.

12

The Know-It-All

Young Dr. Bosewell was an intern with an avid interest in clinical nutrition. He pursued this interest in his spare time, of which there was precious little. Such was his dedication to healthcare that it was the rare week that went by when you couldn't find Dr. Bosewell in the medical school library for a least a few hours, searching literature and reading books and articles. Unfortunately, his clinical supervisor was an elderly physician, Dr. Leavitt, who had made up his mind long ago on these matters. He considered nutrition to be little more than the basic food groups and nutritional therapy to be a form of quackery. In the mind of Dr. Leavitt, real medicine came in only two forms, drugs and surgery.

Time and again, during clinic conferences, Dr. Bosewell would try to suggest nutritional therapies. He was fully prepared to present the research to substantiate his suggestions because he believed this was for the betterment of the patients. But Dr. Leavitt, drawing on years of experience and accumulated wisdom, would always cut off the young intern with a commanding voice, and then he would condescend to set the record straight in short order:

"Bosewell! Have you been hanging out in health food stores again? How many times do I have to tell you this? Let's hear no more of this so-called therapeutic nutritional nonsense! As I've said, the treatment is straightforward. Next case."

Know-It-Alls like Dr. Leavitt are knowledgeable and extremely competent people, highly assertive and outspoken in their viewpoints. Their intent is to *get it done* in the way that they have predetermined is best. They therefore can be very controlling, with a low tolerance for correction and contradiction. New ideas or alternative approaches are frequently perceived as challenges to the Know-It-Alls' authority and knowledge, regardless of the merits of the ideas or approaches. When their decisions and opinions are challenged, they rise to the occasion. And when their decisions and opinions are questioned, they question the questioner's motives.

Know-It-Alls believe that to be wrong is to be humiliated. They feel it is their destiny and their duty to dominate, manipulate, and control. They have no qualms about taking your time to talk, but they will waste no time with the inferior ideas of others. As a result, it is quite difficult and next to impossible to get your two cents in.

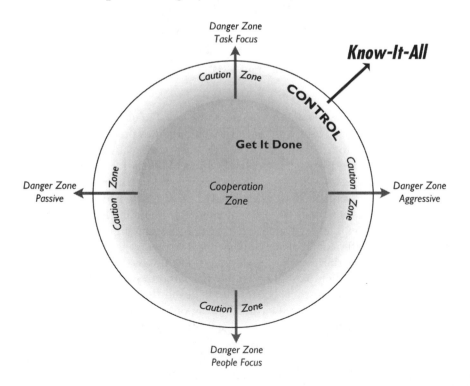

You'd Better Adjust Your Attitude

When confronted by Know-It-Alls, you must overcome the temptation of becoming a Know-It-All yourself. Becoming like them could lead to mental rigidity as well as the musculoskeletal problems that accompany the refusal to bend your neck and yield once in a while.

You also must overcome the temptation to resent Know-It-Alls for their arrogant refusal to get a second opinion. These resentments have a tendency to build up until they blow up into an argument, which is pointless and which you will more than likely lose.

Instead of helping Know-It-Alls to make you miserable, you can retrain yourself to be *flexible, patient,* and very *clever* about how you present your ideas. So, it's your decision. Is it worth it to you to do what it takes to deal effectively with these people you can't stand? If the answer is yes, then reframe your experience by seeing through the eminence front of Know-It-Alls. Realize that these closed-minded difficult people have doomed themselves to struggle with one of the primal forces of life: uncertainty. The most that can be won in this struggle is the booby prize of being right. For, as Marcel Proust once said, "The real voyage of discovery is not in seeking new lands but in seeing with new eyes!" In such a narrow world of their own creation, Know-It-Alls are, no doubt, very unhappy and insecure people inside, no matter how clean the lab jacket or impeccable the résumé.

Next, go into your experi*mental* laboratory, and remember previous experiences with Know-It-Alls. Ask yourself what you could have done differently. Who among the people you know have the resources of patience, flexibility, and cleverness? How would they have handled that situation? When and where in your own life have you had those qualities? Go back, in your mind's eye, to prior encounters with your Know-It-Alls. Replay the incidents several times in a resourceful manner to develop patience and precision. You'll need these resources when you present your ideas and alternative approaches to the Know-It-Alls in a nonthreatening manner.

Your Goal: Open the Know-It-All's Mind to New Ideas

Your goal with Know-It-Alls is to *open their minds to new information and ideas.* A day may come when you have a better idea or the missing piece of the puzzle! When that day comes, and you feel the moral imperative of getting your idea implemented, take aim at the goal and go for it. If Know-It-Alls stand in your way, let your mounting frustration become sheer determination to open their mind to your idea.

Action Plan

Step 1. Be Prepared and Know Your Stuff.   The Know-It-All's defense system monitors incoming information for errors. If there are any flaws in your thinking or if your idea is unclear on any point, the Know-It-All's radar will pick up the shortcoming and use it to discredit your whole idea. Therefore, in order to get the Know-It-All to consider your alternatives and ideas, you must clearly think through your information ahead of time. Since a Know-It-All has little patience for the ideas of others, you will have to know what you want to say and how to say it briefly, clearly, and concisely.

Step 2. Backtrack Respectfully.   Be warned: you will have to do more backtracking with Know-It-Alls than with any other difficult Danger Zone behaviors. They must feel like you have heard and understood the "brilliance" of their point of view before you ever redirect them to your idea. If Know-It-Alls say something and you don't say it back, you run the risk of having to listen to them as they repeat themselves, over and over again, if necessary, until you submit. Obviously, this could be a very frustrating, lengthy, and unpleasant experience. Some call it torture. Whatever you call it, it's better off avoided.

Backtracking is a sure signal to your Know-It-All that you've been listening. However, it's not enough to simply backtrack. Your whole demeanor must be one of respect and sincerity. There cannot be so much as a hint of contradiction, correction, or condescension, or a trace of disagreement. You want to look and sound like you understand that the Know-It-All's point of view is, in fact, the correct one. Patient backtracking can help you to give that impression. If you backtrack too quickly, it can sound insincere, as if you are doing it to lead up to your own point of view. Though Know-It-Alls like to *get it done*, they are usually willing to stop and appreciate their own brilliance when it's reflected back to them.

However, if your Know-It-All seems to be getting impatient with you, then backtrack a little less and move forward. If you hear, "Just get to the point!" complete backtracking and move on to Step 3.

Step 3. Blend with Their Doubts and Desires.   If the Know-It-All really believes in an idea, it is because of specific criteria that make that idea important. If the Know-It-All has doubts about your idea, then those specific criteria, the reasons why or why not, aren't being addressed. You will find it helpful to blend with those criteria, by acknowledging those criteria/reasons before you present your idea. Then show how your idea takes those factors into account.

How can you know the Know-It-All's highly valued criteria? Well, as luck would have it, Know-It-Alls also have a tendency to develop a finite set of dismissal statements that reflect those highly valued criteria. Through time, these statements become extremely predictable to an attentive listener. Regardless of the idea under discussion, your Know-It-All, at some well-chosen point of discussion, may interject a standard dismissal like, "We don't have time" or "We can't afford to make changes at this point." If you suspect that one of these dismissals will be used to undermine the validity of your information, state it before the Know-It-All has a chance to say it to you.

In general you can dovetail your idea with the doubts of Know-It-Alls, by paraphrasing the dismissal statements as a preface to your idea. You can also dovetail with the desires of Know-It-Alls, by showing how your idea meets their criteria:

"Since we can't afford to make unnecessary changes ..."

OR

"Since we have no time for ..."

By backtracking with respect so that they feel like you really understand what they said and by blending with their doubts and desires, you create a gap in their defense system through which you can get their attention and present your information. Since none of your behavior could be construed as an attack, there is nothing for them to defend. You are now at the moment of truth.

Step 4. Present Your Views Indirectly. Proceed quickly but cautiously at this step. You have temporarily disengaged their defense system. The time has come to redirect them to your idea or information. While you redirect, prevent the Know-It-All from raising shields again by remembering these helpful hints:

- Use softening words like *maybe, perhaps, this may be a detour, bear with me a moment, I was just wondering,* and *what do you suppose* to sound hypothetical and indirect, rather than determined and challenging.

- Use plural pronouns like *we* or *us,* rather than singular pronouns like *I* or *you*: "What do you suppose might happen if we ..." or "What might result if we were to ..." Again, this serves as a subtle reminder that you are not the enemy and they are not under attack. It also gives the Know-It-All a bit of ownership over the idea as he or she considers it.

- Use questions instead of statements. When people act like Know-It-Alls, they feel they must know the answers to questions. That means they must consider the question in order to answer it. For example: "Bear with me, but I was wondering, what do you suppose would happen if we were to try [your information and ideas] out in these specific ways?"

- As you ask your question, include how all the Know-It-All's doubts and desires will be handled if he or she acts on your ideas and information.

All of these steps for dealing with Know-It-Alls require extreme patience on your part. You have to think before you speak, you have to backtrack with sincerity, you have to dovetail everything you say with their doubts and desires, and you have to be indirect about new ideas. (And you may have to take your antinausea pills before you do any of it.)

As is true with all difficult people, you must first decide whether or not the end result is worth what it will take to get there. But the good news is that this strategy gets easier to implement as time goes on. It's not that your back gets more flexible. It's just that as you continue to approach Know-It-Alls in this nonthreatening way, you begin to appear on their screen as "friendly." As your ideas get through and those ideas prove to be effective, you develop a track record that gains you respect in their eyes.

Step 5. Establish a Mentoring Relationship. Here is a shortcut to the long-range change that you desire: you can openly acknowledge these knowledgeable problem people as your mentors, in some area of your life that you seek to develop.

Penny, a friend of ours from Ohio, had a stellar track record and résumé. She went to work in a large banking system while quite young, and her goal was to become the youngest executive in the history of that institution. Not surprisingly, Penny had great success in her quest, and in very little time she achieved an executive position. That's when her problems began. She found her every idea, suggestion, and product proposal opposed by a fellow named Dennis, whom she nicknamed "The Menace!" Dennis had been a part of the system, it seems, since its origin. He had been a personal friend of the bank's founder, and his brain contained the collected knowledge and wisdom of every giant that had ever walked the bank's hallowed halls. No sooner would Penny speak up then Dennis would counter, "They tried that 15 years ago, and it was a miserable, expensive failure. No point wasting resources on a failed idea!"

Undaunted—a word that aptly describes Penny's approach to problems—she began looking for her opportunity to change the relationship dynamic. And the opportunity did present itself, in the form of a proposal offered by Dennis at a meeting. Using an astounding number of handouts, charts, tables, and graphs,

Dennis proposed a product that could help the bank profitably weather uncertain times in a struggling industry. And the proposal really was brilliant.

At the end of the meeting, Penny approached Dennis in the hallway, and she asked him for a personal copy of the proposal, telling him that she admired his work and wanted to study the proposal further. Like a farmer gathering in the harvest, Penny sat down with the proposal and a legal pad, and for several days she gleaned as much knowledge, wisdom, and experience from it as she could. Using the proposal as a spring board, she dug deep, tracing ideas back through the history of the bank, examining reference documents, and conducting other research. When she was done, she copied her notes, clipped them to the top of the proposal, and handed the whole stack of it to Dennis in person.

"Incredible," Penny told him. "Remarkable, inspiring, thorough, impeccable," she went on. "I do believe I've learned more from your work on this proposal than any other experience I've had in my time with this bank. Thank you." Penny says that from that day on, the relationship was transformed. When it comes to Dennis, whatever Penny wants, Penny gets.

By letting Know-It-Alls know that you recognize them as experts and that you are willing to learn from them, you become less of a threat. This way, Know-It-Alls spend more time instructing you than obstructing you. It is entirely possible that you will find your way from the "disenfranchised" group into the "generally recognized as safe-to-listen-to" group. Consequently, more of your ideas and information will get heard with much less effort on your part and less resistance on theirs. As your good ideas pan out, you will impress the Know-It-Alls with your wisdom and gain their respect.

Great Moments in Difficult People History

The Case of Young Dr. Bosewell and the Chronic Know-It-All Syndrome

"Laboratory tests indicate that the white blood cell count is elevated, and we are seeing the usual anemia. Liver function tests are abnormal including serum bilirubin, SGOT, SGPT, and serum alkaline phosphate. In theory the treatment is straightforward, though often difficult. Stop drinking. A nutritious diet and perhaps some corticosteroids to control the hepatitis. Any questions?"

Young Dr. Bosewell raises his hand. As Dr. Leavitt peers over his glasses and nods, Bosewell rises to his feet, clears his throat, and begins to speak:

"Dr. Leavitt, sir. If I understand you correctly, the peripheral neuropathy, glossitis, and tender hepatomegaly are all characteristic signs of the start of alcoholic cirrhosis?" [Backtrack with respect]

"Yes," Dr. Leavitt mumbles and affirms with a nod.

"And laboratory tests indicate that the white blood cell count is elevated, liver function tests are abnormal, and we are seeing the usual anemia?" [Backtrack with respect]

"Yes."

"And sir, the nutritious diet you're referring to, I believe the Merck manual recommends 70 grams of protein a day as tolerated by the patient. Is that right, sir?" [Know your stuff]

Dr. Leavitt raises his eyebrows slightly, and with a quick glance around the room at the other students, he says, "Very good, Bosewell. You've done your homework."

Dr. Bosewell clears his throat again and continues, "Thank you, sir. This may be a bit of a detour, sir, but I was reading in the *American Journal of Clinical Nutrition* about some research on the amino acid L-carnitine and its effect on liver function. Now I know your feeling about 'health supplements.' [Blend with doubts] You don't want our patients getting improper treatments. And I certainly remember the story you told us about the patient you saw as an intern, the one who died from treating himself because he didn't want to believe his doctors, and it has always haunted you that maybe you could have done something more." [Blend with doubts]

"But, sir, I am thinking about patient compliance. [Blend with desires] No treatment does any good if the patient doesn't comply. This is a patient who has asked us for information on nutrition. And, well, according to the article in the *American Journal of Clinical Nutrition,* L-carnitine 500 milligrams twice a day may improve liver function. If nothing else, it might improve our rapport with the patient and patient compliance with our treatment. [Blend with desires] I was just wondering what you'd think about our prescribing that for this patient?" [*Note:* By ending with a question, Dr. Bosewell gives Dr. Leavitt control.]

Dr. Leavitt considers what he's heard for a moment. Abruptly, the old man speaks: "Very well. I suppose it could do no harm and may even help. Go ahead. You're in charge of it, Bosewell. Keep close tabs, and report back to us. Who has the next case?"

By backtracking Dr. Leavitt's comments, Dr. Bosewell demonstrated his respect, interest, and attentiveness. He presented his idea as a detour. He dovetailed his idea with Dr. Leavitt's doubts about health supplements in order to prevent a possible objection. He blended his idea with Dr. Leavitt's desires by linking patient compliance to proper treatment. And he redirected in the form of a hypothetical question using the pronoun *our* so that there was no hint of a challenge to Dr. Leavitt's authority.

The long-range change is worthy of comment as well. You see, Know-It-Alls are capable of respecting knowledge in others if you can get them to notice it. As Dr. Bosewell's nutritional therapies panned out, Dr. Leavitt began to respect Dr. Bosewell. By the time young Dr. Bosewell finished his internship at the hospital, Dr. Leavitt was turning to him spontaneously in clinic conference and asking, "Young Dr. Bosewell! Tell the class what the nutritional world holds for this type of patient." Dr. Bosewell told us that Dr. Leavitt's attitude didn't change with anyone else. But rumor has it that Dr. Leavitt was overheard in the faculty lounge bragging, "That young budding Know-It-All reminds me of myself in my med school days!"

The Carpenter's Story

When we were student doctors, we saw a patient named Max whose chief complaint was a stomach ulcer. We couldn't help but inquire in depth as to what was eating him. We also couldn't help noticing the way he carried himself. His every movement was perfectly coordinated with great care. He appeared at all times to be in complete control of himself. We learned that he was a dedicated martial artist and that he had developed himself through this discipline from a very young age.

As his story unfolded, we learned that he earned his livelihood as a carpenter. He worked in a carpentry shop belonging to an elderly Japanese gentleman, Mochizuki, who had trained him in the higher levels of his martial arts discipline. Max had taken the job to honor the request of his teacher. Mochizuki's son, Ishida, also worked in that shop. When Mochizuki wasn't around, Ishida would stand over Max and criticize his work. Sometimes his comments were valid, other times they weren't, but more often than not it was really just a matter of preference. Max was deeply annoyed by this, but Max said and did nothing about it. He didn't want to offend his teacher by complaining about his son.

Instead, Max used the self-discipline he had learned from martial arts to suppress his thoughts and feelings (particularly the thoughts about using Ishida as a practice dummy). As we talked, Max reframed his ulcer as an unconscious mechanism that was forcing him to deal with the discomfort of his work situation. We asked Max if there were some other ways that he could handle the situation, besides suppressing his thoughts and feelings. Max said he could leave, but he didn't want to do that because he learned so much when Mochizuki was around. Another idea was to continue as he had in the past. His stomach actually hurt when he thought about that one. His third option took us all by surprise. Max suddenly saw himself letting Ishida be the expert. He imagined himself thrusting the tools toward Ishida and saying, "Show me." He kind of smiled at that one.

And that, in fact, is what Max ended up doing. Whenever Ishida approached, Max would circumvent the once-inevitable criticism by voluntarily turning it into a learning opportunity. "I want to learn. Show me what you would do." [Turn them into mentors] Ishida had not anticipated this development and was initially taken aback. In time, he was moved by this gesture, and he became less harsh with Max. Though they never became friends, the relationship did become friendlier. Max actually learned some valuable techniques, and Ishida acknowledged the artistry of Max's work. Best of all, Max's ulcer symptoms went away completely.

Quick Summary

When Someone Becomes a Know-It-All

   Your Goal: Open the Person's Mind to New Ideas

   ACTION PLAN

   1. Be prepared and know your stuff.

   2. Backtrack respectfully.

   3. Blend with their doubts and desires.

   4. Present your views indirectly.

   5. Establish a mentoring relationship.

13

The Think-They-Know-It-All

Tony was a "fun-lovin' kinda' guy." He laughed at his own jokes even if no one else did. Wherever there was a party, Tony found it, whether he was invited or not. And whenever someone received an award, there was Tony, claiming it was because of his ideas or suggestions.

To hear Tony tell it, he was the man with a plan, the one in the know, and all you had to do was ask. But in fact Tony didn't wait until he was asked. Instead, he volunteered and interfered, and he drove everyone around him insane, particularly Sally. For her, his overbearing manner was unbearable. She despised his lies, and she rejected his foolish opinions. Time and again, she tried to confront him with his generalizations, distortions, and deletions. Unfortunately, Tony's defenses would go up, he'd dig in his heels, and he'd argue for all he was worth. And the most frustrating part was that others who didn't know better would believe him. After each confrontation, Sally would think to herself, "What is his problem? Why does he have to act like that?"

Like other people who become Think-They-Know-It-Alls, Tony's abrasive behavior results from his desire to get appreciation. When he feels slighted in any way, he is likely to up the stakes and try harder than ever to attract some attention in his direction. Think-They-Know-It-Alls are assertive in their behavior, pushing their way into conversations where they may not be wanted. They have a strong people focus because people are the source of the attention and appreciation they crave.

Think-They-Know-It-Alls do have at least one unique ability: they know how to learn just enough about a subject to sound conversant in it. They also have a particularly bad habit. They are addicted to exaggeration as an attention-getting device. Though you would think they'd know that's exactly how it sounds, they certainly don't think of themselves as liars. They believe what they say, even if they're hearing it for the first time. The more defensive they get, the more they have to repeat themselves. Each time they hear the words that left their mouths come back in through both their ears, they think other people are agreeing with them. In this way, they are able to rapidly build up a consensus of opinion, even though it exists only in their own minds.

At first this misinformation can be fun to listen to and even funny. In times of crisis or change, it becomes annoying at best and dangerous at its worst. After a while, people quit listening. In desperation, Think-They-Know-It-Alls may try even harder to get attention, and this leads to greater isolation and disapproval. Pretty soon, Think-They-Know-It-Alls get nothing from everyone: no attention, no respect, and no encouragement. In fact, people will actually begin to say, "Don't encourage them!" The end result is that even their best efforts and good ideas tend to get dismissed or overlooked. Unfortunately, this causes them to need attention even more, so the Think-They-Know-It-All behavior increases.

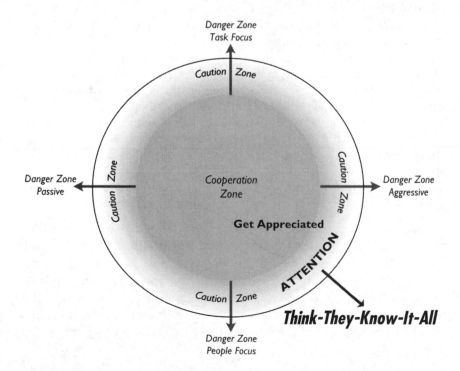

You'd Better Adjust Your Attitude

If you have a low tolerance for people who exaggerate to the point of lying or who traffic in misinformation, there's probably nothing you'd like better than to burst their bubble. But be warned: when you challenge or confront them aggressively, their only way out is to counterattack with grander claims and louder persuasions. Their conviction can sway other people who don't know any better. This in turn can lead to disastrous consequences as Think-They-Know-It-Alls lead people down illusory paths.

Don't be too quick to judge, thinking that you're above this kind of behavior. Haven't you ever defended an idea that you hadn't thought through and didn't necessarily believe in? Maybe you read something somewhere, believed it was true, presented it as if you knew something about it, and found yourself faced with someone more knowledgeable than you, and you just wanted to save face? Have you ever found yourself justifying something you said, that you wish you hadn't said at all, or have you ever exaggerated about something just a little? Whenever you acted like you knew what you were talking about but you were actually uncertain or didn't have a clue, you too were being a Think-They-Know-It-All.

So, no matter how far they stretch the truth, don't give in to the temptation to stretch it in the other direction. If you do, you will lose your credibility, and people will think the same things about you that you think about your Think-They-Know-It-All. You must *restrain* the urge to show Think-They-Know-It-Alls up and, instead, see their interruptions as minor annoyances, to be handled before you can move on. In fact, we recommend using a *go-beyond attitude*. Think, "A hundred years from now, what difference will they make?"

Losing face, appearing the fool, or being labeled a liar is an insecurity shared by many people. When you were growing up, chances are your parents compared you to other children, unfavorably on occasion. Or you may have had the humiliating experience of being picked last in the schoolyard for team play in a given year. We suggest you see the frightened and insecure children within Think-They-Know-It-Alls and have some compassion for these people who must struggle so hard for attention. *Compassion* is one of the attitudes that enhances your ability to deal with them effectively. Life is tough for Think-They-Know-It-Alls because they think they have to maintain a show, and they hide the insecurity they are always feeling. Compassion helps you to give them a face-saving way out instead of wanting to punish them with humiliation.

Another resource that you will need is *patience*. Sometimes Think-They-Know-It-Alls run off at the mouth, holding their audience in rapt attention, and you may have to wait for the right moment before moving things in a different direction. Timing can be important, and good timing requires patience.

Your Goal: Give Their Bad Ideas the Hook

Your goal is to catch them in their act and *give their bad ideas the proverbial hook*, just as bad acts were removed from the stage in Vaudeville days. Only in these cases, you'll want to do so without putting Think-They-Know-It-Alls on the defensive.

Action Plan

Step 1. Give Them a Little Attention.   There are two ways to give a minimum amount of attention to Think-They-Know-It-Alls:

- *Backtrack to their comments with enthusiasm*. Enthusiasm is to Think-They-Know-It-Alls what the spotlight is to entertainers. Backtracking the remarks of these problem people enthusiastically is a surefire signal that you're paying attention to them, while at the same time putting them on the receiving end of their own foolishness.

- *Acknowledge positive intent rather than wasting your time with their content*. For example: You're at a meeting, and a Think-They-Know-It-All starts making ridiculous suggestions and offering useless or regressive information. To acknowledge intent, you can say: "Thanks for wanting to contribute to this discussion."

Notice that you don't have to agree with the content of their communication. Instead, you acknowledge them for the positive intent that you project into their remarks. It is highly unlikely that a Think-They-Know-It-All is going to make an honest confession at this point: "Oh no, that's not what I am trying to do at all. I am a loud-mouthed braggart who just likes attention."

In fact, this positive projection may be enough to end the negative distraction because you are giving them exactly what they want: attention. With the intent satisfied, they may be able to drop back and let others have a moment in the limelight of the discussion.

Step 2. Clarify for Specifics.   If you are certain that they *don't* know what they are talking about and you *do* know what *you're* talking about, then this ought to be easy for you. Ask them some revealing clarification questions for specifics. Since Think-They-Know-It-Alls speak in huge generalizations, you'll want to question the use of universal words like *everybody* with "Who specifically?" and *always* with "When specifically?" and *significant* with "Significant in what way specifically?"

Warning: Be extremely careful with your nonverbals. Asking clarification questions of Think-They-Know-It-Alls can back them into a corner. They may not be able to provide specifics, if they never really had any to begin with. And cornered Think-They-Know-It-Alls can defend by becoming more defensive. So when you ask your questions, look innocent or curious, and resist the temptation to thoroughly embarrass them. Remember that humiliation never works as a long-term strategy.

Step 3. Tell It Like It Is.   Now is a good time to redirect the conversation back to reality. You can tell it like it is from your point of view, and if you remember to use "I" language, you'll be able to keep your remarks as nonthreatening as possible. Preface your facts with "The way I heard it," "What I've read," "I've seen," and so on. To add irrefutable evidence to your spoken word, you can document your information and show it to them as you speak. Even Think-They-Know-It-Alls know that you can't fight printed facts, and they won't try. This is a great time to quote journals, articles, and the like.

Step 4. Give Them a Break.   At this point Think-They-Know-It-Alls are at a moment of truth. It has become obvious that you know what you are talking about and they don't. Resist the temptation to embarrass them. Instead, make them allies by giving them a way out and again minimizing the chance of putting them on the defensive. For example, if you just mentioned an article or showed them a supporting document, you can say, "But maybe you haven't read that article yet?"

Another escape that you can utilize to great effect at this stage of the game is *Junk O'Logic*. Discovered in the 1950s, Junk O'Logic is an advertising principle that says you can give someone any two unrelated ideas and act like they're related, and people on the receiving end of the combined message will make up a connection. Turn on the TV, open a magazine, and look at a billboard, and chances are you'll be seeing an image that has nothing to do with the product. We suggest you take the Think-They-Know-It-All's ideas, hook them together with your information, and then act like they are somehow related. This will confuse Think-They-Know-It-Alls and send them on a transderivational search for meaning from which they may never return, or it will at least keep them occupied long enough to get a meeting back on track.

Here is an example: "Thank you. I'm glad you brought that up! It really does a great job of highlighting …," then change the subject back to the facts. This can confuse the Think-They-Know-It-All just long enough to throw him or her off track, while allowing you to refocus the discussion and get it back on track.

Another way you can use Junk O'Logic to give Think-They-Know-It-Alls an out is to act as if their distortions have reminded you of the facts, and tell them you appreciate them for their efforts: "Thanks for bringing up that subject. You really jogged my memory of those articles."

Think-They-Know-It-Alls wouldn't think of denying any appreciation that comes their way. While they stop to appreciate the appreciation, you just keep going.

The key to all of this is the realization that Think-They-Know-It-Alls are not as attached to their ideas as Know-It-Alls. If you give them a way to go along with you, chances are they will jump on your bandwagon. This strategy has long-range ramifications too. If they constantly see that you know what you are talking about, they will be less inclined to challenge you with others present. In fact, they may try to become your pal because the next best thing to being a winner is to be seen with one. That's where the next step comes in handy.

Step 5. Break the Cycle.   The long-range action step here is first to recognize the negative cycle caused by a Think-They-Know-It-All's behavior and then work to break the cycle. Once these people are perceived as foolish and distracting know-nothings, they will try harder and harder. Then even their best efforts and good ideas tend to get dismissed out of hand or overlooked as flukes, and they don't get the attention they truly deserve. This could cause an unfortunate increase in the negative behavior.

You can break this escalating cycle by doing two things:

- Use the gentle confrontation to tell them the truth about the consequences of their negative behavior.

- Actively look for and notice what these problem people are doing right, and give them credit where credit is due. For some people this is all that is needed and the behavior subsides. For others this educates them in how to properly get recognition, and it may stem the flood of foolishness and turn the tide into more productive channels.

Great Moments in Difficult People History

The Almost Million Dollar Fiasco

Sally was excited about, and at the same time dreading, the upcoming meeting to decide on a new computer system for the company. She was excited because she had put extensive time into her research, and she was certain about the value of purchasing the Bartlett by Pear Computer. She was dreading the meeting because Tony was going to be there, and she knew he could foul things up if she wasn't careful.

When the meeting finally happened, she began making her presentation, and things seemed to be going more smoothly than she could believe. But just as she got her hopes up, Tony butted in.

"Bartlett? We talkin' fruits and vegetables here, or what!? Ha ha! Listen everybody, this decision is a no-brainer! Yer' lookin' at a bona fide computer expert. I've not only done undergraduate work in computers but also overgraduate work too. In fact I have had my own personal computer for, ah oh, about three years now. Yep, there is only one way to go, and that's BMI! The whole world uses 'em, so that proves they must be great! There's so many choices of software and all kinds of virus protection programs and that's important if you are going to be on the interweb. And anyway, if you want to be able to store your input, you have to get a computer that is BMI computable and has lots of K, that is, *if* you want to play in the big leagues of business. It's the only way to go. Everybody knows it."

Sally centered herself. She had mentally rehearsed for this moment, and the moment had arrived.

"Tony," she said, "thanks for wanting us to get the right system for our people. [Acknowledge positive intent] Playing in the big leagues of business is certainly the way to go!" [Backtrack with enthusiasm] Then she innocently asked, "Say, do you happen to recall how many "K" the BMI has?" [Backtrack, then clarify for specifics]

"Well it is, uh, special K." When Tony tried passing it off like this, she simply asked another question.

"Are you aware of the networking and file transfer capabilities between Bartlett and BMI computers?" [Clarify for specifics] He didn't have a good answer for that either. In fact, the answer was so garbled, no one knew quite what he had said as his voice trailed off.

Having reduced Tony's roar to a squeak, Sally then fell back on documentation: "Well, in the latest issues of *PearUser* and *Byte* magazines, I found articles on how easy it is to transfer files with a Bartlett. And as I recall it [Use "I" language to minimize defensiveness], I read that there are over 200,000 viruses for BMIs, which is why there are so many virus programs. The Pear has only had 68 viruses in 30 years and none in the last 10. I read in another article [Documentation] that according to tests run by an independent research firm, it takes a computer illiterate one-tenth of the time to be up and working productively on a Bartlett than it takes on any other system. But maybe you haven't had a chance to read those articles yet?" [Give him a break]

His answer was a resounding, "Well no, but I plan to. That Bartlett sounds like the way to go."

"I agree with you," smiled Sally.

Quick Summary

When People Become Think-They-Know-It-Alls

Your Goal: Give Their Bad Ideas the Hook

ACTION PLAN

1. Give them a little attention.

2. Clarify for specifics.

3. Tell it like it is.

4. Give them a break.

5. Break the cycle.

14

The Grenade

Mark and Margie had been happily married for 6 years. The problem was that they had been married for the last 15 years. And since the first 6 were the happy years, it seemed like they were doomed to suffer if they stayed together. Yet, somewhere inside, each knew that it could be what it was meant to be. So doggedly they stayed together, hoping and praying for a miracle.

Theirs was a common pattern: she blew up and he withdrew. The more she blew up, the more he withdrew. The more he withdrew, the more she blew up. Each felt victimized by the other's behavior.

Mark came home from work tired. All he wanted was a little peace and quiet, a chance to put his feet up, kick back, and let go. But as soon as he walked in the door, Margie hit him with a list of the day's trials and tribulations and demanded that he listen.

"Honey, relax. What good does it do for you to stress yourself out over these trivial concerns? You're making mountains out of molehills!" said Mark innocently.

"Mountains out of molehills? Great! Just great! Do you think I slave around here all day to have you come home and insult me!? Nobody cares how I feel! I might as well *Kaboom!*" Margie exploded!

"Why does she have to act like that?" thought Mark to himself. "What have I done to deserve this?"

When people's efforts to *get appreciation* are thwarted by the indifference of others, they may become Grenades. When the intent is not met, the behavior becomes an inescapable and immediate demand for attention. Blowing up, or losing emotional control, is a last-resort defense strategy against the feeling of unimportance. If the behavior is tolerated through the years, it can become the first line of defense.

Some people hold back their feeling of insignificance for 10 years before blowing up. For others, it is a daily event. Some blow up with strangers, while others save it for their loved ones. But everybody, sooner or later, has a temper tantrum. Almost anything can pull the pin on a Grenade that's ready to go off. It can be a tone of voice, the look on someone's face, something said or unsaid, or some aspect of the situation itself. And if you wait too long to deal with it, it's too late. At that point, anything you say or do will only make the situation worse. Only seconds after the explosion begins, it turns into a chain reaction.

If you, as an adult, have ever lost control of yourself in front of witnesses, we're certain you'll agree that it is humiliating to blow your top and be unable to stop. Grenades hate themselves for their behavior while they're doing it, after they've done it, and whenever they fear they may do it again. This never ending cycle of self-hatred is the timing device that causes the explosion. Often Grenades will leave the scene of the explosion, as soon as they realize what they've done, hoping time will heal the wounds and that the witnesses will forget that it ever happened. Unfortunately, no one ever forgets that it happened. That's why, when the smoke clears, the dust settles, and Grenades return, typically, the cycle immediately begins building up to a critical mass again. Obviously, this is a volatile cycle that can self-perpetuate until the adrenaline supply is thoroughly exhausted. This is a case where an ounce of prevention could be worth more than a pound of cure. It doesn't have to go this far or happen this often. You just have to get involved as soon as you hear the distant thunder.

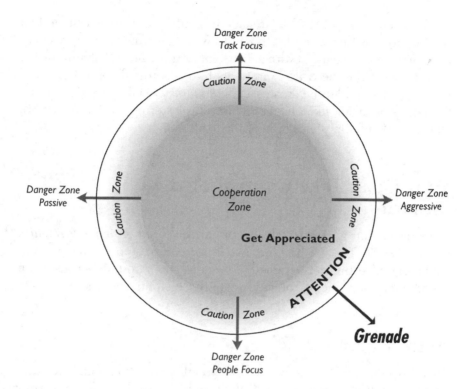

You'd Better Adjust Your Attitude

The two most common reactions to Grenades who explode are (1) to blow up at them for blowing up or (2) to quietly withdraw and hate them from a safe distance. Both reactions are based on disgust and sometimes fear. Hating people who are hating themselves is like offering to pour a little more gas on their already raging fire, when what is needed is some cool thought and fluid action. Instead of saying to yourself, "I don't need this, and I don't deserve this," you can do yourself a favor by forgiving Grenades their moments of temporary insanity. After all, what you fail to forgive, you live. To break the cycle, you must stop blaming them for what they blame themselves for doing.

How does one forgive the almost unforgivable? You just keep breathing in, and with every breath out, release some of those painful reactions. If you're seeing red, let it change to a relaxing blue or green. Or you might try writing an angry letter, venting all your own frustration and disappointment. *Caution: Do not mail this letter. Burn it when you're done writing.*

Then, learn to look at the Grenade in a different way. A woman in a seminar told us that when her boss throws a tantrum, she simply imagines him as a two-year-old with a dirty diaper throwing a tantrum (which isn't that far from the truth) and treats him accordingly. Another seminar participant told us he creates a *funny fantasy* to take the edge off the Grenade's behavior, like imagining himself plastering the Grenade with a cream pie right in the middle of the explosion.

Your Goal: Take Control of the Situation

In essence, your goal is to *take control of the situation when Grenades start to lose it*. Though it is impossible for you to stop Grenades from exploding once the pin is pulled, Grenades can stop themselves given the right circumstances. You can create those circumstances.

Action Plan

Step 1. Get Their Attention.   To get people's attention when they are losing control of themselves, call their name, raise the volume of your voice so you can be heard through the explosion, and wave your hands slowly back and forth in front of you. (This also works, exactly the same way, on the phone.) If you don't know their name, call them by their gender, sir or ma'am, but whatever you call them, raise the volume of your voice until it's loud enough to be heard. You don't want to be misunderstood as being aggressive, so *make sure your tone and language are friendly*. As you do, wave your arms back and forth to attract their attention.

Step 2. Aim for the Heart.   Show your genuine concern for these problem people by saying what they need to hear. By listening closely, you can determine the cause of the explosion, then backtrack while reassuring them of your concern. The first few frustrated statements leading up to it usually have something to do with the present circumstances. Then they quickly diverge into massive generalizations or areas that have nothing to do with the present circumstances.

Take Joe for example: "Nobody cares how long I worked on this! Nobody cares how I feel! That is the problem with the world today!

Neglect! The government, they're all just doing the same thing! The environment is ruined! The crime! Just like my father the ..."

You would respond to this by saying: "Joe, Joe, we care. We care how long you worked on this."

It isn't necessary to discuss world problems, government, the environment, or Joe's father. Speaking to the first few ravings will be enough.

You do have another choice. You can use generic Grenade-interruption statements. You can say: "I don't want you to feel that way! Nobody should have to feel that way. There's a misunderstanding here! Joe! Joe! You don't have to feel this way."

This can work because the Grenade doesn't like feeling that way any more than you do. "Joe, Joe, we care. We care how long you worked on this, Joe! You don't have to feel this way. There's a misunderstanding here!"

In a personal relationship you have another option. You aim at the internal self-hatred by saying: "I love you, I care about you, and it is good to get all that out of your system. Let it out. There is obviously something troubling to you here, and we will deal with it."

The words, admittedly, are simple to say. Backing them up is the hard part. Probably the last thing you want to tell a Grenade is "It's good to get all that out of your system." But the Grenade is usually so far gone that even empty words are better than no words at all. And when you hit the heart, you'll be surprised how quickly the Grenade calms down.

Step 3. Reduce the Intensity. If your aim is true, the Grenade will register the heart-hit by trying to shake off the anger or rapidly blinking his eyes. This is a good sign that you've hit the mark, as it means your problem person is running a systems check to see if anything was damaged before coming back to his senses. When you see this kind of response, you can begin to reduce your voice volume and intensity. You can talk Grenades down from their peak of explosion to a normal level of communication by reducing the intensity in your own communications.

Step 4. Take Time Off for Good Behavior. There is absolutely no point in trying to have a reasonable discussion about the cause of the explosion while a Grenade has adrenaline still coursing hotly through his bloodstream. So this is the time to take time out and to let things cool the rest of the way down. Whether it be 10 minutes, an hour, a day, or a week, time away is necessary to a meaningful follow-up on the episode of temper: "Joe, let's take a break from this. Then we can get back together and work everything out."

Step 5. Prevention: Find the Pin and Don't Pull It.   The fifth action step deals with the long-term relationship, and it is therefore the most important. Find the pin, and don't pull it! If you can find out what pulls the pin on a Grenade, you can act to prevent it from being pulled again. Finding the pin happens at a different time and place from the explosion, when nothing is going on and you're both in the Cooperation Zone. You could simply come right out and ask what makes your Grenade mad. This assumes that you have enough of a relationship with your Grenade to ask.

A good way to start is by stating your intent clearly: "I want to reduce conflict with you." Then inquire as to what made the Grenade so angry that "last time." Use clarifying questions to get specifics. A useful question is, "How did you know when to get angry?" For example, if a Grenade says, "I got mad because no one was listening," do not try to convince the Grenade otherwise. You may know for a fact that people were listening, but based on what the Grenade is saying, it is obvious that the signal that indicates people are listening was not received. Ask the Grenade in a friendly tone, "How would you know if people were listening?"

The response may be, "When people don't just sit there. When they respond!"

You, of course will want to inquire, "What response would they give you when they are listening?" Do not take anything for granted. Be specific. You can even get specific about what you can do to help the situation the next time it gets out of hand:

Laura had a boss who blew up frequently. Most of the time it had nothing to do with her. For a year she felt bad because she didn't know what to do to help him. Everything she said or did seemed to make the explosive episodes intensify. A day arrived when she just came right out and asked him, "How can I support you at those times when you lose your temper?"

He casually said, "Just walk out and ignore me, and do whatever you need to do."

She couldn't believe it! After a year of driving herself crazy trying to help him, the only help he wanted was to be left alone. Proof that it pays to communicate!

You may discover that you aren't the pin puller. If the pin puller is someone else in the office, then one solution is training in team building, interpersonal communication, and conflict resolution. The pin puller may even be at home and the explosion happens at the office.

In this case, helping the problem person to realize the difference and the consequences of failing to understand the difference may prove helpful.

Whatever the cause of the explosion, if you're willing to invest a little time every day in actively listening to the problems the person faces, and if you actively support this individual in talking instead of blowing up, you will slowly but surely have a positive impact, reducing the frequency and intensity of the negative behavior. At the very least, you will be one of the few people around whom the Grenade never loses it again.

Great Moments in Difficult People History

Irant Versus Irave in the Muddle East Partnership

Chet and Dave were business partners in a Chicago creative enterprise. The lifeblood of their business was new ideas. Yet their work sessions resembled a war zone, with Chet being the Grenade and Dave the Tank. Once, in a moment of calm, Dave the Tank asked Chet the Grenade what bothered Chet the most about working with him. Chet replied that Dave seemed closed to new ideas. This really annoyed Dave the Tank, who felt that he was incredibly open to new ideas.

But to Dave's credit, he breathed through his urge to argue, and he asked, "How do you know I am closed to new ideas?" Chet the Grenade explained that whenever he came up with a new idea, all Dave did was find fault with it. Chet the Grenade felt that Dave the Tank was failing to appreciate the value of the idea.

Suddenly, a lightbulb went on in Dave's head. He realized that Chet was in the *get appreciation* mode and that he, Dave, was working in the *get it done* mode. He drifted back through time, revisiting a few instances of conflict. In a blinding flash of the obvious, he realized that when Chet offered an idea, Dave rushed off into the future in his mind to see if it would work, and he came back with a report on how the idea seemed to be flawed. His intent was not to discredit the idea but to make it happen by eliminating the obstacles. The more he liked an idea, the quicker he was to investigate the problems inherent in the idea. Being in the *get it done* mode, Dave had failed to give Chet some simple and deserved acknowledgment. Dave now saw that this was pulling Chet's pin! To someone in the *get it done* mode, nothing is more despicable than a Grenade out of control. So Dave would try to control Chet with Tank behavior, and that's how their work sessions quickly became a battle zone.

Once Dave knew what the problem was, he found a way to solve it. Dave learned to purposely slow himself down whenever Chet offered an idea. He would say, "Thanks, Chet. That's a terrific idea." He learned to wait until his compliment registered before continuing: "Let's figure out the next step to take to make it happen. Are there any obstacles we will have to get past?"

He first blended with Chet's desire for appreciation, and then he clearly communicated his intent to make the idea happen by handling the obstacles. Using his *get it done* know-how, Dave came up with this plan, implemented it, and lo and behold, it worked! That one little change was all that it took to eliminate most of the conflict between them.

The Power of Positive Projections

When Mark and Margie finally decided to seek therapy and hopefully preserve their marriage, they made an appointment with a relationship counselor.

Margie began the session with this angry generalization: "He doesn't love me. When there are problems that need to be dealt with, I deal with them alone." Unfortunately this thought would infuriate her, making her blow-ups even worse.

Mark responded: "She's hysterical and out of control!"

It looked like the battle was about to erupt in the doctor's office, but the Doctor was in: "Margie! Mark! Hold everything. You both have legitimate concerns that deserve to be addressed, and I'm here to make sure that happens."

The counselor pointed out that Mark and Margie needed to reframe the behavior that they each hated in the other. Margie was more sensitive to the problems in the relationship that couldn't be ignored. It is well known that if a couple puts off dealing with its problems too long, they become bigger than they really are. Eventually, such delayed problems have a tendency to become blown out of proportion. Without the explosive warning signals, Mark would never know what happened until he woke up one day and the relationship would be gone. Looked at in this way, Mark could see the advantage of Margie blowing up.

The intent behind Mark's retreat into silence was to protect her from anything hurtful he might say. Mark had a deeply held belief that once hateful words have been spoken, you can never take them back because the damage is already done. He preferred to stay quiet when he was angry, using the quiet time to understand his feelings until he could communicate constructively. Looked at in this way, Margie could see the advantage of Mark's retreats into silence.

As Mark and Margie left the counselor's office, a lot had changed for them. The most significant change was in their understanding of each other's behavior. When Margie blew up, instead of deciding "She is hysterical," Mark could choose to perceive this as an early warning signal, alerting him to issues they must deal with to keep their love alive. His new behavioral response was to lean toward her and say, "Honey, if you feel like this, then there must be something important going on that we need to deal with. I don't want you to feel this way. Let's talk." That is exactly what a Grenade needs to hear, and it really helped Margie to calm herself. In the long run, his new behavior shattered her old belief that he didn't want to deal with their relationship, and that prevented further explosions.

In those times when Mark did withdraw, Margie stopped thinking the infuriating thought "He doesn't love me." Instead, she could tell herself, "He does love me. He doesn't want to hurt me with angry words, and he probably needs time to think this through." That kind of thinking helped her to remain calm, and she would say, "Why don't you take some time to consider this, and we will talk about it tonight."

As she developed confidence that the issue wouldn't be put off forever, she experienced greater satisfaction and calm. Her calm communication pulled him out of his withdrawal, and the discussions became easier, faster, and more fruitful. So Mark and Margie learned to live happily ever after—well, most of the time anyway.

Quick Summary

When Someone Becomes a Grenade

Your Goal: Take Control of the Situation

ACTION PLAN

1. Get the person's attention.

2. Aim for the heart.

3. Reduce the intensity.

4. Take time off for good behavior.

5. Prevention: Find the pin and don't pull it.

15

The Yes Person

During a staff meeting, Ms. Rooklyn, the district sales manager, asked for a volunteer to work with Jamie to coordinate the proposal to be made to Avex in two weeks. As she scanned the room for any takers, she saw Teri, who smiled awkwardly, looked around at the other staff, and volunteered for the job.

They made a lunch appointment to work out the details, but Teri called at the last minute to cancel.

"Listen," Jamie said. "If it's a problem, why don't we just work this out on the phone?"

"That's fine, if that's what you'd like to do!" said Teri obligingly. Teri agreed to pulling together the information needed from the other departments and turning them into a document with graphics, while Jamie would prepare the presentation.

Jamie called Teri one week later. "How's it going?" asked Jamie.

"Oh, fine." replied Teri.

"Have you got the info from accounting?" asked Jamie.

"Um, yes, well, I think I'll be talking with someone about that today or tomorrow."

On the day of the presentation, Jamie was psyched. She bought a new suit for the occasion, and it looked great. Ms. Rooklyn even stopped by her desk with the "old man" to wish her good luck and remind her how important it was to get Avex's business. Jamie kept looking at her watch, and the time seemed to crawl by. Teri was supposed to meet her at one o'clock. That was in 10 minutes. She was surprised that Teri wasn't there already. At 1:03, she began to wonder if maybe she was supposed to go by Teri's office instead of the other way around.

When she got to Teri's office, she found her hunched over the computer typing away. "Hi, Teri? What are you doing? We were supposed to meet five minutes ago. Don't tell me there are some last-minute changes that need to be made?"

Teri looked up. "Oh, Jamie. Hi. I'm so sorry. I forgot the time. Uh, no last-minute changes. This is something that I am working on for Frank in shipping. He is short a person today and asked me if I could help him out. He needs this real soon. Can we wait a few minutes?"

"Frank in shipping!? A few minutes!? Teri, we need to get going or we are going to be late. Where is the proposal?"

Teri rotated her chair to face her desk that was covered with papers at least an inch deep, and she began to shuffle through stuff. "Oh, here is one, ah, and here is another." One by one she pulled out papers, some of them quite mangled.

Jamie's jaw dropped open as she looked at them. "Teri, this looks like rough draft stuff. It is not even in the same font. Where are the graphics?"

"Oh Jamie, I'm so sorry. I didn't get a chance to do them, and Mary's department is undergoing a reorganization, and you know how that can be. I didn't have the heart to put the pressure on them."

Jamie fell into Teri's guest chair. Suddenly she felt sick. They were supposed to leave in five minutes or be late; they weren't ready, and there was no way they would be. Teri was still saying something, but she couldn't really hear it. All she could see were the faces of Ms. Rooklyn and the "old man." She thought, "What am I going to do now?"

By agreeing to coordinate the proposal, Teri had made a promise she knew would be difficult to keep. Her desires to *get along* with the other staff, to please Ms. Rooklyn, and to be helpful overwhelmed any consideration of what the task would actually involve. Like other Yes People, Teri's strong people focus was countered by a poor task focus, which meant she was extremely disorganized in her approach to most tasks. Yes People can easily overcommit themselves as they try to run their life based on the desires of other people. Sometimes they have no clear idea how to follow through on something they've agreed to do because they didn't analyze the task before agreeing to do it. More often

than not, they don't think about the down-the-line consequences of saying one thing and doing another. All they know is that somebody wants
something and they can't just say no. Driven by the desire to fit in and
get along with others, Yes People easily overcommit in order to please.

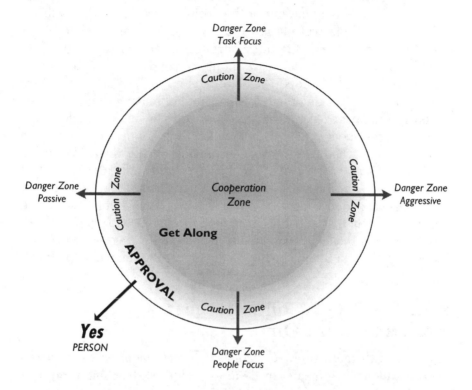

Because they are nice people, Yes People hope it all works out won-
derfully. When it doesn't work out, they honestly feel terrible about it.
Yet they don't feel responsible for not following through because there
is always some set of circumstances beyond their control that has caused
the trouble. Instead, they make excuses and offer explanations, and they
hope that this will somehow make up for their failure to keep promises.

Sometimes, when you are visibly upset with them, they maintain a
pleasant appearance on the outside while slowly simmering in silent
hostility on the inside. Yes People don't want to offend anyone, even
people they are angry with. The *get along* part of them prevents them
from telling you the unpleasant truth. Even if you succeed in extorting
an apology from them and a promise to do better next time, that's no
guarantee that they have any intention of doing what they say.

You'd Better Adjust Your Attitude

When Yes People leave you holding the bag of empty promises, it's easy to feel sabotaged and to want to confront them. Yet blaming Yes People and making them feel shame only perpetuates the behavior. In the moment of interaction and out of the desire to *get along*, they will say whatever they think will placate you, even if it means making more unrealistic commitments. If the confrontation angers them, they are unlikely to express their defensive thoughts aloud, resorting instead to passive-aggressive behaviors. The bottom line: You'll never get people to keep promises by making them feel bad about breaking them.

You may have to reach deep into your heart to find that place that sincerely cares about others. People whose top priority is to *get along* somehow know when your interest is something other than relationship building. You'll also need a lot of patience with Yes People. Recognize that Yes People are simply lacking skill in the area of organization, and they are too disorganized to recognize the deficiency or to do anything to correct it. Remind yourself that you can change the future by helping your Yes People develop their task skills. With patient and caring assistance, Yes People will prove in time to be the best teammates you could hope for.

Your Goal: Get Commitments You Can Count On

Your goal with these problem people is to *get commitments you can count on,* by making it safe for them to be honest, teaching them task management strategies, and strengthening the relationship. As you will see, there is a similar objective for dealing with the Maybe People, who have trouble making decisions, avoid confrontations, shy away from conflicts, and let people down. The difference is that with Yes People, it's fairly easy to get the appearance of a decision. The challenge is to get them to do what they say they will do. Yes People need to learn that, while nice is nice, reliable is twice as nice. Your goal with the Yes People is to get commitments you can count on.

Action Plan

Step 1. Make It Safe to Be Honest.   Make the communication environment a safe one, so that the two of you can honestly examine whether promises being made for the future will be promises kept. Make the conversation comfortable enough that any anger or fear they may have can be discussed calmly, like two friends working out differences with care and consideration. With patience, this could be a one-time, long conversation, or you may require several meetings over an extended period of time. The key to safety is nonverbal blending and verbal reassurance:

Jamie called on Teri a week later. That's how long it took her to get over the anger and frustration she had initially felt when the presentation was cancelled. Jamie believed that it was important to work this out with Teri. Since they were working on the same team, they would have to deal with each other in the future.

"Teri, is this a good time to talk?"

"Um, yes, as good a time as any, I suppose," Teri replied shyly.

Jamie took her time, letting every word sink in. "Teri, I like you. You're friendly, and caring, and I think we can work well together. Ever since the Avex presentation was canceled, I've felt that we need to talk or we're both going to feel terribly uncomfortable around each other."

This kind of people-focused communication revolves around feelings. By approaching Yes People as teammates or friends and speaking to the future of the relationship first, you can increase the comfort level and gently introduce the past into the conversation.

"I'm certain that you did intend to pull together the information for that presentation. [Acknowledge positive intent] And I know that some things unexpected got in the way of that for you. The difficult part for me was that I didn't know what was going on until it was too late to help.

"If our relationship is going to be a dependable one, then I think we need to be honest and open with one another. I want you to know that you can be honest with me. Can I be honest with you?" [Make it safe to be honest] Jamie watched Teri closely, and she waited quietly for Teri's response.

"Well, of course. I'm really sorry about last week, but it wasn't my fault. I don't think you understand."

Jamie nodded in agreement. "You're right. I don't understand, and I would like to. I want to take a closer look at this situation with you and see if we can learn anything from it that will help us in the future."

Realize that every moment you spend with a Yes Person in open conversation is an investment in the future. As the relationship becomes more comfortable, you will be able to find out your Yes Person's true thoughts and feelings sooner. In this way, you can end the sabotage and disappointment, achieve your results, and find relief. Done well, this is a one-time, in-depth conversation about the quality of a promise. Done poorly, you'll have an ongoing struggle. That's why it's important for you to slow down, plan plenty of time for this, and make it count.

Step 2. Talk Honestly.   Yes People may be angry or resentful about something or believe in their excuses, whether justified in your opinion or not. Encourage them to talk it out with you. Hear them out, without contradicting, jumping to conclusions, or taking offense. Then backtrack and clarify. Make sure you acknowledge them for their honesty, and tell them how much you appreciate it.

"Teri, help me to understand what happened last week. What stopped you from having the information ready on time?"
   "I really meant to do it. But I don't think it should have been all my responsibility. There were plenty of other people at that meeting who could have lent a hand. It seems like I'm expected to do everything!"
   Jamie nodded in understanding. "Gosh, that's awful. There certainly were other people at that meeting who could have helped out. Did you feel that way when you volunteered? Did you ask anyone else for help?"
   Teri looked past Jamie and out the window. "Well, not exactly. To begin with, I already had too much going on. And then there were all the unexpected things that came up. Mary's department was undergoing a reorganization, and I didn't have the heart to put the pressure on her. Then there was Frank, one person short and asking for help. How could I say no?"
   Jamie suppressed the urge to confront Teri's excuse making. Instead, she nodded again. "So you really didn't have much free time to do the proposal at all, did you? Why didn't you tell Ms. Rooklyn or me how busy you were?"
   "Well, I didn't want to disappoint you. You know how that is."
   "Teri, it sounds to me like nobody knew what you were going through except you! No wonder you were overwhelmed. Thanks for telling me what it was like. I really appreciate your being honest with me."

   Note that Jamie thanked Teri for being honest instead of rushing to express her own feelings about what Teri actually said. It is always important to acknowledge honest communication with Yes People so you can get more of it in the future.

Step 3. Help Them Learn to Plan.   Once you've listened to your Yes Person's point of view, it will be obvious to you why you can't take "yes" as an answer. This is the time to create a learning opportunity. Since learning to plan comes from experience, this is an opportunity to *change history* with your Yes Person to create a positive experience of keeping a promise in the past:

"You know, Teri, one of the most important parts of being team members and even friends, for me at least, is knowing that my friends can count on me and that I can count on my friends. Just think how it would affect our ability to be friends and work together if something always got in the way of keeping our promises to each other. I want to ask you this: If we could go back three weeks in time to that original staff meeting, what would you do differently?"

Though the answers were obvious to Jamie, they definitely were not obvious to Teri. So Jamie helped Teri to see that she had options that she didn't use. For example, she could have stated at the original meeting that she could be part of a team but couldn't do it all, or she could have called Ms. Rooklyn as soon as she felt overwhelmed and asked for more help, or she could have not volunteered in the first place. If she didn't have the heart to pressure the accounting department because of the reorganization, she could have asked Jamie to do so, rather than putting it off to a later time. There were plenty of options, as soon as the motivation to use them was clear. Reliability and asking for help are both acts of teamwork and friendship.

By using the past experience as a template, you can go back together and approach the task as if it's in the future. What motivation was missing? What could have been done differently? How else could the situation have been handled? Help the Yes People focus in on the specific action steps and processes involved in accomplishing the task. Too quick to please, people whose top priority is to *get along with others* rarely take the time to do this, until someone shows them the importance of it. Make certain to deal with the excuses that they've made in the past about how the phone kept ringing off the hook, how people kept stopping by, how there was too much work in the way that prevented them from getting to it, and so on—all those signs and symptoms of a disorganized people person.

At this point you may be thinking, "Hey, I don't want to have to do their work for them!" And you shouldn't have to. Still, if you are already frustrated from dealing with unkept commitments, you might as well put the energy to good use that you've been investing in feelings of frustration. If you take the time up front to create comfort around honest communication, and then teach your Yes Person some simple task management skills, you won't have to deal with Yes behavior down the line.

Step 4. Ensure Commitment. At the end of the discussion, thank the Yes Person for talking the problem out with you, and ask, "What will you do differently, the next time you've made a promise to me and you are unable to carry it out?" Once you've received your answer, you must follow through and ensure commitment.

Here are five simple ways to ensure commitment and follow-through:

- *Ask for their word of honor.* The simplest of these is to ask Yes People to back the commitment with their word of honor. You look them in the eye and say, "Now do I have your word that you'll do that, no matter what?" When people give their word of honor, that's a deeper level of commitment than saying a simple, "Mmhm, or yes."

- *Ask them to summarize the commitment.* Have Yes People summarize back to you what will be done, while you backtrack and clarify as you let them give you the details. You say something like: "I want to make sure that you and I both understand how this will be done. Could you describe to me what you will do and when?"

- *Get them to write it down.* To help Yes People remember the commitment, get them to commit in writing before walking away. Ask them to write down what they plan to do, post a note by the phone or on the dashboard, give you a copy or put it on the front page of their daily calendar as an affirmative "I will," and then fill in the commitment they are making. Most organized people agree that there is something about the physical act of writing down a commitment that makes it easier to remember and more likely to be acted on.

- *Set weird deadlines.* "So you will have it on my desk by 10:23 a.m. on Wednesday?" Most people round off time. Weird deadlines are unusual, which means that they stand out in the mind.

- *Describe negative consequences.* The fifth way is to point out the possible negative consequences of not keeping the commitment. Your description of these consequences will be most effective if you put them in terms of people and relationships. "Now let's imagine it is Wednesday at 10:23, and this project you've agreed to do isn't done yet. How is everyone who was depending on you going to feel?"

Step 5. Strengthen the Relationship.   Finally, with *get along* people in general, and especially those who have been difficult in the past, look at every interaction as an opportunity to strengthen the relationship. Acknowledge the times when your Yes People are honest with you about doubts and concerns, make an event out of every completed commitment, and be very careful how you deal with a broken promise.

There will still be times when your Yes Person doesn't follow through on a promise. That's because task and time management are skills learned through time and by doing. We recommend that you deal with broken promises carefully. When people make mistakes and you tell them they've done something wrong, they tend to become defensive. Instead, see mistakes and broken promises as opportunities to help them develop their skills further. Correcting people effectively is a powerful means to strengthening the relationship. Here's how to do it:

- Tell them what they did, describing what happened as specifically as possible. Don't give them your opinion, but do give them the facts. Make sure you do this with caring and sincerity: "Teri, you made a commitment to pull together the proposal."

- Tell them how other people were affected, to the best of your ability: "As a result we looked bad in front of an important client. Ms. Rooklyn and the 'old man' were disappointed. They lost confidence in us."

- Tell them how you feel about it: disappointed, angry, frustrated, and so on. Don't exaggerate, but do be honest: "Quite honestly, I'm disappointed and very frustrated over this."

- Project positive intent. Tell them, "That's not like you." Even if it is like them. Rather than denying positive projections, people consistently attempt to fulfill them: "That's not like you to let all those people down. I know you care about doing great work and being part of the team, and I know you're capable of doing what you say. I also know that you don't have to make promises that you can't keep."

- Ask what they learned from the experience or what they would do differently if given the chance to do it again. This is called a *learning moment*, and it changes negative memories into useful experiences: "So, tell me, what would you do differently if you could do it again?" Using this method, you can turn a failure into a success for both of you.

This same strategy can be applied to strengthening a relationship when people *have* successfully done something they promised to do. Normally, when people keep their word, they hear a brief "thank you" and that's the end of it. With Yes People, and with Maybe People, your "thank you" can increase the likelihood that promises will be kept in the future. Here's the same strategy, only applied to a kept promise:

- Tell them what they did right, as specifically as possible. Don't tell them what your opinion of it is, just the facts: "Teri, you promised to pull together the proposal for the presentation, and you did exactly what you promised."

- Tell them how others were affected, to the best of your ability: "As a result, the client decided to do business with us. The 'old man' is as happy as can be, and we made Ms. Rooklyn look very good."

- Tell them how you feel about it—pleased, impressed, grateful: "I am grateful that you took care of this. I'm also impressed with the design of the whole proposal! The graphics were great. You made a whole lot of information easy to absorb. The presentation couldn't have worked out as well as it did without your involvement. Thank you for your caring."

- Project a positive intent. Tell them, "That's one of the things I like about you." You want to build their mental association with keeping their word: "You know, I really like that about you. When you do something, you do it right. That was really terrific!"

- Let them know you are looking forward to more of the same in the future: "It's been a real pleasure getting to work with you on this, and I'm looking forward to more opportunities in the future to team up with you."

By building up your relationship with Yes or Maybe people, you will not only be strengthening your own network of reliable people but you will also have the pleasure of obtaining a lasting reward for yourself. That is, you'll be making a meaningful difference in other people's lives.

Great Moments in Difficult People History

The Case of the Unrealistic Commitments

"I don't know how I will ever get it all done," Kristy said, shoulders slumped. "The Johnson report, the new recommendations." Her spirits seemed to lift, though, as she asked, "So how's Johnny? Did he lose the tooth yet?"

"Yes," Becky replied. "Johnny did, and he looks really cute with that space between his teeth. But Kristy, if you have all that work to get done today, you shouldn't be here with me having lunch. You had better get to it."

"I know, I know," Kristy said, as she scanned the room for familiar faces.

Harry saw her, smiled, and came over. "Hi ladies! Hey, Kristy, can you do me a big favor? I've fallen a little behind on gathering information for the quarterly report. Do you think you could look up the numbers and get 'em back to me by the end of the day?"

"Sure," said Kristy, smiling broadly.

"Thanks. You're a pal. See ya' later."

Becky's mouth hung open. "Kristy, are you kidding!? Do you realize what you committed to just now?"

"What?"

"Well," Becky said, "getting those figures together is not a simple matter of just looking them up. At best this is going to take you two hours! With what you just told me you already have going on today, there is no way you can finish by five!"

Kristy looked down. "Oh, I didn't think of that."

"Well, think of how Harry's going to feel if it doesn't get done—and then there's all the people counting on him. Not to mention all the other people who are already expecting things from you!" [Show the future]

"Well, I guess I could work late."

"What about your family?"

"Oh no. What have I done? What can I do?"

"Well, from now on, when people ask something of you, if you really want to make them happy, train yourself to say, 'Give me a few minutes to check my schedule, and I'll get back to you.' [Help them learn] Then you can make realistic commitments. Everyone likes you, Kristy, and no one in this company wants you to feel overburdened."

"What should I do about Harry?"

"Be honest with him. Good relationships are based on honesty. [Blend with the people focus] He will appreciate knowing *now* when there is still time to do something about it rather than at five when it is too late."

"Okay, I guess I'll talk to him."

"Great. It is 12:49 now. You will be in Harry's office telling him between 12:58 and 1:06, right?" [Ensure commitment]

Kristy laughed, then left. She was honest with Harry, who not only understood but even offered to help her with some of her work.

The Christmas That Almost Wasn't

A real-live dramatization of a fictional incident.

Northpole: With sad eyes, Pinky the elf confided, "Everyone is so depressed! The promised equipment hasn't arrived, and at the rate we're going, we'll be lucky to be ready for next Christmas, let alone this one."

Rachel, the new human supervisor answered, "Has anyone talked to Santa?"

"Oh, sure," Pinky replied. "He says what we want to hear, but nothing happens."

Rachel caught Santa alone in his office. He was his normal jovial self. "Santa, it's been two months since you swore to the elves that you would replace this equipment, and nothing's happened. Now we've got two near injuries a week, and the quality of our work is going to the dogs. I can't believe you didn't keep your promise! Now," Rachel angrily threw the stack of complaints on his desk, "we'll have to suffer another week under these conditions!"

"Now, Rachel, I am going to, uh, replace that equipment. Really I am. It's just that I've been busy, that's all. You'll just have to wait a little longer, but I'll get around to it. Really. Can I get you a cup of tea?"

"Tea!? I don't want tea. I want results!" Rachel stormed out of Santa's office.

That night Rachel's husband told her, "Honey, you can't go in with your guns blazing like that. You probably scared him half to death. Why don't you go in there and give him a chance to explain. Make it safe for him to be honest. Maybe there's more going on than meets the eye?" Rachel could hear that her husband might be on to something. And she couldn't help but notice how easy it was to talk to him because he was so calm and patient with her. Maybe that was just what this situation called for.

The following day, there was a knock at Santa's door. "Ho ho ho! Come on in, it's open!" said Santa, his back to the door, as he fiddled with pictures of children on his wall.

"Santa, I, we need to talk. I'm not going to yell this time, I promise. If I'm going to work for you, I want you to have confidence in me, and I want to have confidence in you. We need to have a heart-to-heart and clear the air. I want to listen. [Make it safe to be honest] So, if you have something to tell me, now's the time. Santa, do you remember promising me that you would replace that broken-down equipment out there on the plant floor?"

"Yes, and as I've told you, I'm going to."

"Santa, tell me the truth. What stopped you from replacing it already?"

"Well, uh, it's on backorder?"

"With whom? When did you place the order?" [Clarify for specifics] Rachel asked with calm determination.

"Well, actually, I haven't exactly placed the order yet. I'm waiting for some money to come in, any day now! And then we'll take care of the problem. I promise."

"So you're telling me that the reason you haven't replaced the equipment is that there's not enough money?" [Backtrack]

Santa sighed, "Yes."

"Why didn't you tell me that when I first approached you about this two months ago?"

"Well, I didn't want to trouble you with it. I didn't think it was a good idea to worry you."

"Santa, I appreciate that. Really I do. That was very considerate of you. [Acknowledge honesty] But working on that outdated equipment worries the elves. Even worse, when you promise something and don't deliver, it demoralizes them. Now, let's have the whole story."

Santa poured out his tale of woe. The factory was in the red, and orders were down. New electronic toys had eaten up their market share. Product was being returned at a rate unequaled in the history of Santa's workshop. It looked like it was only a matter of time before the whole business fell apart. And if it did, the kids wouldn't have a real Christmas, not to mention what would happen to all those loyal elves. And the reindeer! They could be turned into sausage! Santa just didn't have the heart to tell everybody they could be put out of work. Government unemployment compensation did not extend to mythical creatures. He cared so much, and he didn't know what to do.

"Santa, thanks for leveling with me. I appreciate your honesty. [Strengthen the relationship by appreciating honesty] Even if it *is* a little late. But it's not too late to do something about this situation. I need to know, starting right now, can I count on you to keep me informed about everything that's going on in a timely fashion, from here on out?" [Ensure commitment]

"Rachel," Santa sobbed, "I'm so sorry. Of course you can count on me. But what can we do to save this year's Christmas?"

"First of all, you're going to have to do what you should have done when these problems began. You're going to march out of this office and out on to the floor, where you're going to speak to the elves and tell them the truth. Ask each elf to make a commitment to action in quality improvement and innovation. In a dynamic organization, all workers offer their employer a minimum of 24 continuous improvement suggestions each year. What has the average elf been giving?"

"Ahh, I don't know," replied Santa as he stroked his beard.

"I'll give you a hint. It's a lot less. In order to change that, we have to destroy the bureaucracy around here and give everyone the authority and accountability to make changes. You need to empower everyone."

Santa did just what Rachel said. He marched somberly out of office and onto the factory floor, and he gathered his loyal crew around him. As Santa talked from his heart, the elves and reindeer listened. They heard his sincerity and the depth of his caring. Working together now, they reorganized the workshop into powerful small elf-managed teams and quality circles. They brought in trainers who taught them the principles of Total Quality Management. In one year they had increased their quality by a factor of 10, won the Malcolm Baldrige award, and tripled their market share, and they had become so strong they succeeded in a hostile takeover of Nintendo.

The lesson was learned: *When dealing with Yes People, do not take yes for an answer. Be friendly, make it safe for people to be honest, and find out what is really going on.* The team that pulls together, sleighs together.

Quick Summary

When Someone Becomes a Yes Person

> *Your Goal: Get Commitments You Can Honestly Count On*

ACTION PLAN

1. Make it safe to be honest.

2. Talk honestly.

3. Help the person learn to plan.

4. Ensure commitment.

5. Strengthen the relationship.

16
The Maybe Person

The deadline was rapidly approaching. A decision had to be made, and it had to be made fast. There had never been this many marketing plans to choose from before, and it seemed that everyone who had thought of an idea had a vested interest. The pressure was incredible. The chief called in his staff of advisors. "What's the word out there, Ted?" he asked.

"Hard to say, chief. Some say make the change, some say stay the course."

"And what do you say?"

"Whichever way you want to go."

"That's all well and good, but I need your advice as well as your support."

"Well, sir, it's hard to say at this time. It could go either way."

"I know that. I'm asking for your opinion. Bill, where do you stand on this issue?"

"Uh, let me think about it and get back to you later, sir."

"I need a decision now. Mary, do you think the new plan will work?"

"Maybe."

The chief threw up his hands and muttered dejectedly: "Thanks. That'll be all." As they filed out of the room, he shook his head. "Am I the only one I can count on around here for an honest opinion?"

Decisive people know that every decision has an upside and a downside. They develop the habit of making their best decision based on available information and then dealing with any negative outcomes as they occur. When people become Maybe People, however, they can't see their way clear to the best decision because the downside of each option blinds them. They have numerous reasons for not seeking help in making decisions, from not wanting to bother anyone to not wanting to upset anyone to not wanting to be the cause of anything going wrong. So they procrastinate and put it off, hoping an even better choice will present itself. Unfortunately, with most decisions there comes a point when it is too late to decide and the decision makes itself.

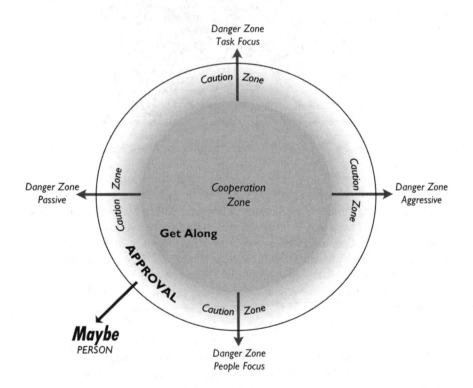

You'd Better Adjust Your Attitude

Irritation with indecisive people is completely understandable and completely ineffective. Impatience with procrastination creates static, and static makes a tough decision even tougher. Anger puts the kiss of death on the decision-making process. If you try to push Maybe People into a decision, they will push against your efforts with more doubts. If you try to drag Maybe People into a decision, they will pull back from it by stalling. So when you're angry or impatient, you had better deal with those feelings before you deal with your difficult people.

You'll need personal *warmth, sensitivity* to the feelings of others, *patience*, and the *desire to help*. Warmth is necessary because it helps Maybe People to trust you enough to relax and think clearly. Sensitivity is necessary because without that, you could lose trust in an instant and send Maybe People tumbling into deeper levels of doubt about having told you anything. Patience is needed because this information extraction takes time and a willingness to allow the process to unfold at their pace. And the desire to help is essential because you're going to have to teach this person a decision-making strategy.

Your Goal: Help Them Learn to Think Decisively

The real problem facing Maybe People is a simple one: they don't have a systematic method for choosing between imperfect choices. Your goal, therefore, is to *give them a strategy for decision making and the motivation to use it.* Perhaps you've heard the proverb, "Give people a fish and they eat for a day, but teach them to fish and they eat for a lifetime." Well, it is also true that "you can lead people to water, but you can't make them fish." So, you are going to create a communication environment within which Maybe People want to stop procrastinating and learn how to make reasonably good decisions.

Action Plan

Step 1. Establish and Maintain a Comfort Zone.   Have you ever told a salesperson that you were going to "think about it," even though you knew you weren't going to buy "it"? Why did you do that? Because the *get along* part of you didn't want to deal with the discomfort of telling the truth?

There's no doubt about it: nebulous fears and negative feelings interfere with clear thinking. Remember that when you are dealing with people in the *get along* quadrant, intensity drives them deeper into the wishy-washy behavior. Even if you could intimidate Maybe People into making a decision, they would probably change their mind as soon as they were pressured by someone with a different agenda. To help them think clearly, you must develop a comfort zone around the prospect of making the decision. Instead of pushing them too hard to make a decision, you're going to take your time and be as considerate as you can possibly be.

Address your first remarks to the importance of a dependable relationship with them, and reassure them that you believe relationships improve with open communication. Since Maybe behavior happens when people are in a *get along* mode, even your boss will respond to sincerity. For example:

"I know that if you haven't made a decision yet, there must be a good reason. If you're concerned about my feelings or opinion, relax. I assure you, your willingness to be honest with me is more important than anything else."

If you think it's prudent, reassure them that the conversation will remain private. Keep your tone of voice and facial expression congruent with comfort and safety.

Marv found Sue when she was alone by the vending machines. She looked as though she would have bolted if she had seen him sooner.

"So," Marv began, with as much warmth as he could muster. "Have you decided who we will be sending to the convention in Hawaii?"

"Well, I'm still thinking about it."

"Sue, I asked you to make this decision two months ago, and now the convention is only three weeks away. You know we always send our best sales rep. I know that if you have been putting off this decision, there must be a good reason. Whatever it is that's holding you back, you can talk to me about it." [Establish a comfort zone]

"Well, here is a list of people. Why don't you choose?" Sue's generally cheery disposition was clouded with concern.

Step 2. Surface Conflicts and Clarify Options. Patiently explore, from the Maybe Person's point of view, all of the options and the obstacles involved in making the decision, as well as any people that might be adversely affected by the decision. Listen for words of hesitation like *probably, I think so, pretty much, that could be true,* and so on, as signals to explore deeper.

"Sue, thanks, but I don't think so. You are the sales manager. There is no one better or more appropriate than you to make the call. Is there something going on for you regarding this decision that I should know about? [Surface conflicts] You really can tell me!"

"Well," Sue hesitated.

Marv kept the initiative going. "If something is disturbing you about this decision, I want to know. [Maintain the comfort zone] Even if it is about me, it's all right to tell me. What's going on?" [Surface conflict]

"Well, maybe the trip should go to Jerry. He has had a record quarter."

"So, it's Jerry then." Marv's heart leapt at the thought that it could be so easy!

"Um, that would probably work."

"Sue, when you say 'probably,' it sounds to me like you're not that certain that Jerry is the best choice. Is there something about choosing him that wouldn't work?"

"It's not that. Well, it is. I mean, how about Lori? Since she used to be your personal assistant and you trained her, and you're always complimenting her work, … Well, I just don't know." [Conflict is found]

Knowing Sue, it occurred to Marv how much she must have agonized over this. "Is that it? Are you worried about my reaction?"

"Well, yes!" [The plot thickens]

Step 3. Use a Decision-Making System. The best way to make a decision is to use a decision-making system. There are plenty of systems already developed so there's no need to reinvent the wheel here. If you have one that works well for you, teach it to your Maybe Person.

If not, a tried-and-true simple system is the old Ben Franklin method of drawing a line lengthwise on a piece of paper and dividing the page in half. Put one of your choices at the top and list all of the pluses of that choice on one side and all of the minuses on the other side, and then repeat the process for each option. Some people can do this mentally, in their mind's eye; others write it down. For Maybe People, writing it down is probably better, clearer, and more useful when it comes to the follow-through. After creating these lists, you compare them. It becomes easier to get an overall feel for which is the stronger choice, or the less negative one, once all the pluses and minuses have been made explicit.

Marv said, "I really appreciate how tough it must have been for you to talk to me about this." [Maintain the comfort zone]

Sue looked surprised. "You do?"

"Absolutely. And in the future, I hope you'll remember that I care more about honesty than I do about agreement. Meanwhile, a decision does have to be made, and soon." Marv led Sue to a nearby table, grabbed a sheet of paper, and wrote "Lori" on top. He turned it over and wrote "Jerry." "So let's look at your choices here. [Use a decision-making system] You could select Lori to please me." He wrote "Make Marv Happy" on the plus side, then drew a line through it. "Which really wouldn't if she isn't the best." He continued, "And, of course, that might send Jerry's productivity into a tailspin." He put this in the negative column. "I want you to pick the person who you believe most deserves it." For the next few minutes, he brainstormed with Sue on all the pluses and minuses of each candidate.

Leaning back, Marv said, "Well, it seems that Jerry is far more productive than Lori, and rewarding him with this trip could even inspire others. But Sue, that's only how I read this. I want us to have a stronger working relationship built on a foundation of honesty, and no choice that you make here could please me more than that. And the choice is still yours. Who do you think is better?"

Sue breathed a sigh of relief. "I'm picking Jerry." The weight seemed to fall from her shoulders, and her naturally sunny disposition broke through the clouds of doubt.

Whatever system works for you, use it consistently with Maybe People, and it will become second nature for them.

Step 4. Reassure Them, and Ensure Follow-Through. Once the decision is made, reassure the Maybe Person that there are no perfect decisions, and that the decision is a good one. Then, to ensure follow-through, stay in touch until the decision is implemented. You can keep things moving along by keeping this small piece of the action in your own hands:

"That's great! I think you've made the right choice for all the best reasons. [Reassure] When will you tell him?"

"As soon as we are done talking. Whew! What a relief."

"I'll bet. Listen, Sue, I'll drop by later this afternoon and follow up on this. I want to know what his reaction was." [Ensure follow through]

Step 5. Strengthen the Relationship. These moments of truth offer you the opportunity to strengthen your relationship with Maybe People so that surfacing conflict is easier in the future. Promote the idea of a better future for the both of you as a result of their honesty with you.

"So, Sue, before I go, I want to ask you one more thing. What have you learned from this?"

"Well, Marv, one thing I've learned is that I can talk to you. I didn't know you could be so understanding!"

"Thanks. I'd really like you to know that you can count on me to listen to your concerns. Can I count on you to talk things out with me in the future? That would mean a lot to me!"

"Yes, you can." Sue paused for a moment and then continued: "As a matter of fact, there's something else that I'd like to talk about with you, if I may. It's a little more personal." As they sipped their soft drinks and walked down the hall talking, what had seemed like a hard decision had become the bedrock of a growing friendship.

Be willing to take a few moments from time to time and listen to your Maybe Person's concerns. Talk on a personal level with your Maybe People, and help them learn the decision-making process whenever the opportunity arises. If you are willing to patiently invest a little time in this kind of guidance, Maybe People will never want to let you down. Then you'll find that former Maybe People have become some of the most dependable decision makers you know.

Great Moments in Difficult People History

To Bat or Not to Bat

Sally Davis walked into Hank's office to see him staring out the window. He seemed to be so lost in thought that she could have stood there for an hour and he wouldn't have turned around. Finally, she threw her baseball glove in his lap, and he jumped as if it had fallen out of nowhere. "So, do you have the starting lineup yet, captain?"

His hand rubbed the furrows in his brow as he said, "Well, um, not yet."

Sally's jaw dropped a little. "Hank, the softball game is in an hour. When do you think you are going to do it?"

"Soon, I guess."

Sally shook her head. "Hank, this is not like you. [Positive projection] Knowing you, you've been thinking about this all week. If you haven't decided, then there must be a good reason. Talk to me. Hey, this is Sally

Davis, your catcher. If a pitcher can't talk to the catcher, whom can he talk to? [Make it safe to be honest] Come on, conference on the mound between you and me. Nothing leaves this room. What's going on?"

Hank put his arms on the desk, laid his chin across them, and sighed, "I've got a dilemma."

"What is it? C'mon, out with it!" encouraged Sally.

"Well, I don't know what to do with Johnson. I don't know where to bat him."

Sally looked confused, "Hank, eighth or ninth is where you bat him. He's a .250 hitter at best. How is this a problem?"

"Well, you know how much I want that promotion, and Johnson is on the committee that decides. I don't want to take the chance of offending him. But then again, I don't see how I could bat him earlier either. The team is counting on me to do the right thing, and I don't know what to do."

Sally took a breath to calm her own reaction to the situation and then calmly said, "I see you have a real problem here. On one hand, if you bat Johnson where he deserves, you take a chance of offending him and losing the promotion. On the other hand, if you bat him anywhere else, you are letting down the team that made you captain. Do I paint an accurate picture?"

"Yeah, you got it. There's no way out."

"Maybe," said Sally. She walked over to the white board on Hank's wall.

"What are you doing?"

"We are going to look at your choices." On one side she wrote, "Bat Johnson eighth" and on the other side she wrote, "Bat Johnson earlier." Then she drew a vertical line under each choice to make two columns, and she put a plus and minus sign on each side of each line. "Okay," she began. "Let's see what the positives are of batting Johnson eighth." [Help them decide]

"Well, ah, it is better for the team. And I wouldn't let my teammates down. I guess that's all."

"All right," said Sally. "What's wrong with Johnson batting eighth?"

"Well, I might jeopardize my promotion. I could offend him." Hank sighed. Then his head jerked up, his eyes opened wide, and he said, "Johnny Blanchard."

"Huh?" said Davis.

"Johnny Blanchard hit .305 and 22 home runs with the 1961 Yankees as a *sub*. He couldn't even break into the starting lineup with those kinds of numbers because they had Mantle hitting 54 homers. Maris hit 61 that year."

"Of course," said Sally. She wasn't that much of a baseball fan and had no idea what this had to do with the starting lineup that day against their arch rivals, Arvy Plastics, but she listened and nodded anyway as if she understood. [Blending]

Hank went on, in a world of his own: " Blanchard was a catcher, but so was Elston Howard and Yogi Berra. Howard hit .340, and both he and Berra hit over 20 homers. Skowran hit 27 homers. They hit 240 homers as a team. A record that stood for 36 years!"

She had to clarify: "Hank, so the 1961 Yankees were good. What does that have to do with where Johnson bats?"

"I'll tell you. Johnny Blanchard could have started for any other major league team, but he would have rather been on the bench for the Yankees. You never heard him complaining. When he was finally traded, he actually cried into his Yankee hat." Hank looked out the window, his eyes glistening. "I'll never forget the picture on the back of the *Post*. There he was, right in the newspaper, cryin' into his hat! Now, that's a Yankee. That's a team player! Thanks, Davis. We don't have to go any further. The team trusted me to be captain, and I am going to do my job. Johnson is part of this team, and I'll count on him to do his job. Johnson is batting eighth. That's where he belongs. If he chooses to hold that against me, too bad." And with that he grabbed his glove off the coat rack, poked Sally playfully in the shoulder with it, and said, "Thanks, Sal. Glad you're on my team. Now let's go warm up."

"No problem," smiled Sally.

They Love You, Yeah, Yeah, Yeah

A real-live dramatization of a fictional incident.

The musical group was taken by surprise at their sudden success. Crowds now gather at all their concerts, and media people compete for interviews. In the midst of all this public clamor, a TV spot opens up that is guaranteed to take the lads to a level of recognition beyond their wildest dreams. There's only one small problem: a member of the band is having second thoughts about it all, and he can't make up his mind about going on the show. Let's listen in:

"I mean really, John, are you or aren't you going to make the grade?"

"Paul, I'll, uh, get back to you later."

"John, try to see it my way, only time will tell if Ed finds another band to play."

"Well, Paul, there will be an answer. Let it be."

"Listen, John. I know you, you know me, one thing I can tell you is we can work it out. [Establish a comfort zone] All you need is love. Just give me some truth: What is it, me old chum, about performin' on Ed's show?" [Surface conflict]

"Paul, I feel hung up, and I don't know why. Now that I'm older, I feel so insecure. You know it ain't easy."

"John, there's nothin' to get hung about. Don't carry the world upon your shoulders. Let it out and let it in. Hey, John, begin. Well, you know that it's just you. Hey, John, you'll do. You can talk to me. What are your choices?" [Clarify options]

"Well, Paul, you say yes, I say no. You say so, I say I don't know. What if I'm the biggest fool that ever hit the big time? Methinks I'm gonna let you down. I'm as blue as I can be!"

"I see, John, you don't want to let me down, is that it? [Backtracking] This decision's really got a hold on you." [Blending]

"Paul, yer lookin' through me."

"All right, then. Try to see it my way. There *will* be a show tonight. Picture yourself on the tube, on the telly, with a black-and-white screen and the CBS eye. They'll love you, yeah?" [Mind's eye decision system]

"Yeah, yeah. If I could stop me mind from wanderin'. Paul, can ya whisper words of wisdom?"

"You know it's gonna be all right. Let it be. Let it be." [Ensure follow-through with reassurance]

"I suppose I'll get by with a little help from my friends. How will we get to the studio, Paul?"

"Let me take you down, John, cause I'm goin' too." [Strengthen relationship]

Quick Summary

When Someone Becomes a Maybe Person

Your Goal: Help the Person Learn to Think Decisively

ACTION PLAN

1. Establish and maintain a comfort zone.

2. Surface conflicts and clarify options.

3. Use a decision-making system.

4. Reassure them, and ensure follow-through.

5. Strengthen the relationship.

17
The Nothing Person

WAITING FOR THE NOTHING PERSON TO RESPOND...

Ray walked into Sam's office, and he sat down on the couch across from him. Sam didn't even look up to acknowledge Ray's presence. "Look, Sam, you can't keep this up forever. Talk to me. Whatever it is that you're upset about, we can work it out if you'll just give it a chance!"

Sam continued to browse through his journal. Ray thought he saw a flicker of interest on Sam's face, but then it passed. Impatiently, Ray shouted, "Come on, Sam! The whole project has stalled out because you're sitting on the numbers. I can't keep putting people off. I've run out of excuses and interest is flagging."

Sam slowly pushed his chair away from his desk, rose to his feet, and started across the room. Ray, believing that a breakthrough was at hand, rose to meet him. But as Sam neared the couch, he veered to his left and walked over to a pencil sharpener on top of his bookcase. "Too bad!" he muttered.

Ray glared at him, shook his head and thought, "Why does he have to act like that? What did I do to deserve this?"

Sam is the person you find yourself waiting to hear from at one time or another. And what do you get for your patience and perseverance? Generally, nothing. No verbal feedback. No nonverbal feedback. Nothing. Mouth sealed shut, the Nothing Person stares past you as if you're not there.

When you look through the Lens of Understanding, Nothing People's behavior begins to make sense. Nothing People are passive, but they can be task focused or people focused depending on the thwarted intent—*get it right* or *get along*. When the intent to *get along* is threatened or thwarted, shy, quiet, or thoughtful people tend to withdraw and become ever more passive. Silence is, after all, the ultimate passive response. Some *get along* people withdraw out of their fear of rocking the boat, stirring things up, making waves, and getting thrown overboard. We all have those moments when we bite our lip and say nothing, when we convince ourselves it will accomplish nothing to speak up, when we fear that someone's feelings will be hurt if we speak, when we stop ourselves from saying something that we'll later regret. Everybody knows if you don't have something nice to say, you shouldn't say anything at all. *Get along* Nothing People don't and won't.

Get it right Nothing People seek perfection, but nothing measures up. They may decide that no one else cares about avoiding mistakes as much as they do and that nothing will change that condition no matter what they say. They get frustrated and finally withdraw with the thought, "Fine! Do it your way. Don't come crying to me when it doesn't work out." Then they shut up and shut down. They can think of nothing that can be done.

Although Nothing People *seem* to withdraw from conflict, inside they can be a boiling cauldron of simmering hostility that occasionally boils over. Perhaps you've been around people who were breaking pencils or throwing them and slamming drawers and doors. When asked what's wrong, they answer, "Nothing!" Another person asks, "Is everything all right?" and they answer, "Everything is *fine*," a passive-aggressive acronym for *frustrated*, *insecure*, *neurotic*, and *emotional*. While passive-aggressive Nothing People may be furious about what's going wrong, they are considerate enough to try to prevent their emotional hostility from damaging anyone else. This explains their abuse of inanimate objects like pencils and doors. Silence, then, can be a kind of aggression kept under wraps.

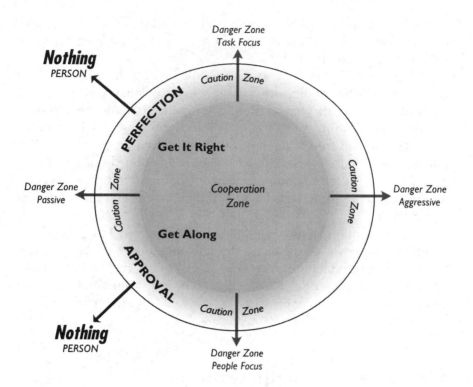

You'd Better Adjust Your Attitude

To make certain that nothing you do makes matters worse when Nothing People are at their worst, you must find a way to slow yourself down. The biggest challenge is to find and take the time when you're in the *get it done* mode and there isn't much time. Perhaps you've experienced the frustration of wanting to move quickly toward a goal, only to have Nothing People slow you down. That frustration can easily turn into aggressive communication, which will guarantee that you'll get nothing out of them. And impatience with *get along* Nothing People, who are trying to avoid conflict and disapproval, will likely defeat your purpose and drive them further into nothingness.

That's one of the most common mistakes parents make with their children. Nothing behavior is the best trick children have. Intense communications directed at children by frustrated parents are likely to silence the children and further frustrate the parents, who may then escalate with greater intensity, which drives the children further away. The children become too preoccupied with finding shelter from the verbal bombshells to pay much attention to what is actually being said. In the short term, nothing is accomplished, and in the long term the fallout damages the relationship.

The same principle is at work in adult relationships. If you lose your temper with people who have low assertiveness, you can count on diminishing returns in communication. Since impatience and frustration drive Nothing People deeper into nothingness, it is essential that you look and sound like you have all the time in the world. The internal resource that produces that outward appearance is *relaxation*. Take the time to compose yourself before attempting to communicate. To get something from Nothing People, you must be *calm and relaxed*.

Another helpful resource is *intuition*. The best way to develop your intuition is to try to see the world through another's eyes. Another way to develop intuition is to assume a similar body posture and facial expression as another person, and then you observe your emotional state and thoughts. You may be surprised at how well you can understand and communicate with Nothing People using this method.

Your Goal: Persuade Nothing People to Talk

Regardless of why Nothing People tell you nothing, your goal is to *persuade Nothing People to talk*. That is not only possible but it is also probable because when you use this strategy, nothing *can't* stop you.

Action Plan

Option 1. Plan Enough Time.   Hostile Nothing People may push you up against your deadline. You need information badly, they've got it, you want it, so they won't give it to you. For this reason, protect yourself if possible by planning ahead. Dealing successfully with Nothing People may take a long time. If you are tense and intense because of limited time, it's the wrong time.

If you have committed yourself to open communication with people who are closed, your time allotment may have to include more than one slot on your monthly calendar. We recommend that you plan a few 15-minute "communication opportunities" with your Nothing People. That way, if at first you don't succeed, you can keep coming back to try. Once they get the message that you are not giving up, they may open up just to get you to quit showing up.

Option 2. Ask Open-Ended Questions Expectantly.   The best kind of question to ask Nothing People is one that can't be answered with a yes, a no, or a grunt. We suggest that you use questions that begin with the words *who, what, where, when*, and *how* because they tend to open topics for discussion, with a request for specific information about Nothing People's thoughts. For example, "What are you thinking?" and "How do you want to proceed?" and "Where shall we go from here?" have a greater chance of success than "Do you like that?" or "Are we going to get your information soon?" or "Can you tell me?"

However, it isn't what you ask but how you ask it that makes all the difference in the world. When you ask the question, make certain that your nonverbals are also asking for a response. We recommend that you look and sound like you are about to get an answer. We call this the *expectant look*, and it is a nonverbal skill based on the idea that you get what you expect (even though it often takes more time than you would prefer).

Try this now if no one is looking. Raise your eyebrows, open your mouth slightly, tilt your head to the side, and lean forward a little as if you just asked a question and at any moment you expect an answer.

When you ask the Nothing Person your open-ended question, you may have to persist in looking at them expectantly for a longer period of time than you would with normal human beings. It may help you to pass the time if, in your mind's eye, you imagine that you can see the words marching up the back of their throat, through their mouth, and out to the tip of their tongue, where—any second now—they are going to open their mouth and give you that answer!

Beware: You won't want this to become a staring match. If at first you don't succeed, review what's happened so far, which isn't much, and then, ask your question again. Here's an example. "A moment ago I asked you what's going on, and you didn't answer. I'm still wondering, what's going on?"

At last, the pressure builds to a point where the Nothing Person feels compelled by your behavior to answer you. You see their mouth open, and out comes the typical response, which is "Nothing" or "I don't know."

If a Nothing Person says "Nothing," then you can say "What else?"

If the Nothing Person says "I don't know," then you can say "Guess!" or "Make something up!" or "If you did know, what would it be?" Give the Nothing Person your best expectant look. You will be surprised at how effective this can be with both adults and children. Try it the next time anyone says, "I don't know." It is amazing how quickly people come up with something to say, only moments after claiming that they knew nothing.

Option 3. Lighten It Up.   When nothing else is working, a little humor carefully used can go a long way. Making absurd, exaggerated, and impossible guesses about the cause of the silence has cracked a smile and broken down the armor of some of the most intransigent Nothing People you can imagine. If you can get Nothing People to laugh, it ruins the mood.

Your next line of offense against an "I don't know" could be exaggeration. At a couples seminar, a participant claimed her husband left too many glasses in the sink. We asked her, "How often and how many?" To which she replied, "Too often and too many." We laughed and asked for a number, and she said, "I don't know." We were ready for that, and we asked her to guess, and then we gave her our very best expectant looks. She couldn't resist the look and said (again), "Too often and too many." Since we're convinced that if what we're doing isn't working, we should do something else, that's what we did. We exaggerated: "Well, would you say it is 30 glasses a day seven days a week, 52 weeks a year?" And she said, "No, it is probably about 4 glasses, three times a week." We had to wonder, "Where were those numbers a moment ago?" We still don't know, but we do know that if you exaggerate, people get specific.

Or you might begin guessing yourself. You could say, "You're mad because I beat you to the watercooler and it's a full moon, right?" Or you could say, "I'll talk, and you blink once for agreement, twice for disagreement." We've found that with some Nothing People, the more outrageous your guesses and suggestions, the sooner they will speak up and get specific.

Be careful with this because humor is a two-edged sword. It can inadvertently cut Nothing People and yourself, and there's nothing funny about that. Consider yourself warned. If you proceed to use humor and Nothing People take offense, don't keep trying to make light of what has become a serious situation. Apologize immediately and sincerely. Then remind them that your intent is to have a dialogue, not a monologue. Like many kinds of communication, the use of humor is not guaranteed to work in every situation. It is a judgment call on your part, so use it with caution.

Option 4. Guess.   If the Nothing Person remains silent and nothing else has gotten results, or you want an alternative to Option 3, try this: Put yourself in the Nothing Person's shoes, and think back on the course of events as you understand them. What was the sequence, and how else might you interpret that sequence to make positive sense out of this negative silence? Once you've come up with an idea, suggest it to the Nothing Person, and watch for a reaction. You may think of several possibilities. Just rattle them off. Don't worry about trying to figure out the right one. It won't matter if some of them are inaccurate, so shotgun a bunch of them. Always preface your guesses by saying, "I don't know what is going on for you" or "I am just guessing here, but ..." People hate to be told that you know what they are thinking, but they love it when you guess correctly. If you can hit on or near the reason for the silence, you may actually get these people to start talking. At least you'll notice a definite change in their posture or expression.

A state agency referred Becky, a troubled teenage client, to a counselor named Gideon. Becky had dropped out of school, was sleeping all day, and wouldn't talk to anyone—including the counselor. She just sat in his office, shaking her foot, and staring out the window. She wouldn't answer any of his questions. Worst of all, she was ignoring his very best expectant look.

So the counselor started guessing about the cause of her behavioral change. He said, "I don't know what is going on for you, and you certainly aren't going to tell me, but you've got me wondering. If I were a teenager, sleeping all day, what would be going on for me? Hmm, I think I would be avoiding something! Well, what would I be avoiding? Maybe something at school, maybe something at home. At school, let's see. Maybe I wouldn't fit in, maybe I don't have any real friends, maybe I think the whole clique thing is dumb. The state urges me to go back to school, but maybe I'm so far behind I will never be able to catch up. Maybe I am missing some basic reading and math skills that I am embarrassed about."

Gideon continued, "Now, what could I be avoiding at home? Maybe I don't feel cared about. After all, if I dropped out of school and I was sleeping all day but my parents didn't say anything, well, I guess I'd figure they just didn't care very much. After all, it's the state that's making the big deal out of it. And I heard you do have a new step-parent. I can sure see how you would feel left out of that relationship."

How did Becky respond to this guessing game? On the counselor's second guess about school, her foot stopped wiggling. That was a good sign because it was the first change in her practiced nothingness in 20 minutes. As Gideon continued, Becky looked up and locked her eyes on his. Then tears welled up in her eyes. And within moments, she was speaking the fears that had been hiding in her heart.

If you notice a change in behavior while you're guessing, that's an indicator that you're on the right track. Continue along the same lines, and before you know it, they will be talking with you. Best of all, even if your guesses miss, people sometimes start talking anyway. It's as if they feel sorry for you because you haven't got a clue about what is really going on, and they decide to give you a break. By walking a mile in the footsteps of another, you reveal the common ground of your humanity.

Option 5. Show the Future. Sometimes, the only way to get Nothing People talking is to take them out of the moment and into the future. There they can see the consequences of continued silence, and perhaps they can find enough perspective and motivation to open up. The actual words you use may change depending on your relationship to the Nothing Person:

- For the *get it right* Nothing Person, you might say: "Fine, don't talk. [Blending with what is happening] Just imagine how many things can go wrong and how much time we are going to waste on this project because we didn't have your input."
- For the *get along* Nothing Person, you might say: "Okay, you don't have to talk [Blending], but in the long term I don't see how our relationship can survive if we don't start to communicate."

- For the *get along* Nothing Person at the office, you might say: "Okay, you don't have to talk [Blending], but it sure won't be any fun to work around here if we are all in our own little worlds. That will certainly kill the team spirit and make for a lot of bad feelings and misunderstandings."
- For the hostile Nothing Person who is trying to "get you" by closing you out, talk about the negative consequences, like grievance procedures, going over their head, filling out paperwork, and the like.

Warning: Don't make promises you won't keep. Idle threats teach people that you're idling. Your goal is to make something out of nothing, not nothing out of something, so that it becomes uncomfortable for Nothing People to remain silent.

Sometimes, when a Nothing Person finally does speak up, you may find that it's a case of "all or nothing." If you get a lot of seemingly disconnected information, instead of interrupting for clarity's sake, go with it for a while, so they can get used to talking aloud. Don't try to control it. When Nothing People start talking, that's when you need to start listening.

Great Moments in Difficult People History

The Power of Persistence
Ray fought the urge to leave. Instead, he relaxed and told himself he had the time and this was worth it. He seized upon this scrap of verbiage, and he returned it in a question: "What's too bad, Sam?" [Ask open-ended questions expectantly]

Sam looked at Ray with eyes of steel. Those eyes seemed to soften for a brief instant. Then, he braced himself and replied, "I don't know." Sam .returned to his desk and his journal.

Ray said, "If you did know, what would it be?" [Ask questions expectantly]

Sam looked away, and after a moment of silence he said, "I don't see how anyone thinks we can do the job around here the way we were treated. It's just …" he muttered and faded out into silence again.

Ray sat there mentally reviewing recent events at the company, and that's when it dawned on him.

"Sam, I'm just guessing here, but three months ago during the reorganiza-tion, two of our departments were downsized significantly, and budgets were axed. What effect did that have you?" [Guess] Ray saw Sam's body language go through an incredible shift. Sam was practically squirming in his seat, and it looked like the pressure was building inside him to speak. But again, Sam braced himself, and he glared steely eyed at his journal.

Ray felt that Sam needed a little motivation to open up and talk about whatever had caused him to go silent. So Ray spoke to the future, as he said, "If I've guessed right about this, and you found that shrinking budget and loss of personnel to be tough to deal with, then think about this! Without that information you're withholding, more people will lose their jobs, and people right here in this company who you've known for years are going to have their futures put at risk, all because you didn't do the right thing. You may think you have a good reason for being silent now, but how will that reason of yours hold up later? [Show the future] Come on, Sam. What's going on?"

Sam opened the flood gates, and a torrent of bad feelings and apprehen-sion washed through the room. It was obvious that Sam had been suffering in his silence. Ray let him talk. And when it was all said, Sam yielded the badly needed information like a shy little boy. Ray, happy to have brought a little light to the situation, thanked him for his honesty and left him alone with his thoughts.

The Great Foot Fire

The speaker was brought in by a state agency to give a motivational presen-tation to eight of their most hopeless cases. None of the speaker's audience involvement strategies was working very well. As far as these teenagers were concerned, he was just another authority figure, and when he looked around the room, all he saw were eight hostile Nothing People with no interest in hearing a word of it. He had his back to the writing on the board when he suddenly smelled smoke. He turned around to find their ring leader, Eric, grinning at him. Eric had set his own shoe laces on fire. The laces were burning like incense, and the teenager was sitting there with his legs crossed, grinning.

The speaker didn't want to be another authority figure in a long line of authority figures whom these kids had rebelled against. So instead, he looked the boy right in the eyes, smiled, and said, "I heard you were hot but you're smokin' today, dude." [Lighten it up] Then the speaker went back to writing on the board, picking up where he left off as if everything were normal. The kids all laughed, and the boy put out the fire. When the speaker turned around again, he had eight allies who were ready to participate and learn.

Quick Summary

When Someone Becomes a Nothing Person

   Your Goal: Persuade the Nothing Person to Talk

   ACTION PLAN

   1. Plan enough time.

   2. Ask open-ended questions expectantly.

   3. Lighten it up.

   4. Guess.

   5. Show the future.

18

The Whiner

"It was terrible," Cynthia whined.

Joann took a deep breath, looked up at Cynthia, and forced a smile. "Yes, terrible you said."

Joann began doodling on the pad of paper in front of her. This was the fifth time Cynthia had interrupted her this morning. And if that wasn't bad enough, Joann had 16 more in her department just like Cynthia. She had heard that the manager before her had taken an early retirement because she couldn't stand these people any longer. Joann had mistakenly believed the other managers were kidding about that. Painfully, she had discovered they were not. It seemed that she couldn't concentrate on any one item for longer than 10 minutes without someone whining about something. "How will I ever get any work done?" she thought to herself.

"Wow, Cynthia, that's an awful shame about the box and the grill." Joann thought that if she agreed with her, Cynthia would stop. She was wrong.

"You have no idea how awful it is!" said Cynthia with renewed enthusiasm. "Why ...," and she started the whole story again, with new embellishments to amplify her pain.

These complaints were a complete waste of time. Joann just didn't see the point of it. And as the whining drifted in and out of her consciousness, she began whining to herself: "Why do they have to act like this? Why is this happening to me?"

There are three different kinds of complaints that we all hear in the course of our lives: *helpful, therapeutic*, and *obnoxious*.

The *helpful complainers* draw attention to problems that ought to be addressed and offer options or solutions along with the complaints. This can actually help businesses, systems, and relationships to grow, develop, and improve. Most people with a problem, the silent majority, do not complain to the offending party. The few people who speak up about a problem while working to find a solution are a blessing to their coworkers, families, employers, and the companies they do business with.

Another type of complaining can be downright *therapeutic*. We all need to vent, to unload, to give voice to our frustrations once in a while. A little whining on occasion can actually help us unwind from the stress of modern living. Telling someone about your stress can provide a valuable release valve for otherwise-pent-up concerns and backed-up energy.

Wallowing in their worries and woe is the behavior of the Whiners. It has very little to do with releasing stress. Wallowing just goes on and on. Cynthia was this kind of complainer. She never offered solutions, and her complaints were not geared toward change of any kind.

As you look through the Lens of Understanding, you can begin to make some sense out of this difficult behavior. Negativity occurs on a spectrum, ranging from the helplessness of whining to the hopeless certainty of a No Person. Both behaviors emerge out of the intent to *get it right*. No People can see what could and should be, then look at what is, and when what is doesn't measure up to what could and should be, they give up and become hopeless. The Whiners, on the other hand, become helpless, while hoping that someone else can close the gap. Perhaps that is why they let anyone in earshot know what's wrong with everything.

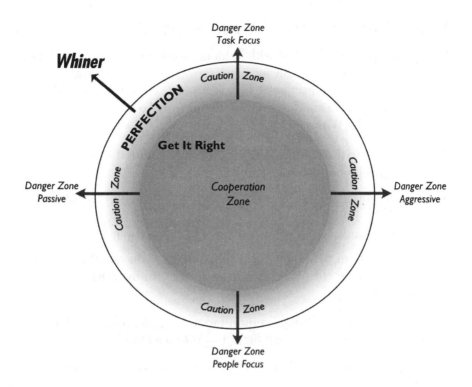

Whiners may have a vague sense that events should be different from what they are, but they have no clue about how events ought to change. This leaves them utterly helpless to deal effectively with what they don't like, and that's why they come to you. In other words, if there's a plan for their lives, they're not in it! Because of this feeling of helplessness, Whiners are vocally less assertive when compared to No People. Three elements contribute to giving their voice that characteristic whining sound: the weight on their shoulders from carrying their burden of collected woe, which only grows heavier as they continue to find and collect problems; the effort required to talk about all that's wrong when there's nothing they can do about it anyway; and the feeling of futility, since you probably won't offer any useful ideas or right the wrongs.

Expressions of negativity can be virulent, spreading like the flu through teams of people. Before you know it, everyone is doing it. If these behaviors become habits, morale and productivity are dragged down into the quicksand of inaction. Not to sound negative, but if you don't deal with these behaviors, morale and productivity may never return.

You'd Better Adjust Your Attitude

Like Joann, people who deal with Whiners sometimes become Whiners themselves. This exponentially increases the agony of dealing with them as it becomes difficult to distinguish between whose complaints are whose.

There are four acts of desperation that only make the situation worse. We call them the *Whiner Don'ts*:

1. Don't agree with Whiners. If you agree with them, it just encourages them to keep complaining.
2. Don't disagree with them. If you do, they will feel compelled to repeat their problems.
3. Don't try to solve their problems for them. You can't.
4. Never ask them why they are complaining to you about their problems. They hear this as an invitation to start all over again from the beginning.

There are three attitudinal requirements that will help you deal with these problem people. We call them the *Whiner Dos*:

1. Do have *patience* with their impossible standards and seemingly endless negativity.
2. Do have *compassion* for the pitiful Whiners whose lives seem beyond their control.
3. Do have *commitment* to the lengthy process of getting them to focus on solutions.

The goal and strategy that you are about to learn for dealing with Whiners is also the first thing you try with negative No People.

Your Goal: Form a Problem-Solving Alliance

If you must deal with Whiners, your goal is to team up with them to *form a problem-solving alliance* (and if that doesn't work, then your goal is to get them to go away!). The difference between problem solvers and Whiners is in the way they approach a problem: the problem solvers look at the specifics of a problem with an eye toward finding solutions; the Whiners look at the problem, feel helpless, and then generalize that the problem is worse than it actually is.

So the best you can do with people who are whining, and for the sake of everyone around them, is work with them to diminish their feelings of helplessness by helping them to identify solutions. Done consistently through time, this strategy can sometimes cure Whiners once and for all. As the feeling of helplessness diminishes, so does the need to whine.

Action Plan

Step 1. Listen for the Main Points.   We know! The last activity you want to engage in when someone is whining to you is listening! Yet that's just what you need to do with Whiners. We recommend that you listen with paper and pen in hand so you can write down the main points of the complaint. We make this recommendation for several reasons.

First, Whiners love this because it shows them that you are listening. They may even infer that you're accepting delivery on the bag of woe and signing for it. Second, this will help you backtrack and clarify, which is the next step of this strategy. Last, by writing down the main points of the complaint, you'll never have to listen to a complaint more than once because you can recognize it immediately if they begin to recycle the complaint!

Step 2. Interrupt and Get Specific.   Take command of the conversation through a tactful interruption. Then ask clarification questions to get the specifics of the problem, because generalizations are rarely solvable. But be ready for generalization stacking.

When you ask, "What's wrong?" They say, "Everything."

If you then say, "But what specifically is wrong?" They say, "All of it."

Ask when it happens and they say, "All the time."

Ask who is doing it and the answer is, "Everybody."

And of course in response to the question, "What have you tried?" he answer is "Everything."

Be ready for it, because after three generalizations are thrown on the stack, your growing frustration with getting nowhere may tempt you to jump to offering a solution. Don't do it. At this stage, your goal is simply to outlast them.

It is normal human behavior to generalize. You know how this works. If you stop at two or three red lights in a row, you say, "All the lights are red today." If you meet two or three people in a bad mood, you say,

"Everyone is in a bad mood today." The same thing happens for Whiners and No People, but on a grander scale. So when asking questions of negative people, you may find it helpful to think of this as being on a sort of archeological dig. Buried under all those generalizations lies some truth. If you keep digging, even asking questions you've already asked, you will eventually hit something specific.

There will be times when Whiners are simply unable to get specific, because they've put the problems in their bag of woe without examining them first in detail. If that's the case, then you can assign (if you outrank them) or suggest (if you don't) that they go out and gather more information, with instructions to bring that information back to you at a specific time. This gives them something to look forward to, instead of leaving them in their helpless condition.

Step 3. Shift the Focus to Solutions.   Once you begin to get specific about Whiners complaints they find themselves face-to-face with the specifics of a problem. Although you may know what should be done, don't say it. Instead, ask them, "What do you want?"

For some Whiners, this simple question has the potential to move their mind in a direction it's never gone before, and they will actually come up with a practical solution. You may find yourself wondering, at that point, why they didn't just suggest the solution before. The answer is that they couldn't do it before. Human beings can only pay attention to so much at any given moment in time. If their attention is locked into generalizations instead of specifics, solutions are nowhere to be found. But once attention gets refocused on the specifics of a problem, solving the problem becomes possible.

Their response to your inquiry may be a simple "I don't know," in which case you use the standard, "That's OK. Guess, make something up. If you did know, what would it be?" type of response, and look at them expectantly.

Still other Whiners, upon pondering your question, may come up with a list of wants that is completely unrealistic. For example, if the Whiner says, "I'm doing the work of three people. I want three more people hired."

You may have to say: "Yes, you are working hard. But we both know that Ebenezer isn't going to hire three more people. So the question remains, what do you want?"

When a Whiner's answers to your questions are impractical, absurd, or unlikely, it's important that you provide a reality check. Tell it like it is, and inquire again: "Based on these facts, what do you want?"

If the Whiner comes up with a reasonable answer, then ask what the next steps are or should be to make the solution happen.

Step 4. Show Them the Future.   When people have been feeling help-less, it is helpful to give them something to look forward to. If solving the problem they've brought to your attention turns out to be your responsibility, then you must keep Whiners informed about progress.

If the complaints are about other people, you can offer to help set up a meeting with the people about whom they are complaining. Or, you can ask them to track and document the problem in writing. With employees, coworkers, or family members, you can then schedule a time to get back together and discuss the information they've gathered.

For example you could say, "You obviously know more about this problem than I do. I recommend you track this problem for the next two weeks. Then come back to me with three possible solutions and a rec-ommendation on such-and-such date. Then we'll take our next step."

Step 5. Draw the Line.   If backtracking, clarifying, and asking for a direction has not produced the desired result and your Whiner refuses to think solutions, then drawing the line on the interaction is a necessity. But how you draw the line varies according to your relationship to the Whiner.

- If you are the manager of the Whiner, it is important to take control and draw the line firmly on whining, because negativity, perhaps more than any other behavior discussed in this book, can undermine and destroy morale and team spirit. You might say, "If you don't want to talk solutions, that's your decision. But I don't want to hear any more complaining. And I don't want you distracting the people around you by whining about problems to them. If it continues, I will be forced to …" and then promise them specific negative conse-quences they will suffer if they continue to demoralize others.

- With a coworker or friend, drawing the line must be done more consid-erately: "Mary, our friendship is important to me, but there's no point in complaining if nothing can be done. If you want to talk to me about solutions rather than just identifying problems, my door is open."

Do not allow them to draw you back into the cycle with their "But …" and "You don't understand" and the like. Stonewall your Whiner by repeating the closing statement: "As I said, if you change your mind and come up with some solutions, let me know." If they don't get the message, add a little nonverbal communication by placing your hand on their shoulder and guiding them to the door, or turn around and walk away.

Great Moments in Difficult People History

The Trouble Book

We met Katherine at one of our seminars, and she told us she inherited 17 chronic Whiners. The previous manager took an early retirement due to illness and fatigue (she got sick and tired of dealing with those people). Katherine was determined not to let that happen to her. She created the *Trouble Book*. She instructed her team that if they had problems, they were not allowed to whine about them. Instead, they had to use the *Trouble Book*.

The instructions were simple, and they were posted by the book:

1. Enter your name and today's date.

2. Write a complete description of the problem. [Get the specifics]

3. Suggest three possible solutions to the problem. (If there were no suggestions, Katherine wouldn't read the complaint. She didn't care if the suggestions were outrageous as long as there were three of them.) [Shift the focus to solutions]

4. The fourth column was for Katherine's initials, which would indicate that she had read each complaint and the suggestions.

5. The last column was for follow-up. Katherine became the champion for their solutions in the hospital bureacracy, and she kept them up to date as to what she was doing about the problem and it's ongoing status. [Show them the future]

After a while, people started noticing that their complaints were addressed and suggestions implemented. Their feelings of helplessness gradually disappeared, and when they encountered problems, they began to take the initiative rather than even bother with the Trouble Book. Katherine proudly told us, "They became an inheritance of 17 useful problem solvers."

The Great Positive Wallpaper Caper

Joe was the manager of a state government office. He didn't have one specific Whiner to deal with. He had numerous negative and whiny people who, on any given day, took turns demoralizing the office. The big generalizations that circulated his office were along these lines: "This is government," "Nothing ever changes," and "Nobody listens to our recommendations anyway."

Joe decided that disproving those generalizations could be the solution to their attitudinal problems. So Joe took a page from a flip chart and put it on the wall, and he labeled it "Things Changing for the Better." For the next several weeks, whenever he implemented a suggestion, he wrote it on the chart. In three weeks' time, the page filled with evidence of change, so he left that one on the wall and put up another piece of paper next to it. He continued to list changes for the better as they occurred. Two pages became four, which became eight, until the walls were literally wallpapered with changes.

Still, the biggest change was one that wasn't written on the wall. The attitude in the office changed. People saw that they weren't helpless and that change for the better does occur—even in government! Instead of noticing where the glass was half empty, people began to see where it was filling. The helplessness that had once plagued their operation gave way to high morale and innovations.

Quick Summary

When Someone Becomes a Whiner

   Your Goal: Form a Problem-Solving Alliance

ACTION PLAN

1. Listen for the main points.

2. Interrupt and get specific.

3. Shift the focus to solutions.

4. Show them the future.

5. Draw the line.

19

The No Person

Ever since his childhood, Rick had loved to play hockey. And though he no longer played on ice, he managed to pull together a group of regulars for floor hockey at a local gym, including a few recent immigrants from Russia. The first day they played, he had a run-in with one of them, a guy named Vladimir. Rick soon learned that Vladimir was the official No Person of the group. He would always tell the other players what they did wrong, not what they did right.

"Vat? You half brro-ken leg? Can you run?"

"Vat language am I to speak to get a pass vrom you?"

Each game degenerated into an argument sparked by Vladimir's negative comments.

"Darn," thought Rick. "It could have been such fun."

No People are task-focused individuals motivated by the intent to *get it right* by avoiding mistakes. Perfection is their standard for what should be done, where it should be done, when, by whom, and most importantly, how it should be done. When the shortcomings, weaknesses, and failings of others get in the way of perfection, then nothing measures up, mistakes loom on the horizon, and No People feel despair. Seeing themselves as the only ones willing and able to look at what did, is, or will inevitably go wrong, the No People find the negatives in everyone and everything else.

Some No People put considerable energy into grumbling aloud, while others fall into a completely passive and apathetic hopelessness. Through thoughts, words, and occasionally deeds, negative No People have the uncanny ability to extinguish hope in others and smother creative sparks before they catch fire. It is almost as if they protect the people around them from disappointment, by preventing them from getting their hopes up. "What goes up," they tell us, "must come down." And what comes down, one could infer, must never get back up.

As we said in the previous chapter, negativity has an insidious effect on others. It undermines motivation, stifles development, and leads to depression and hopelessness in others. Whereas the root of whining is the feeling of helplessness, the root of the No Person's behavior is the feeling of hopelessness. And just like whining, this behavior is contagious. Allow it to keep happening, and before you know it, everyone starts doing it.

Yet, No People do not intentionally try to make everyone miserable. They really do believe it is as hopeless as they say. They have all the certainty and arrogance of a Know-It-All seduced by the dark side of the force. Extremely negative people build their lives on and around disappointments from past situations. The difficulties pass, but the bitterness lives on. So it is, that negative people can develop deeply held assumptions about life that will paint all of their perceptions in the colors of despair.

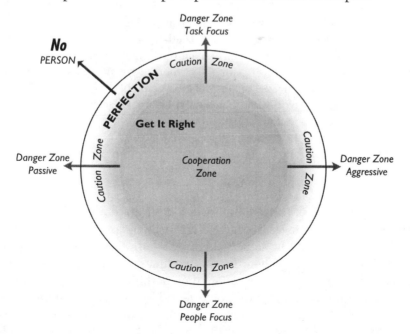

You'd Better Adjust Your Attitude

The key to dealing with No People is to have compassion instead of contempt. You'll also need perspective and patience for the long haul ahead.

You may never know, and you don't need to know, what trials and tribulations they've faced in their lives, what obstacles they've had to overcome, or what circumstances they have survived. Suffice it to say that when people turn sour, there is usually a negative history that preceded the behavior change.

We recommend the dissociative techniques in Chapter 9, "How to Change Your Attitude," to help you regain *your perspective*. Compare your dealings with No People to something even more unpleasant (you can think of something, unless you've turned sour yourself). Or ask yourself, "In 100 years, what will their negativity matter?"

Though it may sometimes appear that, despite your best efforts to influence the behavior of your No Person, nothing has changed, be patient with the process. Some behavioral change takes place at a snail's pace, yet there is a payoff for patience with the process. There are few outcomes in life as gratifying as when a negative person gains the courage to let go of fear and begin to live. This new framework will change your response to their negativity.

Your Goal: Transition to Problem Solving

When dealing with No People, your goal is to *move from fault finding toward problem solving*, from stagnation toward innovation, from decline toward improvement. You may not stop the flood of negativity completely, but you can succeed in turning the tide back to its proper course.

Action Plan

Option 1. Use the Whiner Strategy. Your first option for dealing with negative people is to use the Whiner strategy in order to get them to be specific. No People, like Whiners, are adrift in a sea of generalizations. But where Whiners' generalizations cause them to feel helpless, the No People's generalizations make them feel hopeless. How does this work? The thing about generalizations is that once you make them, you start noticing only the evidence that matches them, while leaving out any evidence to the contrary. Once No People give up all hope, they notice everything that fits their negative generalizations, thus reinforcing them and increasing their sense of certainty. That's why the motto of a chronically negative person is, "I'm not being negative, I'm being realistic."

Don't waste your time trying to convince No People that things are not so bad, or pointing out that things can always be worse. Instead, listen, backtrack, clarify for specifics, ask for solutions, and set future focused action, just as you learned to do with Whiners in the previous chapter.

Option 2. Use Them as Resources. No People can potentially serve two valuable functions in your life: they can be your personal character builders, and they can serve as an early warning system for problems.

If you want to build muscle, you push against weight. Adversity builds character. So if you want to build character, hang out with No People and remain positive. Rather than trying to turn negative people into positive people, which would inevitably turn you into a negative person, maintain a positive attitude. Tell yourself that you are in training for the big challenges of your life and your No Person is on a mission to help you build your character. After all, this is a challenging world. Inner strength will be your reward for accepting the challenge, and character is an essential resource for a happy life.

If you want to have some fun, the next time your No Person starts to overwhelm you with negativity, place your hand gently on their shoulder, look them in the eye, and say, "Thank you for the wonderful work you're doing." It will probably confuse them, it may stop them, and you'll probably feel better for messing with them.

No People also can serve a similar function to a smoke detector: they give you an early warning for potential problems. We know of one company that has a No Person on its executive staff. The executives run every new idea, every plan of action past her, asking her to critique it before they move ahead. "I've got this great idea, but I'm sure it's seriously flawed. Sue, break it down!" This is strategic because if you ask, listen, and then dig deep enough, you will find some truth to the negative person's concerns. Such knowledge can lead you and others to preventive action. Often No People are the first to become aware of problems that others have overlooked. While it is true that the No People generalize about these problems, it may also be true that what you don't know can hurt you far more than their negative behavior.

All people generalize on occasion, and all communications (including this sentence) are generalizations to some degree. Negative people generalize about problems. They begin by observing details that suggest something has, is, or will go wrong, and then expand out from the details to encompass all the world: "Everything is wrong, nothing is right, and it will never work." That is the point where you must backtrack and clarify to get back to the specifics. The more clearly you define the problem, the more likely that you will find adequate solutions.

A woman attending one of our seminars told us a story involving her husband Bob, whom she described as a classic negative person. The cub scouts were planning a trip to Washington, D.C., and the two people responsible for organizing it began to get nervous, wondering if anything could go wrong. They decided to bring her husband in on a meeting, figuring that if anything could go wrong, Bob was most likely to identify and point out any problems with the plan in advance. Sure enough, he did. He started with big generalizations, too, but by backtracking what he said and then clarifying for specifics, they were able to identify in advance several real potential problems and took steps to prevent them before beginning the trip.

Option 3. Buy Some Time.   No People tend to operate in a different time reality than other people. Any effort to rush them to a decision will force them to slow down. Push them for action, and No People will put enough drag on things to bring a group to a complete stop, or they will become the sand in the gears that eventually destroys the machine. It may be tempting to throw them out, exclude them, or slam a door in their face, but the wiser course of action is to give them time to think and leave the door open so they can come back in when ready.

You can indicate that the door will remain open with statements like "If you change your mind, let us know" or "When you think of a solution, get back to me" or "Why don't you think about this for a while, and report back any ideas that you have for preventing or solving the problem." While the modern world provides pressure on all of us to get more done in less time, sometimes patience wins the race—not by going the fastest but by identifying a clear and unobstructed way forward. If you can buy some time, your willingness to hurry up by slowing down at the starting line may gain big rewards.

Option 4. Go for the Polarity Response.   What do you get when you tell a two-year-old to go to bed? A polarity response! "I don't want to go to bed!" The more you insist that they go, the more they insist that they won't. You can actually use this attempt at staying opposite to you to your advantage, by telling the child, "You can't go to bed, and you have to stay up all night!" The two-year-old is likely to say, "But I'm tired."

You find this same pattern in teenagers, who hate being told what to do and want to define themselves as being different from you. Tell them their ideas are bad and they'll go to great lengths to prove you wrong by acting on those bad ideas. If it seems adversarial, that's because it is. It's also predictable, and you can deal with it by using it yourself.

The single worst thing you can do with No People is try to convince them that things aren't so bad. This forces them to polarize more deeply into their negativity. The deeper they go, the more insistent they become that things are worse than you think. Attempting to convince No People to be positive is like struggling to climb out of quicksand: the harder you struggle, the more embedded you become. But when you meet them at the edge of their polar response, and go just a little further, the only way they can stay negative to your negativity is to go positive.

We once had an opportunity to observe a brilliant therapist use the polarity response on a depressed client, who was doing his best to convince the therapist that he was completely hopeless. When all his other attempts failed, the therapist gave every impression of agreeing with the client, saying, "Okay, you win. Of the thousands of unhappy people that I have worked with, you have convinced me that you are the most hopeless, worthless human being I have ever seen, and there is no hope that you will ever get better!"

The client looked shocked as he considered that for a long moment, then replied, "Come on. I'm not that bad."

We know of a CEO who was complaining to his assistant about how the employees in his company were inefficient, incompetent, and utterly incapable of doing a single thing right. His assistant, with a look of utmost earnestness on his face, suggested, "You're right. Let's take them all outside, shoot them, and burn the building down!" The CEO laughed at this idea, then admitted, "All right, it isn't that bad!"

There are two ways to apply this polarity response when dealing with No People. The first is to bring up the negatives before they do. "Here's my idea, and here's where I see it has problems." When No People hear that you are approaching your idea realistically (seeing what's wrong), they often point out how to make it right.

A second way to use this polarization principle is to agree with the hopelessness of the situation, and take it one step further. Throw down the gauntlet by insisting that even they would be incapable of finding a solution to this problem. "You're right. It is hopeless. In fact, not even you could find a way to solve this problem." Don't be surprised to see your No Person go in the opposite direction, telling you that it can be done and how to do it.

Option 5. Acknowledge Their Good Intent.   If you are willing to project good intent onto negative behavior, No People may come to believe it themselves. Then their analytic perfectionism can be expressed in a more useful way that is actually helpful. (See Chapter 8, "Get What You Project and Expect.") Here are some positive intentions you can project on to No People.

> "I appreciate that you have such high standards."
>
> "Thank you for the willingness to speak up and point out problems so we can come up with solutions."
>
> "Thank you for making us aware of the pitfalls we will have to avoid."

Remember when you project positive intent onto another person, you need a degree of authenticity for it to be believable, and a lot of patience because you may need to keep at it over a long period of time. Think of each positive projection as giving the No People a push in that positive direction. Even negative people prefer to think of themselves in a constructive way rather than in a destructive way. They are unlikely to deny your positive projections regarding their negative behavior, and if you stick with it, they may eventually internalize your projections as their own, and then adjust their behavior to be more constructive.

When something does work out that the No Person said would not, avoid the temptation to say, "I told you so." Instead, include the No Person in the victory celebration. Even if the No Person was a dead-weight on the entire project, speak and act as if the No Person was part of the team effort that led to the victory. This not only effects the No Person but can sometimes have a remarkable effect on other people's perceptions of the No Person.

We know a team leader who used this strategy. After the team had been recognized at four different award banquets, the No Person pulled all of them aside and said,

"You know, I've been moved by all of this recognition for the work our team has done. I'm no longer certain about many of the things I've long held to be true. And I've been thinking, maybe you're right, after all. Maybe this proves that some things can work out; that disappointment isn't inevitable; that people can rise to a challenge and overcome. Maybe it does, and I still have my doubts, but maybe."

Hey, even the biggest changes start with such small beginnings!

Great Moments in Difficult People History

The U.S.-Russian Hockey Détente

At his first game with a new group of guys, Rick really tried not to react to Vladimir's negativity, but before you knew it, they were having words, and he left the game feeling bad that he had finally met his first Russians and he was already at war with one of them. Since peace begins with individuals, and since he *was* the coauthor of a book about bringing out the best in people at their worst, he decided to put in the effort to bring about the goal of peaceful coexistence. During the next game, Rick suggested to Vladimir that they play on the same team together.

To their surprise, the two of them had complementary skills and good chemistry together. Vladimir was somewhat of a perfectionist about hockey, as was Rick. They both didn't care as much about winning as about having a good game, and they both loved combining to make the pretty play. Rick was now able to understand Vladimir's frustration with everyone else. Half of the other players just wanted to win and didn't care how, and the other half didn't know what they were doing, and that was the source of Vladimir's hockey negativity. It was ironic that Vladimir, who Rick thought was going to be his most difficult person, turned out to be the most fun to play hockey with. They did great together. Their only problem now was getting other people to play on the same team with them because no one wanted to deal with Vladimir's constant negative criticism.

One day Rick said to Vladimir, "I think it is great how much you care about others learning to play well."

Of course, Vlad's answer to that was a confused, "Vat?"

Rick explained, "Well, it's obvious that you care a lot about people playing better because you spend a lot of time telling them what they do wrong. Why bother if you didn't want them to learn what to do right? Right?" [Project positive intent]

He said, "I suppose."

For positive projection to be effective, you must be consistent over time. So whenever they played hockey and Vladimir started to criticize someone, Rick would approach him and say, "Thanks for helping him." Or "Good, now he knows what to do next time." Or "Soon we will all be passing the puck."

After three weeks of persistent positive projection, twice a week, two hours a night, Rick and Vladimir were in the locker room, and Rick decided to test his results. He said, "Vladdy, you're a guy who cares a lot about people learning, aren't you?"

And he said, "Da, dis is true. So?" Once No People accept a positive projection about their intent, they are ready for some feedback.

So Rick said, "Have you noticed that nobody is getting better around here?"

There was a moment of silence as he got thoughtful, and then he said with deep concern, "Da. Rick, do you tink maybe, vell, could it be dat dey are all stupid?"

Rick stifled a laugh and said, "I don't know about stupid, but when it comes to communication, I believe that if what you are doing isn't working, try something else. We have told them what they're doing wrong. Why don't we tell them only how to do it correctly for two weeks and see if it makes a difference?"

Well, not surprisingly, Vladimir wasn't too hopeful about that idea, but he was willing to try it. And a funny thing happened. He noticed that when he told people how to do something correctly, they did it correctly. When he told them what they were doing wrong, they repeated the mistake. His behavior became increasingly focused on the positive and therefore more constructive to the others. And as the others' game improved, Vladimir, the former No Person, became a valued member of the team.

The Negativity Jar

A manager we know who was hired to run an office with chronically low morale devised and implemented a brilliant policy for dealing with complaints and negativity. If an employee uttered a negative word, thought, or an entire complaint without a suggestion, he or she had to put a quarter into the "negativity jar," which was nothing more than a large pickle jar with the label still attached and a bit of pickle fragrance left in it. All money put in that jar was to be used for a "Thank God It's Friday" company party to be held once a month.

Two notable outcomes occurred: First, as the jar quickly filled up, people started to take notice of just how negative they had been. This perspective had a profound impact on the employees. They gradually realized that they had developed a collective "weaned-on-a-pickle" look, and they saw what a pickle that had put them in. Second, the monthly party was an excellent morale builder that everyone enjoyed. As a result, employees would exaggerate the negativity of different events as an excuse to put more money into the jar for bigger and better parties. As the cloud of negativity dissipated, the workplace atmosphere improved dramatically. The party was moved from Friday to Monday and renamed the "Thank God It's Monday" party. The manager convinced the company to pay for it based on increased productivity. Oh yeah, and the pickle jar yielded its place on the cabinet to a memorial cookie jar with the words "Every Cloud Has a Silver Lining" printed brightly on the lid.

Quick Summary

When Someone Becomes a No Person

   Your Goal: Transition to Problem Solving

   ACTION PLAN

   1. Use the Whiner Strategy.

   2. Use them as resources.

   3. Buy some time.

   4. Go for the polarity response.

   5. Acknowledge their good intent.

20

The Judge

Fable: Olivia Owl and Robin Robin
"Hi there, Auntie Olivia." Robin chirped.
    "Well, whoo, whoo is this," Olivia Owl replied, "but my favorite niece Robin Robin."

Robin landed on a branch perpendicular to Aunt Olivia's so she could look into her big yellow eyes without having to turn her own head. Although Robin had known Auntie Olivia all her life, there was still something disconcerting about the way she looked at you directly, with both eyes at the same time. It was almost … human, and it made Robin's neck feathers tingle. But one thing was certain, Olivia Owl had a penetrating gaze that could, and usually would, look right through you.

"So, Auntie, I heard you went to a flock party? How was it?"

"Well, the food was terrible. The nuts were so hard that everyone had problems getting them open. Except, of course, that old bird Tara Toucan. Can you believe the beak on that bird? And you should see her colors! Why I never! Perhaps that's what they wear in the jungle, but she will never make it in this forest dressed like that."

"Well, Auntie Olivia, wasn't there anything you liked about the party?" Robin Robin chipperly inquired.

"How can you like a party with food like that? For one thing, everyone knows you don't serve worms at a flock party. They simply won't stay fresh. And all those seeds, seeds, seeds. Not a single field mouse. I am a carnivorous bird, you know. I think they were just being cheap, cheap, cheap."

Before Robin could reply, Aunt Olivia went on: "You remember Daisy and Dahlia Duck, your distant cousins? They were there too. I know they are amphibious birds, and yes, they do have to float, but you can't tell me their backsides have to be that big! I just don't understand whooo, whooo could let themselves go like that."

Robin fidgeted nervously on the branch. She didn't like hearing Aunt Olivia putting down any of the many members of her extended family. But Olivia didn't notice and continued her commentary.

Suddenly Olivia Owl became very focused, gazing off into the distance. Robin didn't see anything, but Olivia said, "Don't look now and don't say anything, but here comes Betty Blue Jay."

From a distance, Robin heard Betty's unmistakable loud screech. "Hello, Olivia Owl! Hello, Robin Robin!"

"Hoo, Hoo to you Betty," they replied as Betty flew into view and then flew away. "My, aren't you looking nice!" Olivia called after her. As Betty disappeared from view, Olivia turned to Robin and said, "What blue trash!"

But Robin could barely hear what her auntie said because of a deafening noise overhead. She looked up to see a flock of at least 30 crows. They circled a few times, squawking loudly, then rumbled off toward the horizon. Aunt Olivia Owl muttered, "Yech, that's all we need, a gang of crows stirring up trouble around here. There goes the forest! A bunch of avian hooligans, that's what they are. Making all that noise. Do they think our auricular areas are ornamental? Look at them. Common crows, and they think they're so tough, flying around in those black feather jackets."

Robin Robin's fidgeting intensified. She didn't want her auntie to know that she was dating the leader of the flock. Perish forbid that Olivia might turn her critical eyes on her! "Well, Auntie," she said nervously, "it was nice visiting with you, but I must fly!"

"All right, Robin. Wait, turn around and let me adjust your tail feathers. You are the symbol of spring, and you have a reputation to keep up. You shouldn't fly around all ruffled, as you so often do."

And as Robin Robin flew away, she couldn't help but wonder what Olivia had to say about her when she wasn't around.

Judges set a standard that *no one* can meet, then pronounce judgment along with a running commentary of criticism.

Critical to a fault, picky to the point of perfection, and certain of their criticism, Judges declare you GUILTY and then sentence you to time in the jail of their disapproval.

In our Lens of Understanding, Judges' behavior originates out of the positive intent to *get it right*.

There are two ways that the intent to *get it right* can lead to this difficult behavior:

Threatened intent: Fear of being wrong

Projected intent: Identifying what's wrong in others

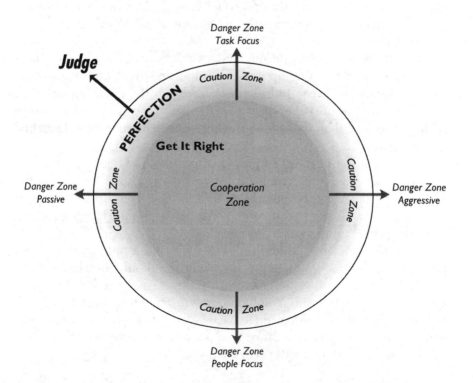

The Judge's behavior begins when someone who wants to *get it right* rises to the bench in the courtroom of discernment to determine what is truly proper in a given situation. The observation is made that someone or something is out of place, out of step, out of accord, or has failed to conform to the high standards of Judges. Something is wrong! That's when the good intention of Judges becomes a relentless nitpicky perfectionism that manifests as criticism and condescension.

In general Judges become critical, finding fault in everything and everybody. The internal demand to criticize keeps growing in intensity. Then Judges can be perceived by others as disgruntled perfectionists, hopeless cynics, or relentless nitpickers.

The Range of Judgmental Behavior: Innocent or Guilty

In the court of Judges, you're either innocent or guilty. There are few shades of gray to interfere with their judgment, but there are several ways to hold court.

There are the Small Claims Judges who complain about the failings of every person to every other person. These Judges present evidence, pass judgment, and then pass the judgment along to others as gossip and rumor.

Then there are the Nitpicking Judges who, much like the neatness freaks who keep cleaning up after cleaning up, fixate on details of no real consequence. These Judges prefer order in the court. In an effort to build a wall against the chaos, they cover the carpet and furniture with plastic, and then they close off the room so it cannot be disturbed by human touch.

There are also the Hanging Judges who throw the book at you if you disagree with anything. Hung up on one narrow point of view, the Hanging Judges impose rules and pound the gavel to drown you out if you keep trying to argue your case. In the courts of the Hanging Judges, the rulings of the Judges are supreme.

Then there are the Cynical Judges who look up only to tear something down and believe that others are motivated only by selfishness.

Finally, there are the Probation Officer Judges who like to look over your shoulder because you're in their domain. The Probation Officers will tell you what not to do as you do it, what will go wrong before it happens, what doom awaits you if you take unapproved-of action, and what never was or will be right, no matter how hard you try.

These problem behaviors cause harm to both Judges and to those who must deal with them. Judges may wind up in constant pain because the world refuses to conform to their standards. And those being judged may become cynical and apathetic, deciding that there's no point in trying, because no matter how hard they try, it will never be good enough.

You'd Better Adjust Your Attitude

Get defensive, and you condemn yourself. Say nothing, and you seem guilty. But you don't have to correct the Judge, not if you correct yourself to yourself instead. If your highest priority is self-defense and you don't want to be found in contempt in the courtroom of the Judge's opinion, then let go of the need to correct the Judge when he or she is wrong about you. Instead, correct yourself. The attitudinal key to dealing with the Judges is to counter the negative rulings, whether stated directly or implied, in the privacy of your own mind. You do this by telling yourself the positive corollaries to the negative judgments:

> If the Judge says or implies: "You are a lousy friend."
>
> You say to yourself: "I am a good friend, and that's why I'm still on the phone."

> If the Judge says or implies: "You totally screwed it up."
>
> You say to yourself: "I know I did the best I could."

> If the Judge says or implies: "I was waiting for you for a half hour, and I put my package down, so it's because of you that I forgot about it."
>
> You say to yourself: "It was not about me. She put the package down."

Doing this will help you to keep your perspective. Offering encouragement to yourself is the ray of light that keeps your thinking bright in the otherwise gloomy presence of criticism.

Your demeanor must indicate that you have nothing to defend and that you do have a case to make. Be wary of making big leaps of logic. It is essential in your approach that you go slowly, step-by-step. A wry amusement may be useful in this regard because it indicates that the charges don't really apply to you. Avoid saying anything sarcastic, though. When you present your case, you must build it in a way that says, "A careful examination of the evidence is all that is required of you.

I'm certain that when you've considered what I have to say, you'll draw a just conclusion." Be dispassionate, at least until your closing argument. A calm, methodical, logical, and consistent approach is the best way to get past the guards and get your day in court.

Don't question the court's judgment. If you do, the Judge will likely fine you for contempt. If you tell the Judge that he or she is wrong, by inference if not by intent, you are out of order! Instead, recognize that what the Judge has said reflects his or her view of the facts. You aren't there to contradict the Judge. You are there to offer new evidence or to interpret the facts in a new way.

Your Goal: Get the Judgment Dismissed

When the *get it right* Judge rises to the bench, if the accusation is that you have somehow failed to measure up to the perfectionistic order of the court, prepare your defense but without getting defensive. Your goal when dealing with the Judge is to get the judgment dismissed.

Action Plan

Option 1. Acknowledge the Judgment and Move On. This option works great with the Small Claims Judge. Sometimes you're better off acknowledging the judgment and then moving on, rather than taking the time and expending the energy to try and change the Judge's mind. If you choose this option, give thanks for your Judge's good intentions, and then go your own way:

"Thanks for being honest with me about how you feel."

"Thanks for bringing that to my attention."

"Thanks for your thoughtful suggestions."

If the judgment is about someone else in your family:

"Thanks for wanting their life to work out."

"Thanks for letting me in on what you're thinking."

"Thanks for your insights."

Then change the subject, get up and move, or offer to get them something. As you deflect the judgment with your positive projection about the Judge's intention, the Judge may wind up having to reflect on himself and the conclusions he's drawn because you're not getting in the way.

Option 2. Return to Sender. This option works well with the fault-finding Nitpicking Judge. If you're tired of hearing the Judge passing judgment on other people whom you care about, you can return the judgment to its owner by asking the Judge to own the judgments. It may be obvious to you that the criticized person doesn't want to go by the Judge's laws. However, it may not be obvious to the Judge. That's because Judges refer to an internal lawbook of their own making, and they mistakenly assume everyone has a copy. The best way to let a Judge know that nobody else has the book is with a gentle backtrack and then a question regarding the authority by which the Judge is passing judgment.

First, backtrack the judgment, so the Judge will know what you are specifically referring to. Use as many of the Judge's words as possible, so there's no mistake about it.

> "When you say, people that look like that shouldn't be seen in public, I'm curious to know how you came to that conclusion. According to whom?"

> "When you say that the proper thing to do is keep your mouth shut and don't talk back, how do you know that? It's the proper thing according to whom?"

If the response you get is a generalized, "Everybody knows it," then ask for specifics. If the Judge says, "Everyone," ask, "Who specifically?" If the answer is, "Always," ask, "When specifically?" If the Judge says, "It's just common sense!" bring it back around by asking, "Common sense to whom?" If the Judge says, "Any thinking person," ask, "By whom specifically is this regarded as common sense?" Keep bringing it back around until it lands squarely in the Judge's court. You'll know it's back in the court when the Judge says, "By me!"

Option 3. Appeal the Sentence. Here's the situation. Suppose you're dealing with a Hanging Judge. A negative comment is made about you or about someone in your family that you care about who is having a hard time with the Judge because of all the judgments. The judgments follow the comparison format of "You're too much" or "You're too little" or "You're not enough" or "You're not even close." In any case, you can either appeal the decision of the Judge or you can take your appeal to a higher court (the court of your own opinions!).

Bringing your appeal to the Hanging Judge's court applies only if you have specifics about new or unexamined evidence that directly contradicts the Judge's opinion. For example, if the Judge says, "Your daughter isn't even trying to lose weight," yet you happen to know what steps she's taking to lose weight, you can introduce what you know as new evidence. Ask a leading question, while suggesting an explanation for why the Judge was unaware of the information you're presenting. The information you offer reveals to your Judge that the Judge's generalization isn't accurate:

"I can tell this is important to you. [Positive projection] I guess you didn't know that she's cut out sugar and simple carbohydrates from her diet the last three weeks? [Leading question that introduces new information] She's been talking with me regularly, and she is very frustrated with how difficult this is for her. Yet she perseveres, and I'm proud of her because I understand how much effort this is going to take to see it through."

Then, if you have an alternate sentence to suggest, offer it, in order to shift the Judge from judgment to constructive actions. If your information is solid and your references as a character witness are good, this may be enough to influence the thinking of the Judge, reducing the sentence to time served, or at least diminishing the harshness of their criticism for the moment.

If a public judgment is happening to other people and you want to help them out of the awful situation, then try making your appeal public. Say something nice to the people being judged, and ask them to account for their success or progress. To the people being judged for appearance, you might say, "You look really nice. What have you been doing? Whatever it is, keep it up." To the people being judged for performance, you might say, "I've noticed that you've really been doing some terrific work lately. What are you doing differently?"

If, however, the judgments are directed at you, take your appeal to the higher court of your own opinion. This is the attitudinal approach we recommended earlier in the chapter. Place yourself under the influence of your own attitude by introducing counterexamples of the Judge's judgments upon you. If a Judge criticizes you for the way you look, say something in the privacy of your own mind to encourage yourself. "I'm making a big effort to deal with this, and I'm making progress." If the Judge says, "You are to blame!" say to yourself, "I'm doing the best I can.

These accusations are about him, not about me." Maybe you can't tell the Judge because the Judge can't handle the truth. But *you* can handle it, so make sure to tell it to yourself! This keeps you free of your Judge's negative characterizations, strong in your knowledge of the facts, and focused in your Judge's presence in spite of the judgmental behavior. It's bound to influence your Judge's opinion of you in the long run, and it keeps you in charge of your own destiny.

Option 4. Go for the Polarity Response. A common mistake made with Judges is trying to change their mind. Unless you've been granted an appeal, you are wasting your time. However, you can use Judges' judgment intentionally to get the Judges to go from prosecuting what they find offensive to defending it!

Lucky for you, the Judges, like No People, have strong polarity responses. While it's both ironic and paradoxical, the fact is that people who judge others tend to strongly dislike being judged themselves. Simply crowd them out of the role of prosecutor, by taking what they said and saying it in an even more polarizing manner, offered in the form of a question. Here are two examples:

Example 1

Judge: "Jeff doesn't apply himself in college. He just plays and runs around all the time, and he acts like it doesn't matter. He is a disgrace to the family."

You: "You think Jeff is intentionally trying to disgrace the family? Do you think he's stupid?"

Judge: "No, I'm not saying that."

Example 2

Judge: "Loretta doesn't care how other people see her. She always looks like a mess, and it's embarrassing."

You: "You think she doesn't know how she looks? You think she likes looking that way? You don't think she hates looking that way?"

Judge: "Well, no, of course she hates it!"

In both of these cases, notice that the Judge goes opposite to the question and affirms something opposite to his or her own original judgment. That's the beauty of the polarity response. You don't have to convince people. You get them to convince themselves.

Then you can provide some reinforcement for the Judge's new position:

You: "I'm relieved that you know that."

This has the potential to put the Judge back in the Cooperation Zone. Typically, the Judge will then express regret over his or her own helplessness to bring about a change for the better. If ever there were a time to offer a suggestion, this is it!

Judge: "I just wish she would listen to me."
You: "I've found that what works best in this kind of situation is to offer encouragement. When people feel bad, they don't change. When people feel successful, they accumulate successes."

Option 5. Give Them a Glimpse of Greatness. Sometimes you have to draw a bigger line and tell problem Judges the truth about how their behavior is self-defeating and what you think would work better instead. Begin by appreciating that their intent is positive, that they care about you, about quality, about *getting things right.* Then show them how the way they are going about it defeats their own purpose because of how people react to it. Then quickly switch to what they could do instead that would work better. The overview is the same for honesty with any of the problem behaviors. (See the "Tell Your Truth" section in Chapter 7, "Speak to Be Understood.") Your goal of honesty is to give Judges a glimpse of greatness:

> State your positive intent.
>
> Be specific about the problem behavior.
>
> Show them how their behavior is self-defeating.
>
> Suggest new behaviors or options.
>
> Reinforce behavioral change.

Of the actions listed above, two are especially important to Judges:

1. *State your positive intent.* Appreciating Judges' attention to right and wrong is a key element to gaining access to their willingness to change. You can tell them you appreciate:

   "... wanting her to do the right thing."

   "... the way you care about his appearance."

   "... wanting this to turn out well."

   "... wanting me to have a good life."

   "... wanting me to have a fulfilling relationship."

2. *Be specific about the problem behavior.* Show Judges the benefit of change by revealing the self-defeating consequences of their behavior.

It is likely that Judges are looking at a detail and failing to see the big picture. You want to offer a clear example of how their behavior is self-defeating:

"When you did this, here's what happened."

"You're losing the people you care about because when you say critical things to them about others, they worry about what you'll say about them behind their back. Then they want to stay away from you."

"Because she tries to be nice, she doesn't say anything to you when you say these things to her. But I know she internalizes your feedback and uses it to feel bad about herself. This lowers her self-esteem even further, which makes it even less likely she'll make the right choices that are so obvious to you."

Great Moments in Difficult People History

Olivia Owl and Robin Robin

The day had arrived for the big migration to the south. The migratory birds had packed their nests and were saying their goodbyes to the nonmigratory birds.

Robin Robin had prepared for this moment for over a month. It wasn't the migration that concerned her. She had done that many times before, and she could do it with her eyes closed. But today, when she said her good-bye to Aunt Olivia Owl, she planned to talk with her about her critical behavior.

Robin landed on a nearby branch and chirped, "Greetings, Auntie Olivia!"

Olivia Owl sat silently staring, her big yellow eyes focused unblinkingly on Robin Robin. Feeling intimidated, Robin's resolve briefly wavered.

Finally, Olivia Owl spoke. "Well, I'm glad someone had the decency to fly by to say goodbye. Dahlia and Daisy Duck are already gone. Of course, given how plump they are, they probably need an extra day to fly. Have you seen your brother, Ray Robin? I haven't. Maybe he flew into a glass window and knocked himself out, the way he did last time. Sitting there on the ground unconscious for all that time, he could have been gobbled up by somebody's house cat. But it serves him right for zooming around so recklessly. Whooo knows! Perhaps the impact is what made him forget his manners. I heard the geese have already left too, and I haven't even heard a word from Gabby or Gertie Goose. As Canadian geese, I expected them to be a little more polite than some of the locals!"

Robin Robin knew she couldn't be a chicken. She had to talk to Aunt Olivia because she could no longer stand the constant stream of critical comments, but she loved her aunt and knew she meant well. Robin didn't want to become one of the many birds that were permanently migrating out of Aunt Olivia's life. She took a deep breath.

Olivia seemed to stare at her more intently. "Why are you fidgeting so much? Are you in hurry? If you need to fly off, go ahead."

Robin looked directly at Olivia, "No, I'm not in a hurry. It's just that I love you, and I have something to tell you that is very important for me to say and you to hear. But it is difficult to say it."

"Well, whoo, whoo, I love you too, Robin. What could be so difficult? Just say it!"

"As you wish. Auntie, I know how much you care about everyone. And because you are nocturnal and carnivorous, you have exceptionally good eyes, so you see the details that others often don't see."

Robin paused, as Olivia sat in silence with those big yellow eyes staring at her. Then she continued.

"But the things you say sound so harsh to me. You have so much wisdom to offer, but some of the things you say sound harsh instead. So I have to ask you. Do you really think Dahlia Duck doesn't care about how she looks? Do you really think she is trying to be a disgrace?"

"No! Of course not."

"I am relieved to hear that."

"I just wish she would listen to me. She really doesn't have to be that large."

"Have you influenced her at all, Auntie?"

"It doesn't seem so. I swear, she must be preparing herself to become a dish of Peking duck at a Chinese restaurant."

Robin went on, "Well, I find that encouragement works better than criticism in these situations. Because if you tell her only what is wrong, she feels bad about herself. And when she feels bad, she heads straight to the park and starts quacking to the humans for more bread. And it isn't just her. Do you really think that all the migratory birds just forgot to say goodbye? Is it possible that some of them didn't want to? Because when you tell birds critical things about other birds, the birds you say it to worry about what you say about them when they're not around. They may stop coming around to avoid your criticism. And if they stop coming around, you lose the opportunity to help them."

Olivia blinked her big yellow eyes and shifted her position on the branch. Robin thought to herself, "Wow, Auntie is actually uncomfortable. I didn't know she was capable of discomfort!" Robin knew there was no turning back now. "Auntie, I know a secret way to get people to like you and listen to you. Would you like to know what it is?"

Olivia blinked again and said, "Pray tell, Robin, what is it?"

"All you have to do is say nice things about others when someone comes around. And instead of telling others what's wrong, ask them how you can best be of assistance to them! You have a lot of help to give, but you have to say it in a way that others can hear." They sat there in silence for what seemed like an eternity, until Robin said, "Well, Auntie Olivia, I am really going to have to fly. I love you! Have a nice winter." She then turned and said, "Do you want to help me fix my tail feathers? I can't go flying around all ruffled."

Olivia Owl blinked her big yellow eyes, "That's all right, Robin Robin, you look fine just as you are."

They sat for another moment, and then Olivia said, "Thank you, Robin."

Then Robin flew south for the winter, looking forward to returning in the spring more than she ever had before.

The moral of this story is that a little bit of encouragement goes a longer way than a lot of criticism.

Quick Summary

When Someone Becomes a Judge

Your Goal: Get the Judgment Dismissed

ACTION PLAN

1. Acknowledge the judgment and move on.

2. Return to sender.

3. Appeal the sentence.

4. Go for the polarity response.

5. Give them a glimpse of greatness.

21
The Meddler

Sally Squirrel arrived at the branch where she was supposed to meet the new squirrel guy in her life. She hoped it was sufficiently far from home to keep her mother Suzie from finding out.

But then came a demanding voice from a tree away. "Sally, where are you hiding? Show yourself." And just like that, her mother was on the same branch, facing Sally.

"So how's the chipmunk?" Suzie demanded. "I heard that you were seen with one."

Sally sat silently stunned, not only at how quickly the news had gotten around but also at how twisted it had become. "Who told you I was seeing someone?" she asked. Someone must have seen her, she thought, because she hadn't told anyone, particularly her mother. She didn't want to have to deal with the relentless questioning she knew she was about to undergo. It was like an interrogation, only without the bright lights.

"A little bird told me," her mother replied. "Why would you give a chipmunk the time of day? Do you plan to live in a hole in the ground? Chipmunks are nothing but hoarders, if you ask me. They never amount to anything."

Sally didn't want to tell her a thing. Yet she felt compelled to say something. "C'mon, Mom! He's not a chipmunk. He's a wonderful southern squirrel, and I'm just getting to know him!"

"Southern? What kind of family does he come from? What are his plans for the future? Did you know that stylish Sammy Squirrel hops by our home every week, asking after you? He is so bright-eyed and bushy-tailed. I told him you would have acorns with him tomorrow at the big oak tree."

"You told him what?" Sally screeched.

"You heard me. He looks like a solid provider, not another one of the nutcases you keep getting involved with!"

"But I'm seeing Red tomorrow," Sally squealed—and smacked herself in the head with her tail for revealing his name.

"Red, is it? In which tree does he live? I'll let him know that you can't make it."

"Mother! You will do no such thing."

Suzie didn't even flinch. "Red? What kind of squirrel is named after a color? What does he do, this 'Red'? Does he have any plans?"

Sally was now so off balance from the onslaught of questions that she stuttered out a feeble, "I don't know what he plans to do. I'm just getting to know him myself."

"Don't tell me he's another dropout, or that he's just a gatherer. Anyone can do that. You know what they say. Eventually, even a blind squirrel finds the nuts."

"No, as a matter of fact, he's not a dropout. In fact, he's a flier! He can glide, he's cute, and he's funny. For all I know, maybe he'll go into entertainment. He gets his picture taken every day. He's the most downloaded squirrel on the Internet! He's going to be somebody!"

Suzie twitched her tail in disgust and pressed on. "Not a high-flying dot-com squirrel! And where will you be when he crashes and burns? How do you know he isn't just trying to weasel his way into your nest for a season? After all, why buy the feeder when you can get the seeds for free?"

Suddenly, horror crossed Sally's face as she looked a few branches beyond her mother and saw Red! She covered her face with her tail, hoping he wouldn't see her, but a hop, bounce, and flying jump later, he was right there with them.

"Hi, Sally, ma'am." He tipped his head to Suzie. "How ya'll doin'?"

Sally still hadn't uncovered her face. From behind her tail she mumbled, "Hi, Red."

Suzie looked him up and down. "So you're Red. I'll have you know I'm Sally's mother."

With a gentle sweep of his tail and a bow of his head, Red drawled, "A pleasure to meet you, Mrs. Squirrel."

"I hear you and my daughter are dating," Suzie said.

Sally was still hiding her face behind her tail, when the situation went from bad to worse.

"So, Red, what are your intentions toward my daughter? Are you going to marry her?"

Red's mouth began slowly to open, but before he could answer, they heard an urgent voice cry. "Mother, Mother!"

It was Sally Squirrel's sister Sarah, who hopped, leaped, dropped when she missed a branch, made a good recovery, then jumped, and joined the three of them on the branch.

"Mother, I think the chipmunks may be raiding our nest."

Without a word Suzie bolted from the branch and was gone.

"Do ya'll need muh help?" Red asked.

Sarah Squirrel gave them a wink of her eye and a shake of her tail, and they realized that she was helping them out.

"Thanks so much, Sarah," her sister said. "I owe you."

"Yeah, you do. But right now you two better get out of here before she gets back."

As the two squirrels leapt, jumped, and scampered off, Sally wondered, "Why does Mother have to do that? The last thing I need right now is her interference in my life!"

Meddlers think they know what's best for you. So they use unwanted questions and advice, to try to manage your life.

A Meddler's behavior begins when the intention to *get it done* combines with the intention to *get it right*.

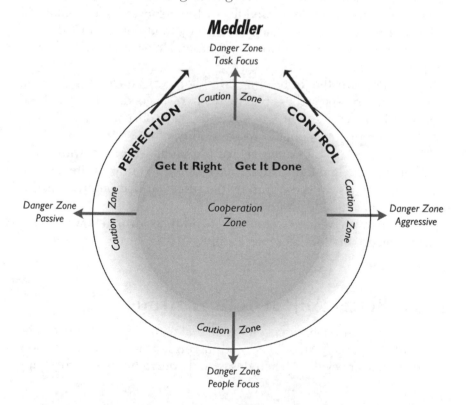

Meddler

When the intent to *get it right* is combined with the intent to *get it done* and is projected onto other people, Meddlers feel compelled to intervene. They seek to get others to change what they're doing and how they're doing it by pointing out what needs to be avoided and directing people toward what needs to take place. Their behavior indicates that they have no confidence in the ability of people to make it happen. They criticize others and tell them what to do instead, in order to assure the right result. "When are you going to get married?" they'll want to know, and then give you the third degree. By prodding instead of persuading, their attempts to have influence are treated like unwelcome interference.

The Range of Difficulty: Nosy to Manipulative

There is a range of difficulty among Meddlers. There are your basic Nosy Meddlers who look over your shoulder in order to get a glimpse into your life. This involves poking around in subjects that are no one else's business, in order to find out what you're doing.

There are the Controlling Meddlers who look over your shoulder in order to make sure you do exactly what they want done. Don't do this. Do that. Watch out for that. Don't touch that. Do what you're told or be judged a failure.

Then there are the Interfering Meddlers who do things for you, against your express wishes, but for your own good. After all, these Meddlers know what's right for you. And you're obviously not going to take the appropriate amount of responsibility.

Finally, there are the Manipulative Meddlers who mess with a key detail of your life in order to affect some other part of your life. You, of course, are the last to know. And by the time you find out, the deed is done, and you get to deal with it.

From what you wear, to whom you spend time with, to how you talk, to what you do, the Meddlers are keeping an eye on you.

You'd Better Adjust Your Attitude

Of all the problem behaviors you could deal with, the Meddlers can be the most perplexing. Meddlers' good intentions, no matter how badly implemented, are evident. Their desire to do the right thing is, for them, an irresistible call to action. You're not going to convince them that meddling is wrong because in their frame of reference nothing could be more right.

- *In your behavior and manner, approach Meddlers with caution and a strong sense of responsibility.* This blends with both their intent to *get it right* and *get it done.* Enter into the dialogue from a place of commitment, strength, and determination, while knowing that they must do what they think is right and responsible. A little bemusement, kept to yourself, is a plus. It will help you not to take their behavior too seriously, no matter how invasive or personal they become.

- *In terms of your demeanor, be relaxed and reflective in the presence of invasive and even hostile questions.* Just because they ask a question doesn't mean you have to answer it. Instead, ask them a question back, and then be curious enough to look and listen for whatever's behind what they've said. If they ask about your diet or weight, be curious about their food and appearance issues. If they ask about your love life, be curious about their relationship issues. If they ask about your finances, be curious about their money issues. Speak with self-assurance, so that you send the clear signal that you're responsible for yourself and alert to making your best choices. Your nonverbal response must also convey that you're responsible and want to do what's right.

- *Don't answer questions that have not specifically been asked.* If they don't ask, don't tell. Just recognize human nature instead of spilling the beans. And if they do ask specific questions, remember, you still don't have to tell them the answers. Instead, rather than deal with the content of their questions, focus on their intentions and the pattern of their relationship with you.

- *Don't volunteer details or reveal anything that you don't want them involved with.* Once the cat is out of the bag, it's difficult to put it back in. (Although why the cat was in the bag is something we've never really understood.) Realize that they may not know where to draw the line and may go further than you want them to.

- *Don't involve them unless you know they have something to offer.* If they do have something to offer, let them know what it is as specifically and narrowly defined as possible, rather than leaving it open-ended or subject to interpretation. By exercising some responsibility over their input, you may be able to maintain an appropriate boundary between you.

Your Goal: Preserve and Protect the Boundary

When dealing with meddling Meddlers who seek to first invade and then remotely run your life, your behavior must send an unmistakable signal that there is a boundary between you that will not be crossed. They must come to understand that while you appreciate their concern and interest, you have the outcome under control and a clear view of the details along the way. The best thing they can give you is their support, and the best thing you can give them is a well-defined boundary that they cannot cross.

Action Plan

Option 1. Appreciate Their Intentions. The behavior of meddling is often adopted as a solution to the problem of loneliness. More often than not, Meddlers are older than you, with too much time on their hands. Add to this the feeling of being unwanted and unneeded that sometimes comes with age. The result? You have people trying to have some responsibility somewhere by applying what they think they've learned from their own life to targets of convenience. Essentially, that's whoever happens to be around.

When Meddlers occupy their thoughts with the business of others, they can experience being with others, even if they're alone. When they see you, they can't help but offer you what they came up with for your benefit.

Other times, Meddlers meddle to compensate for the guilt they feel over their own failures. They didn't figure out what to do until it was too late for them, but it isn't too late to help you!

Telling Meddlers that what they're doing is wrong, verbally or non-verbally, will likely trigger a wave of self-justification and defensive communication that could damage the future of your relationship. Obviously, this is better avoided.

While you may hate what they're doing, there's no reason for or value in hating them for doing it. Instead, you can express appreciation to them for their interest and concern. In this way, you meet them where they are. And with a little luck, you may relieve a good deal of the pressure that drives their behavior by receiving it as an intended gift rather than interference or imposition. That's why it's hard to go wrong when you thank Meddlers for their intentions.

If possible, you can even thank them for their actions, based on your understanding of their intentions. Thank them for visits, for gifts, for advice, for time spent, for interest. Let them see you as someone who respects their desire to *get it done* and *get it right*, and they will remain open to your influence down the road.

Option 2. Give Them a Place to Meddle.   Sometimes people meddle because they have nothing else to occupy their time. With all that time on their hands, they get to thinking about ways to meaningfully contribute to the people they love, and they arrive at the idea of making other people's lives their hobby. They'll offer their good advice, keep an eye on things, and watch out for preventable problems, trying to make sure that nothing goes wrong.

If they're determined to meddle, put the behavior in context and give the Meddlers a place to meddle. Ask their advice on an issue of lesser consequence. This may create a diversion from the subject you would prefer them to leave alone. Pick an area where their meddling is harmless and possibly constructive. Invite their assistance. Let them help you with something, even if it's something you can do more easily without their help. This gives them the feeling of being responsible and appropriate, and it may satiate their need to be involved in your life.

If a Meddler is meddling with your wedding preparations, put the Meddler in charge of something, even if it's just making the place cards. Count your blessings that you have someone willing to help, and take advantage of the offer!

Option 3. Meddle with the Meddling.   There are many ways to meddle with the meddling, like taking control, having a canned response, or creating a diversion.

- *Take control.* You can stop being a victim by taking control of the meddling. Become fascinated with it, and try to find out everything you can, from the source—the Meddlers, of course! Find out their interests. Find out how they define the words they use. Find out by asking questions! Ask enough questions and you may even reveal to them that they know less about the subject than they thought. If that's the case, they'll back off and get out of your way. Let their behavior be your cue. The next time they ask about your private life, ask them what they want to know and then probe their answers.

Meddler:	"Are you dating?"
You:	"What is it you want to know about me and dating?"
Meddler:	"Well, I want to know what kind of person you're seeing."
You:	"What kind of person would you like me to be seeing?"

Meddler:	"You shouldn't wear that. It makes you look fat."
You:	"It makes me look fat to whom?"
Meddler:	"People."
You:	"What is it about looking fat that matters this much to you?"

Meddler:	"All that butter will raise your cholesterol."
You:	"How much will this butter raise my cholesterol?"
Meddler:	"I mean in general."
You:	"How much butter in general will raise my cholesterol?"

- *Have a canned response.* If Meddlers meddle in predictable ways, and you can anticipate the kinds of things they'll say, then having predictable responses to say in response may be all that's needed to derail the meddling. For example:

| Meddler: | "Dear, when are you going to get married?" |
| You: | "Aunt Ellen, I'll get married just as soon as I find someone to love me as much as Uncle Harry loves you." |

That one is particularly effective because it has two possible reactions. If Aunt Ellen is unhappy with Uncle Harry, she isn't going to keep rushing you into something you might regret. And if she is happy with Uncle Harry, she's going to want you to wait until you find the right person.

Predictable responses are best thought of ahead of time. The next time Meddlers meddle in that predictable way, what do you want to remember to say? Write it down, practice it, and then when the opportunity presents itself, use it!

- *Create a diversion.* You could also use Junk O'Logic to create a diversion. Junk O'Logic makes an artificial connection between what Meddlers say and what you say in response. (You can read more about it in Chapter 13, "The Think-They-Know-It-All.")

| Meddler: | "That coat is not going to keep him warm. Why don't you buy him a decent coat for the winter?" |
| You: | "Thanks for mentioning the winter. I was in town the other day, and I saw this lovely window display that you would have enjoyed so much!" [Then just keep going, for at least a minute!] |

| Meddler: | "If you get fat, no one is going to like you, and you'll end up alone and miserable, like your father's brother. Is that what you want?" |

You: "I'm so glad you mentioned him. Have you talked with him lately? The last time we spoke, he ..."

Once you start talking, keep going, for at least 30 seconds to a minute. This may be enough to distract them and make them forget their attempt to meddle. You can also employ a visual distraction:

Meddler: "I can't believe you wasted your money on that car. What were you thinking?"
You: "I was thinking. ... Look! Over there!"

Then point somewhere, suddenly, and start talking about what you see at the end of your finger. Watch them get confused! On the phone, say, "Oh my! Amazing!" And then start talking about anything else. This sort of sudden and strange behavior is called a *pattern disruption*. If you do it regularly in the presence of a behavior you want to discourage, your Meddler may find it harder and harder to remember to bother meddling at all.

One woman told us of the time her mother demanded to know of her boyfriend, "When are you going to marry my daughter?" Her sister jumped in just then with a distraction. "When are you going to pass the potatoes?" Then she quickly changed the subject to something else, and they made it through the rest of the meal without any further meddling.

Option 4. Negotiate the Boundary.   What's usually missing with meddling is a clearly defined boundary between you and the Meddler. When you find that a Meddler in your life is working toward an apparently different life for you than the one you're living, it may be time to negotiate a boundary that you both can live with.

- *Plan a meeting.* Set a formal appointment to talk with your Meddler about the role he or she is playing in your life. Agree together on a time and place where you can talk, preferably someplace neutral where you can both feel relaxed and free of your normal day-to-day responsibilities—like a restaurant or a walk in the park. By making this a planned conversation instead of a casual one, you're more likely to bring the problem behavior into focus:

  "I appreciate all your efforts to look out for me over the years. I have a problem that I would like to discuss with you. Could we make a lunch appointment to discuss the role you play in my life? I have some ideas that I think will make it less stressful and more productive for both of us. I'd like you to bring your ideas about this to our meeting too."

■ *Be prepared.* Know yourself. You have to know your own limitations going in or you'll wind up with a boundary you can't live with. Then there's the problem of being so determined to get your Meddler to agree to your terms that you wind up alienating the Meddler. If you're in a hurry to get the conversation over with, your anxiousness works against you. And this isn't a "have to" situation either. If it doesn't work out, you still have power. If the Meddler continues to interfere in your life, you can always walk away. Knowing that you aren't trapped, that you have a tenable fallback position, gives you some breathing room to hang in there and work your way through the process, even when the going gets tough.

Examine the problem, and determine what your issues are. Is it about time? Does the Meddler spend too much time around you and your family? Is the problem unsolicited advice? Do you feel you're being treated like a child? Does the Meddler actually interfere in your life, doing things expressly against your will? In any case, to make your case, you'll need to know what the specific issue is for you. What is your interest? How do you want it to be if it changes from the way it is? Clarify this in your mind so that when you communicate, you communicate clearly.

You also want to know something about your Meddler's needs and interests. If your Meddler doesn't want you to get hurt, that is valuable information. If the Meddler thinks there's some way you should improve, understanding why this matters to the Meddler gives you valuable information. If the message your being given is that you'd be happier if only you did what your Meddler says, that's valuable information. And the more you know, the more you can do. Information is power, and as in any negotiation, it makes the difference in how well it turns out for you.

■ *Behave wisely.* On the day of your conversation, be pleasant throughout. If you're feeling frustrated and stuck, take a break to regroup, then come back fresh and start again. Keep your conversation focused on specific behaviors (see Chapter 7) and interests, instead of talking about your Meddler. Be looking and listening for a solution that gives your Meddler something to feel good about when he or she gives you what you want.

If you can identify your Meddler's motivation and then show how helping you get what you want will help your Meddler to get what he or she wants, you will have closed the deal and redefined the boundary in your relationship. Here are some pointers to bear in mind.

1. *Open with a positive.* Though it's only an opening phrase, it serves the purpose of placing a positive framework around a potentially difficult conversation: "I know you care about us, and that you really mean well when you …," Project positive intent. "I appreciate that …"

   "… you care about my relationship."

   "… you want me to be happy."

   "… you care about my personal hygiene."

   "… you care about how I look."

   "… you care about how I dress."

   "… you want us to have a nice wedding and get the right gifts."

2. *Describe the problem.* This is where you state your position. If the Meddler is demanding too much of your time, be honest about it. If your Meddler is doing things against your wishes, like spoiling your children or talking to significant people in your life without your permission, be honest about it. Always preface your honest statement with the words, "I know you mean well when you …" or "I know you're trying to be helpful when you…"

3. *Talk about the effects.* This is where you tell your Meddler the part that's hardest on you, and therefore it's the hardest part of the process. Do it in a pleasant manner, but do it well because everything depends on giving your Meddler an accurate understanding of your problem with the meddling behavior. Make sure your description includes yourself, so that your Meddler is hearing about the effect on you rather than your opinion of the Meddler:

   "I felt so angry and frustrated, I could barely talk to you. It really bothered me that you went ahead and did something that I asked you not to do. The result is that I feel afraid to trust you, and I'm anxious about having you spend time with the kids. And I feel awful about that, so it's getting worse for me, not better. Though your intentions are good, it's your actions I'm having trouble with."

   "I feel put down, and I feel ashamed, hopeless, and discouraged. And I want to protect myself from feeling that way so I ignore you. It doesn't have to be that way. This is something I can't change right now. I'm not married, I am fat, and I'm working on these things."

   You can also talk about what might happen if the behavior continues. Many people are motivated to change out of fear of negative consequences. This may prove to be the missing piece in your Meddler's understanding of the situation.

4. *Let the Meddler reply*. This is where you listen to your Meddler's position. Let your Meddler explain, defend, and justify as much as he or she wants. Look and sound like you completely understand, while listening for possible interests that could give you some options. When you give your Meddler the chance to account for the meddling behavior, you may be surprised to learn that the underlying reasons for your Meddler's behavior were actually better than the ones you had thought.

5. *Describe a desired boundary*. If you've been listening well, chances are you've now thought of a way to have it work for both of you. But even if you draw a blank on options, you have to tell your Meddler what it is that you want. If you ask for more than you expect to get, you have room to back down a bit and let your Meddler feel that something has been won. If you like, you can ask your Meddler for a solution before you offer yours. But you must get some option on the table in order to draw the line somewhere.

   Say what you would like to experience around the issue. What works for you? What doesn't work for you? Are there subjects where you would welcome the Meddler's interest? Indicate what those subjects are. Is there another way your Meddler could show interest? Indicate what it is. Be as specific as possible, and communicate in a calm, responsible way so that you are setting a good example of how you want your Meddler to respond.

   "You can help me, and here's how it would work. If you see clothing that would work for me, I would be interested in hearing about where to find it. If you know someone who you think would be a good partner for me, I would be willing to consider that person, but only if you tell me and not him. Showing an interest in my life is not off limits to you. But this is the way in which you can be successful with your interest in helping me with my life."

6. *Establish a signal*. Once you've agreed upon a new boundary in the relationship, it would be nice if you could walk away from the conversation knowing that it was firmly in place. But that isn't likely. The Meddler's behavior was automatic and unconscious, at least in part. You can expect some backsliding. It helps both of you to have a signal system in place so if the behavior reoccurs, you can bring it to your Meddler's attention without creating a conflict. The signal could be something small, like holding up your first finger and slowly moving it from side to side. Or if the problem happens on the phone,

a word or phrase may be helpful. When you have a way to keep the boundary defined, your relationship can improve through time.

7. *Reinforce the boundary*. Catch your former Meddler in the act of doing it right and show appreciation for this. Make it your responsibility to pay attention in order to reinforce the behavior you want.

Great Moments in Difficult People History

The Life and Loves of Sally Squirrel

Sally Squirrel sat on a branch shyly sharing some nuts with Red. She knew it was only a matter of time before her mother showed up. Sure enough, a leap, a scamper, and a jump later, and her mother was on the same branch with them, suspiciously checking them out.

"Hello, ma'am," Red said politely.

"Hi, Mom," said Sally.

Sally turned to Red and said, "I'll see you later." Red took the hint, but no sooner had he turned tail, hopped, bounced, and leaped away than Suzie began the interrogation.

"So, you're still seeing that Red!" she said intensely. "What are your plans? Where is this relationship headed?"

This time, Sally was ready. She chuckled inside, and she reminded herself that just because her mother asked a question, it didn't mean she had to answer it. Instead she said, "Thanks for wanting the best for me! I appreciate how you're willing to use valuable nut-gathering time to check in with me."

Suzie just twitched her tail and said, "That doesn't answer my question."

Sally had spent a lot of time mentally preparing for this. She spoke calmly and directly. "Mom, I really do appreciate that you want me to have a good relationship. But we have a problem here."

"Really?" her mother said. "What is it?"

"I know you mean well, but when you follow me around and snoop on my relationship, it drives me nuts! I feel like running away from you. Sometimes, I even consider doing something nutty just to spite you, like seeing a squirrel that really *is* no good for me. You don't want that, do you?"

"Of course not! But ..."

Sally was determined not to let her mother control this conversation. "No buts, Mom. I have found that by getting to know different squirrels, I am able to better define what I'm looking for in a relationship. This is my business, not yours. If I tell you about any of my relationships, it will be when I'm ready to do so. Now, if you like, there is a role for you to play. If you want to tell me about squirrels that you think I might find interesting, I'll consider them. But I don't need a matchmaker, and if you insist on trying to be one—by setting up meetings with them or prying into my affairs—I will ignore you and scamper off the other way. Do you understand?"

Suzie was taken aback. "But I'm simply looking out for what is best for you," she replied defensively.

"I know you are, and I appreciate your intentions. I'm telling you how you can do that successfully. You may not hunt me down and intrude when I'm with someone. But you may ask questions privately. I may choose not to answer them. If you think there's someone I ought to meet, you can tell me. But whether I choose to act upon your suggestion is entirely up to me. All right?"

Suzie looked at the branch beneath her, then said, "You know, I was young once. And my mother did the same thing to me. I can' t believe I am doing it to you. I used to hate it."

"Then you agree to these conditions for your involvement in my love life?"

"Agreed. I promise to do my best to change. But it's so automatic—what if I forget?"

Sally smiled, "Then let's have a signal. If I swish my tail from side to side, real fast like this," and Sally demonstrated, "that means you are crossing the line. Okay?"

"Okay," her mother agreed.

Then Sally said, "There is one area where I really would like your advice."

"Oh, Sally, nothing would make me happier. What is it?" Suzie asked, excited about an opportunity to help her daughter.

"How do you get at those seeds in the bird feeder? I've seen you do it, and you're quite good at it!"

"Yes, I am. Come on. It's not hard. I'll show you."

And with, a leap, a scamper, and a bounce, Suzie and Sally were happily on their way.

The moral of this story is that when you're feeling nuts and seeing Red, take the leap and build a boundary.

Quick Summary

When Someone Becomes a Meddler

Your Goal: To Preserve and Protect the Boundary

ACTION PLAN

1. Appreciate their intentions.

2. Give them a place to meddle.

3. Meddle with the meddling.

4. Negotiate the boundary. Plan a meeting, be prepared, and behave wisely.

   a. Open with a positive.

   b. Describe the problem.

   c. Talk about the effects.

   d. Let the Meddler reply.

   e. Describe a desired boundary.

   f. Establish a signal.

   g. Reinforce the boundary.

22
The Martyr

Winter was in the air. Hibernation day was tomorrow. But tonight all Papa Bear could think about was his final meal of the season. As he sat in his big chair, his mouth watered at the enticing thought of his favorite food, fresh hot porridge.

Mama Bear brought her bowl to the table first, so her porridge would have a chance to cool off. Baby Bear was served next, so that by the time Mama Bear and Papa Bear were served and they started eating, his would be just right. Papa Bear liked his porridge piping hot, so his was served last.

As he took the first whiff of his porridge, Papa Bear was distracted by the antics of his bear cub, who was rocking back and forth in his chair with glee. He gently reprimanded Baby Bear. "Sit still or you'll break the chair!" Then he turned to Mama Bear, "That chair is barely holding together. Grampa Bear doesn't know how to make furniture! He should stick to gathering honey and leave the carpentry to the beavers."

Mama Bear nodded knowingly. Then she remembered. "Speaking of your dad, he stopped by earlier. He wants you to come over to help with some last-minute projects."

Papa Bear's jaw dropped. "Help him with projects? 'Honey-do' time is over. Tomorrow is hibernation day!"

The phone rang then. Mama Bear pushed her chair back and reached behind her to answer it. Papa Bear and Baby Bear listened as she said, a little loudly, "Grampa Bear! Yes, yes! I gave him the message."

Papa Bear mouthed, "Tell him I'm already hibernating!"

Mama Bear tried to smooth this over before it got out of paw. "Well, I'm sure there's a very good reason, … tomorrow *is* the beginning of hibernation and …"

"He's going to hibernate without stopping in to see his parents?" They could all hear Grampa Bear's depressed voice coming through the phone's earpiece. "All right. If he can't spare a few moments to help me out or have a meal with us, tell him I understand. Me, I'm not ready to hibernate because I spent all that time making that nice chair for Baby Bear and those big beds for you and my boy. But if he's too busy …"

Papa Bear rolled his eyes, bared his teeth, and then, in an exasperated whisper to Mama Bear, said, "I didn't ask him to make that furniture! Not to mention that my bed is too hard and yours is too soft."

"Mine is just right!" Baby Bear laughed and jumped up and down in his chair with delight.

Papa Bear turned and whispered loudly, "That's because I made it! Now quit jumping around. That chair your grampa made is falling apart!"

Mama Bear didn't want to be in the middle of this, so she gestured to Papa Bear to come to the phone. "He's your father," she mouthed.

Papa Bear reluctantly rose from the table, knowing his hot fresh porridge would soon be cold stale mush. Feeling grumpy, he grasped the phone in his paw and said, "Hello, Dad. Listen, we're just sitting down to eat …"

"Hey there, big bear! " said Grampa Bear, as if he hadn't heard a word. "Ready for a nice winter's hibernation in that new bed I made you? Must feel good to be able to hibernate in your own home. That's why I worked so hard all those years doing tricks at the circus, traveling from town to town, living life on the road, so my cubs could have it better than I've had it. Now, if it isn't too much to ask, why don't you all come over here, right now? Your mama prepared a special meal for you—fresh fish."

"Aw c'mon, Dad!" Papa Bear said. "You know I don't like fish."

Grampa Bear said, "It would kill your mother to hear you talk that way after she went to so much trouble. Here, your mother wants to talk to you."

Grammy Bear's voice was sweet as honey. "Hi, my favorite teddy bear. I went fishing all day today and caught some fresh salmon, and it's all ready for you when you get here."

Papa Bear groaned, "Aw, Ma …"

"Don't 'Aw, Ma' me! Last time I saw you, why, you were nothing but fur and bones. Not to mention that I spent the whole day fishing, even though I just had my fur done. But of course if you're too important to spend a little time with us, or our food isn't good enough for you, we'll understand. Don't feel obligated just because we won't see you for months, and we haven't seen Baby Bear all season. He probably doesn't even know who we are at this point anyway!"

Papa Bear sighed, "Okay, Ma. We'll be there shortly." He hung up the phone and looked longingly at the porridge. "Grrrr. I love porridge. And I hate fish. I was so looking forward to one last bowl of piping hot porridge before we go into hibernation!"

Mama Bear tried to reassure him. "Don't worry, the porridge will still be here when we get back."

Papa Bear whined, "Well, that's easy for you to say. You like your porridge cold. But I like mine hot. It's not the same when it's reheated. And besides, I haven't even fixed the lock on the door yet. I was planning on doing that after my porridge."

"Oh, don't be a worry bear," Mama Bear replied. "The forest is safe. Besides, we're bears! Nobody will come into our home uninvited!"

And with that the Three Bears left the house and lumbered down the path, with Papa Bear grumbling every step of the way.

Martyrs are needy givers, giving gifts whether you want them or not. Each one comes with an obligation.

Martyr behavior begins when the intention to *get along* combines with the intention to *get appreciation*.

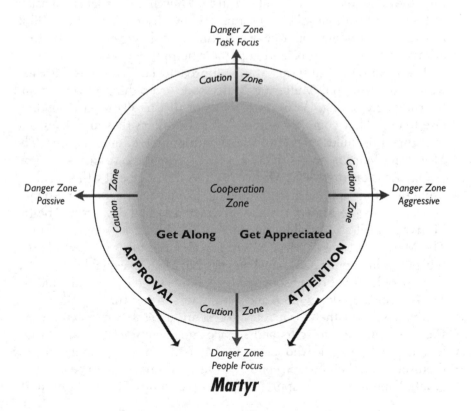

When the intent to *get appreciated* is thwarted and the intent to *get along* is projected onto someone else, Martyrs try harder to matter in your life in order to feel loved and become needy givers. This can happen between people when there is competition for affection or Martyrs feel ignored or taken for granted. Then their good intentions grow in intensity and become a need for *approval* along with a need for *attention*.

Needing approval, Martyrs don't ask for what they want, and needing attention, they fail to find out how to do so.

The Range of Difficulty: Mild to Muttering

There are a number of ways for Martyrs to distress and disturb other people. First, there's the Mild Martyr approach. Mild Martyrs start with the obligation inherent to any family relationship and build on that as a base. They do what is asked of them, just as most people would. And then they do more, and without question. They also do what is not asked of them, and without asking questions. They observe a need and fill it, thinking, "I'm doing you a favor." In this way they gain favor by their efforts and build the expectation of their help.

There's also the Muttering Martyr approach. The pattern is the same, with one exception. Muttering Martyrs do everything obviously and begrudgingly, saying, "Yeah, sure, why not. It isn't like I have anything else to do." They complain out loud, yet they do as they are asked, and over time this builds up their sense of entitlement, of quid pro quo. The Muttering Martyrs say, " I'm doing you a favor. You owe me."

On occasion there is a Martyr Meltdown. Maybe it's the result of using the other approaches for too long, or maybe it just occurs spontaneously, after the Martyr has had a particularly bad day. Or maybe the Martyr is dealt a reversal in the game of life, and it all seems so unfair. The Martyr screams "WHAT ABOUT ME?" and turns into a puddle of self-pity, which pulls hard on whatever obligation is available.

As people tire of the unsolicited help, bouts of self-pity, and guilt, the Martyr winds up doing more and getting less in return.

Martyrs harm their own self-interest in at least two specific ways. First, the unasked-for gifts and services go unappreciated, and others feel no pity for people who seem so capable of providing enough pity for themselves on their own. Second, the Martyrs' gifts come to be taken for granted and again go unappreciated. People figure, "If they want to do it, let them!" This locks the Martyrs into a try-and-fail loop from which there is no exit. The harder Martyrs try, the more they fail. The more they fail, the harder they try. The more they give, the less they are appreciated. The less they are appreciated, the more they give. And no one gives back because the neediness and annoying behavior are both unattractive qualities in a person. The attempts by Martyrs to tap into obligation and to invoke guilt result in no one wanting to give them anything ever.

You'd Better Adjust Your Attitude

Martyrs will play on any vulnerability detected in you, so keep your shields up! Keep reminding yourself that the Martyrs' need for significance is the drive behind the moaning and struggling, rather than someone else's failure to appreciate them, as they claim. Keep some emotional distance on the inside, so you don't get hooked into feeling guilty.

Your demeanor is important. The need for validation in Martyrs is so intense that you *must* feel some appreciation for them if you hope to gain their trust and influence their behavior. Approach them as if they deserve gratitude for something, and if you can't think of anything for which to be grateful, then be grateful that their impact on your life has its limits. Appreciate them for all that they *don't* do. Or appreciate them for all they "try" to do. Or appreciate them for all they "want" to do. One way or another, your demeanor must come across as genuinely considerate and appreciative. At the same time, you must empathize with how unappreciated they feel.

Here are some cautions to be aware of when dealing with Martyr behavior:

- *Don't call them "Martyrs."* Doing so is a guaranteed recipe for starting a conflict. Martyrs want your gratitude and empathy, not a label for their behavior.
- *Don't defend yourself.* It serves no purpose since the problem is about Martyrs rather than you. If Martyrs are trying to hold you accountable for their feelings of insignificance, you need only thank them for being honest or for bringing their feelings to your attention, without engaging in a dialogue about what is and isn't true regarding you. Any defense you might offer will sound like you are making excuses, so you might as well excuse yourself from this futile exercise.

- *Don't try to fix the problem.* It doesn't exist anywhere except in the mind of Martyrs, and any attempt you make to fix it simply affirms and strengthens their commitment to having the problem.

- *Don't let them carry the entire burden.* If you see Martyrs taking on all kinds of things about which they can complain later, get engaged and insist that they should do only their fair share, and that if they take on more, they'll have no one to blame but themselves. By letting them know this in the moment, you create something to refer back to when the Guilt Trip starts again.

Your Goal: Sever the Strings, Keep the Connection

Martyrs try hard to matter in your life, and they become needy givers. There's always a string attached, and you'll feel the pull as they invite you to feel the guilt. But this is an unhealthy and unhappy way to win approval or gain recognition. When dealing with the Martyrs, your goal is to sever the strings of guilt, while keeping the connection and the relationship positive.

Action Plan

Option 1. Look for a Chance to Give.   By handling the Martyr's need for significance preventively, you might be able to avoid the latest episode of "Poor me!" While it may or may not cancel an ongoing soap opera, it can give you welcome relief. And it very well might change the foundation of your relationship with the Martyr. Such things have happened before.

Danny told us:

It started about five years after I moved out on my own. My father used to call my sisters whenever Mother browbeat him. He'd say, "I can't do anything right for her. Everything I do is wrong. She's never happy no matter how hard I try. I don't think we're going to make it." But when they asked him why he kept trying, his answer was always the same. He felt like he owed it to her.

It's easy to understand why he felt that way because she was always at him about what she'd done for him. Why did she do all those things for him? I asked her, and she said it was because she owed it to him! And he was always after my sisters about what he had done for them. And why did he do those things for them? I asked him, and he said it was because he owed it to them! And my sisters were after me about what they had done for him! I asked them why they did all those things for him, and they said because they owed it to him!

One day it occurred to me that here are all these people that I care about, and they all do wonderful things for each other, and yet they don't give each other any real appreciation because everyone feels so unappreciated. And so they're all driven by guilt! So now I make it my work to give all of them the appreciation they deserve. And why do I make that my work? Because I love them, and it is my pleasure to appreciate them. And they do deserve a lot of appreciation! My appreciation may not mean that much to them, but at least this way they're all getting some. And maybe someday they'll follow my example. You never know! In the meantime, I get to enjoy all of them, and they seem to enjoy me too.

Let Martyrs know you don't take them for granted, and they'll be less likely to assume that you've forgotten them. You can do so in the following ways.

- *Tell them what you love.* When they do things or say things that you don't appreciate, tell them that you appreciate their positive intentions. Then tell them what they could do that you would appreciate even more. By directing them to an area where they can know it matters, they learn how to play a role in your life that truly matters to you.
- *Take their side.* If you do something that crosses them and they blame something you said or did for their hurt feelings, there is no amount of explaining that will change the way they feel. But if you apologize or acknowledge their view of the situation, they may let go of their hurt and choose love.

Harry told us:

My mother, Sybil, learned from my wife's sister that I had not told her about a significant event involving my daughter. Sybil was so furious that she stopped talking to me completely. Whenever I called, she would shout at the phone, "You don't care about me!" and then hang up. If I came to her door, she would yell from the other side, "Go away. You don't care about me!" This was difficult for me because I had withheld the information initially in order not to upset or worry her. But after the fact, it was having the opposite effect.

One day, I sent her a huge bouquet of flowers with a note that read, "I see your point. I was thoughtless. I love you. Please forgive me." The result? She called me and thanked me for the wonderful flowers, and she told me that she loved me too.

- *Speak to the child within.* Like children going to extraordinary lengths to win approval, Martyrs often try harder than anyone to win your love and appreciation. When you see this behavior as childlike, you can speak to the child within. Using the same facial expressions and voice tones that you might use with children, give Martyrs the attention they desire. When a Martyr says a pathetic "Poor me," you can lift the burden from the Martyr's shoulders by saying, "Oh, you poor baby! You need a wittle woving wight now, don't you?" Such a playfully loving communication may be just what is needed to soothe the Martyr's soul. Several of the people we interviewed described this effect as a worthy one.

Option 2. Disrupt the Guilt Trip. The Martyr is visiting you. The phone rings, and as you excuse yourself and reach to answer it, the Martyr says, "That's all right, take the call. Though I'm only here for a little while, don't worry about me. I'm sure whoever it is has something more important to tell you than what I was talking about." That's your invitation to go on a Guilt Trip, a field trip into the fantasyland of If/Only, If/Then, Shoulda-Coulda-Wouda, and I Wish! The feeling of guilt is your ticket to ride. Board the bus and away you go. But you don't have to get on the bus. When you understand the dynamic of guilt, you can avoid it.

- *Strip it.* When you understand the nature of guilt, you can strip away the veneer of obligation to see exactly how the Guilt Trip works.

  So what is guilt? It is the emotion that you feel when you do something that violates your values. If you value family but your job keeps you away from them, you feel guilty. If you value loving kindness but yell at your child, you feel guilty. If you see someone suffering and do nothing to help and you value being of service, you feel guilty. Even if the action or inaction that violates your values is your best choice under the circumstances, you still feel guilty.

  Guilt is not inherently a bad thing. People who don't feel it at all tend to end up as criminals. When it doesn't debilitate, it can motivate. Guilt helps us moderate bad behavior, it induces introspection, and it even contributes to the process of creative thinking. You can resolve guilt feelings by taking action or refraining from action. So the feeling of guilt has the power to make us consider our actions and change our behavior in order to restore our values to their rightful place in our lives.

How does guilt hook into your sense of obligation? When you feel in the wrong, you want to set things right! People who grew up with constant criticism or who got blamed for things they did not do may feel in the wrong even when they are not. These people may intentionally do something "bad" as an act of rebellion, and then they live with the fear of being found out. They are ready to go on the Guilt Trip. People brought up to believe that doing nothing is the worst thing they can do may feel guilty every time they try to relax. Such guilt feelings are the price for an E-Z Pass on the Guilt Trip Turnpike. All that remains is to punch your ticket, and they oblige you. They create a link between your sense of regret and obligation and your doing what they want. In effect, the Martyr says, "If you were more responsible, you would do as I want." "If you were more caring, you would do as I want." "If you were more appreciative of me, you would do as I want." "If you were more effective, you would do as I want." Or the Martyr might use the negative corollaries: "If you weren't so irresponsible, you would do as I want." "If you weren't so unappreciative, you would do as I want." And so on. Recognize the pattern for what it is, and you don't have to internalize it at all.

- *Flip it.* When Martyrs directly say something intended to make you feel guilty, you can flip it around to make them feel guilty for saying it. Flipping the guilt requires you to notice it and turn it around. If Martyrs accuse you of not caring, tell them they aren't caring about your caring. If they tell you that you don't appreciate them, tell them they must not appreciate your appreciation. By refusing to accept their explanation of your behavior and by calling their behavior into question, you flip the guilt back where it belongs, and thus you free yourself of any obligation to do or not do what you do or don't want to do.

Martyr:	"You don't appreciate all I've done for you."
You:	"I do appreciate all you've done for me. But I don't think you appreciate my appreciation!"
Martyr:	"That's not true."
You:	"Well, it isn't true for me either."
Martyr:	"If you really loved me, you would help me with this."
You:	"If you really loved me, you would understand why I can't."
Martyr:	"But I do really love you!"
You:	"And I do really love you too."

- *Snip it.* Another way to take you on a Guilt Trip is to encourage you to do what you want to do, with the attached condition that you should feel bad about doing it while you do it! Martyrs attempt to attach the consequence of guilt to your determination to make your own choices. Why? Because guilt becomes obligation. By building the sense of obligation over time, they can invoke it at a future time to get what they want or to stop you from doing what they don't want you to do. Obligation, even when it's manufactured in this way, can be just the kind of access they need to keep you in check on the larger issues of the relationship. The best protection is to snip the connecting cord they've attached that ties your choice to guilt. First, snip the cord inside yourself. Then thank them for their support, as if support was what they had to offer. This disconnects their access and frees you to move on without any chains of obligation to bind you.

Martyr:	"Go ahead. Don't worry about me."
You:	"Okay. That's great. Thanks!"

Martyr:	"Here, let me get the check. I'll find a way to cover it."
You:	"All right, if you insist!"

Sometimes Martyrs assign value to your choices, and they make a negative comparison to their own value in your life, in either caring or appreciating them:

"You care more about him than you do about me."
"You care more about yourself than you do about me."
"You think that is more important than I am."

The best response is to snip the connection between doing what you want and the motives assigned to it by Martyrs. You can easily do this by telling them that caring or appreciation is the reason you're doing what you're doing. Give them credit for the value; then appreciate their understanding.

Martyr:	"Go ahead. You obviously care more about that dog than you do about me."
You:	"Actually, I'm taking care of the dog because I gave my word, just as you would if you were in my place. So thanks for your understanding."

Martyr:	"Go on, if your husband and children are more important to you than your own mother."
You:	"Actually, I am attending to my family's needs, just as you attended to ours. So thanks for understanding because I know you can appreciate that."

Martyr: "You don't have to come visit if you have more important things to do."

You: "You're right. It would be wrong to spend the money to make the trip right now. I appreciate your looking out for us like this."

- *Nip it in the bud.* What is the hook that obligates you with the Martyr? What do you feel guilty about, and how does your Martyr use it? To stay off the trip, you have to free yourself of the guilt that isn't yours and act on the guilt that is.

  If someone gives you feedback in an honest and nonmalicious way and that feedback makes you feel bad about yourself, then there are no Martyrs involved and the Guilt Trip is your own. Identify the undermined value, do something to restore it, and the burden of guilt will evaporate. If you feel obligated because of something someone has done for you, balance the equation and be done with it. Take an inventory of what you've done in return for what the Martyr has done for you, and see how it looks on the balance sheet. If you owe the Martyr and haven't paid the debt, come up with a plan and implement it. Or identify how you're repaying the debt and give yourself credit for it by knowing what it is. Then, when the Martyr pulls on the obligation strings, they will be attached to nothing, and they will come off in the Martyr's hands.

Option 3. Hit the Reset on Their Upset.   Sometimes, people are upset because they keep upsetting themselves!

Emotional problems, irrational thoughts, and difficult behaviors are often the results of taking external events personally. The best thing you can do to improve other people's sense of self-worth is to see and treat them as intrinsically valuable human beings.

- *Respond to exaggerated badness.* Have you ever had something bad happen to you, and you played it over and over in the privacy of your mind so you wouldn't miss out on any aspect of the badness of it? While everyone does this at some point in life, Martyrs tend to make a habit of it. A glass of wine is spilled at an otherwise wonderful family gathering, and the Martyr says, "The whole evening is ruined." If there isn't enough food or some detail was inadequately planned, the Martyr says, "This evening is a disaster!" But was the whole evening ruined? Or was believing so what ruined it for the Martyr? Was the gathering a disaster, or was the Martyr's response the disaster? When people exaggerate the badness, you can exaggerate their exaggeration and then ask for a counterexample.

Martyr: "Nothing could be worse!"
You: "Nothing? You can't think of a single thing that could be worse?"

- *Counter the frustration.* Martyrs tend to express frustration with generalized self-pity, even though they are referring to specific external circumstances outside of their control. They say *always, never, everybody*, and *nothing*. If you have a specific counterexample (and there are probably plenty for you to draw on), here's how to use it:

Martyr: "You never come over to visit."
You: "Never? What about when we stopped by last week? Doesn't that count?"

Martyr: "I know nobody cares about me."
You: "Then I wonder why we threw that birthday party for you last year?"

- *Upgrade to preferences.* Life is change, and it cannot be controlled. Preferences work better than rigid demands in dealing with people and events in a healthy way. People with preferences have some control over their own thoughts and feelings. People with rigid demands of life try to control events and people, and when their demands are not met, they become miserable. They could find a way out of their misery if they upgraded their demands into preferences, so that instead of focusing on how something "should" work out, they could focus on how they prefer it to work out, based on how it is. While Martyrs may be unable to make this shift, you can offer an upgrade:

Martyr: "You should have been more thoughtful about my request."
You: "You would have preferred me to be more thoughtful about your request?"

Martyr: "I would have done anything for you, if you had just asked."
You: "You would have preferred to do whatever I asked?"

When this kind of pattern is repeated over and over, it may make an impression on the way Martyrs think about the woulda-coulda-shouldas.

Option 4. Say No to Unreasonable Requests.   Saying a clear no is an important skill, particularly for people with a well-rehearsed *get along* approach to conflict avoidance. Saying no makes you into a more authentic person, and it lets people know how you actually feel about things. And when you agree to help or be helped, they'll know it's sincere and meaningful, not grudging or given with hidden, ill feeling.

Saying no does not make you selfish either, since in this case you wouldn't be focused on your self-interest to the exclusion of others. When it comes to saying no, it isn't what you say—it's how you say it that makes the difference. Say it calmly and simply, like it's the most normal thing to say in all the world. Repeat it if you have to. Keep it simple. If you encumber it with excuses, out of concern that Martyrs might get upset with you, your no will be easier to challenge and undermine. And if you become aggressive in saying no, Martyrs will get very upset and will remember only how they felt when you said it, rather than focusing on what you were actually talking about.

To add some power to your no, shake your head no at the same time. This makes it a congruent message, which carries more force than the mixed message of saying no while looking tenuous, uncertain, or confused. To make your no more palatable to Martyrs, you can preface it with a cushioning phrase, like "Thanks for asking, but no" or "I'm sorry but I have to say no" or "Unfortunately, the answer is no." If you like, finish with another cushioning phrase like, "Thanks for asking" or "Thanks for thinking of me" or "Perhaps another time."

If you're uncomfortable with saying no, practice on empty elevators. At each floor, act as if you're being asked to get off before it's time and say, "No, not here" and "No, not now" and "No, it's too soon." Then, when it is time to get off, say, "Yes, here it is!" and feel how great it is to say yes only when the time is right.

Option 5. Give Them a Glimpse of Greatness.   Sometimes you have to draw a bigger line and tell your problem people the truth about how their behavior is self-defeating and what you think would work better instead. The overview is the same for honesty as it is for any of the problem behaviors: plan it, write it, rehearse it, and pick your time and place. (See the section "Tell Your Truth" in Chapter 7, "Speak to Be Understood," for more details.) Your goal in being honest is to give the Martyrs a glimpse of greatness.

State your positive intent.

Be specific about the problem behavior.

Show them how the behavior is self defeating.

Suggest new behaviors.

Reinforce behavioral change.

However, there are two aspects of honesty that are especially important when dealing with the Martyrs:

1. *Project a positive intent.* Tell them, "Thanks for …"

   "… taking care of things."

   "… putting all that work into it."

   "… making such a wonderful dinner."

2. *Be specific.* Remember to use language like "I am sure you can appreciate" before showing them the self-defeating nature of their behavior.

Great Moments in Difficult People History

The Three Bears
It was one week before hibernation day when Papa Bear announced to Mama Bear and Little Bear (who wasn't a baby anymore!) that they were going to visit Grampa and Grammy Bear. Mama Bear looked at Papa Bear curiously, and he answered the unspoken question, telling her, "I don't want any last-minute calls ruining my prehibernation day porridge, like last year."

Papa Bear entered the secret code into the new alarm system he installed, double-checked the locks, and off they went. A short while later they arrived at his parents' den.

"Hi ya, Dad!" he called.

"Hello there, son! To what do we owe this pleasant surprise?"

"Well, I felt bad that last year's hibernation goodbyes were rushed and last-minute. I thought we'd come earlier this year to see if you need help with any projects. At least we can have a nice visit and wish you a good winter's rest."

"Well, that's darn nice of you," said Grampa Bear.

Then Grammy Bear came out of the cave. After exchanging hugs with everyone, Mama Bear gave Grammy Bear a freshly collected jar of honey. "Here," she said. "Just a little thank you present from all of us for all you do."

"Isn't that special!" said Grammy Bear, holding up the honey so her honey bear could see it.

Grampa Bear slapped Papa Bear on the back and said, "So what should we do, sonny boy? Build some more furniture?"

"Ah no, no!" Papa Bear replied quickly, adding, "I mean you already made us plenty of furniture, which we appreciate. But I think the time would be better spent if you played with your grandcub!"

So Grampa Bear showed Baby Bear some of his famous circus tricks. Meanwhile, Papa Bear decided to handle the dinner issue with his mom before it became a big deal. "Mom, can we talk about dinner?"

But before he could go further, Grammy Bear said, "Don't tell me you're not going to eat salmon. You never appreciate the good food I make for you." Papa Bear growled, which stopped Grammy Bear short. Then Papa Bear softened and said, "I don't think you appreciate just how much I appreciate you."

Grammy Bear's eyes widened. She was clearly confused by Papa Bear's relaxed posture and caring tone. Papa Bear continued, "I love you, Mom. I know you go to a lot of trouble to get salmon. You also prepare it with such love, and everyone else loves it. So I don't mind if you serve it. It's just that I don't care for salmon, no matter who makes it, and that's why I'm not going to eat it. Still, I can enjoy everyone else enjoying your wonderful salmon, and I'll enjoy all the other delicious dishes that you have on the side."

After a moment's pause, Papa Bear added, "However, there is one area where I would love the help of your culinary expertise."

Grammy Bear was feeling the love. "Sure, my little cubby, what is it?"

"Well, I love porridge so much. And if you could figure out how to reheat it and still have it taste good, it would mean a lot to me."

"Figure it out? That won't be necessary. Tonight while everyone else eats salmon, you're going to be eating a bowl of fresh, hot porridge, made the way your mama makes it."

And with that, they gave each other a big bear hug.

The moral of this story is that a firm no, a big hug, and a jar of honey make for a happier hibernation.

Quick Summary

When Someone Becomes a Martyr
   Your Goal: Sever the Strings, Keep the Connection
   ACTION PLAN
   1. Look for a chance to give.
   2. Disrupt the guilt trip.
      Strip it.
      Flip it.
      Snip it.
      Nip it in the bud.
   3. Hit the reset on their upset.
      Respond to exaggerated badness.
      Counter the frustration.
      Upgrade to preferences.
   4. Say no to unreasonable requests.
   5. Give them a glimpse of greatness.

23

What If People Can't Stand You?

Correspondence with Difficult People

By now you have probably recognized that you too have days when you are at your worst. So what can you do about it? You may find the answer in the following exchange of letters with difficult people.

1. What If *You* Are the Tank?

Rick[2],

You've got guts, and you shoot straight from the hip. I admire that. Since your seminar, I have come to the conclusion that I am the difficult person. The people I thought were difficult are difficult from having to deal with me. Yeah, I lose patience when I think people are wasting time. But I have a lot to do, and when I have the future in my sights, people keep getting in the way and slowing me down. What do I do? Don't mince words. Just be honest. I can take it. I have a pretty hard shell.

Joe Sherman

Dear Sherm,

Well, for starters, recognize that flattening people is probably the most time-consuming and least effective means of getting things done. Stop wasting time. Consider the answers to the following questions: Are things really getting done when you act like that? What kinds of things? At what cost? Do the people around you live in fear of you? Is that what you want? Are you a true leader who can motivate and inspire people? Or are you just a two-bit dictator? Why not get things done without leaving a trail of bodies in your wake?

We understand that you're a man on a mission. You've built something, and you want to keep it going. You don't want anything to slow you down. You're afraid that it will all unravel. If being a leader, instead of a dictator, seems to you like a great result to achieve, use the attitudinal adjustment strategy found in Chapter 9. If you're serious about *getting things done*, study the biographies and autobiographies of people with proven track records of getting results, make an example out of them, and build on their success. Use them as models, change your own history, and get used to the idea.

2. What If *You* Are the Sniper?

Dear Frik and Frak,

Some people grow on you; others turn out to be crop failures. Some people practice what they preach; others practice preaching. Some shepherds feed the flock; some shepherds fleece the flock. Not that I'm trying to say that you guys are failures or liars, but hey, you must be twins. No one person could be so stupid.

Ms. Tree

Dear Ms. Tree,

Did we detect a note of sarcasm? No, no. It was a whole symphony, and it was playing your song. Bad dog! Go lie down in the corner. Actually, as a Sniper, you already have fewer real friends than an alarm clock. Every time you snipe, people probably think you just had your first beer. The fact is, you have a severe speech impediment. It's called your brain. But making you feel bad won't help you change. So how do you change?

If there is some grudge or grievance you are holding against the person you snipe at, you may want to save yourself a lot of trouble: tell your victim, and get it over with. We recommend first, that you admit to responsibility for your sniping; second, that you take responsibility for your perceptions and reactions to the original situation; and last, that you describe what you're upset about and ask for what you want.

It is possible, however, that you do not have a deep-seated grudge against anyone in particular. Your sniping may find its source in a moment of impatience with people who take too long or irritation with people's obviously inferior ideas. It may be impatience with people who generally waste time. Or you may be accumulating miscellaneous irritations over the course of the day that finally cause you to seek revenge by taking it out on others.

In any case, take a good look to see how the sniping behavior is defeating some other important purpose of yours. Perhaps you're a manager and you want the opinions of your people, but you're not getting them because they live in fear of becoming your target. Seeing this clearly may create the motivation to change.

If you are the entertainer Sniper who really doesn't mean anything by your rude and (to you) funny, remarks and you figure, "Hey, if you can't laugh at yourself, laugh at other people," remember that the meaning of your communication is the response you get. Put another way, knucklehead, if you're trying to be friendly and the other people are not perceiving it as such, then they don't get it and you should try something else. Ask them what they would prefer, then commit to it, and give them permission to remind you if you "happen to forget."

3. What If *You* Are the Know-It-All?

Sirs,

When I attended your seminar, I was certain that you would not have anything worthwhile to tell me. After all, I have several business degrees and run my own medium-sized business quite efficiently, thank you. But I must admit, a few of your ideas seemed remotely reasonable, though I doubt most people are intelligent enough to employ them successfully. In your opinion, which part of your program, if any, would be most valuable for me to take personally?

Cordially,
I.M. Pompous

Dear Mr. Pompous,

As you must know, those who value knowledge can obtain it only by keeping their minds open. No doubt you have spent a considerable amount of time learning all you know. Perhaps you have also discovered that the more you know, the more you don't know, and the more there is to know.

Every person has the potential to add to your wealth of knowledge because everyone has a unique perspective. When discussing ideas, remember this, and instead of shutting out others, find out what they are really talking about. Someone can suggest a totally bonehead idea that will never work, but the criteria that makes that person suggest it may be worth its weight in gold.

As far as your attitude is concerned, we recommend that you become curious about and then fascinated with the differences in perception and in behavior between people. In an age of information, where an entire encyclopedia can be accessed in microseconds at the touch of a computer key, wisdom has greater value than knowledge. Wisdom does not come from age, for from the mouths of babes can come great wisdom. Wisdom is the product of an inquiring mind that's connected to the heart.

4. What If *You* Are the Think-They-Know-It-All?

Dear Guys,

Hey, what a blast. I got some great jokes from your class. I can't wait to use 'em on the gang at the office. But I gotta tell ya, there's a much simpler way to deal with difficult people. Just look at 'em right in the eye when they're being difficult, and tell 'em, "Sounds like a personal problem!" Get it?

But seriously, the only problem I have with people is their attitude about me! I never run out of conversation, only listeners! Even when I make mistakes, I have very good reasons for guessing wrong! But I don't get no respect from anyone. Any suggestions?

Till the kitchen sinks,

Wise or Other-Wise

Dear Other-Wise,

We can think of at least three things that you don't already know:

(1) There is no disgrace in admitting a mistake, unless you first try to cover it up. As soon as you realize that your information is inadequate or that your idea has been poorly thought through, a simple admission of that will suffice to regain your esteem in the eyes of your peers.

(2) If exaggeration is a slight problem for you, then it will be fruitful to deal with its cause, which is the frustrated desire to be liked and appreciated. You may want to do a few things to increase your self-esteem because low self-esteem is often at the root of Think-They-Know-It-All behavior. Work with a counselor. Get on a steady diet of high-fiber information on topics relevant to your work and personal relationships. Read books, and listen to and watch tapes that deal with the issue of self esteem.

(3) Most important, stop trying to impress people for a while. People may think you are a fool, or you can remove any question by opening your mouth. Practice being comfortable with silence, and wait to speak until you really have something to contribute. And remember that the surest way to gain appreciation is by giving recognition and showing genuine appreciation to others.

5. What If *You* Are the Grenade?

To the two jerks that presented that program on difficult people,

You guys really [expletive deleted] me off. I sat through your whole program watching you swagger around spouting your philosophy. I kept asking myself, "Who do they think they are?" But the things that really pulled my pin were all your remarks about Grenades' hating themselves. So what if I do? That's my business. Right? So what if I'm not perfect, like you? I have a lot of stress to deal with, like three bratty kids, an arrogant boss, an unappreciative staff, and a wife who doesn't like my attitude. In fact, my wife says she's going to leave me unless I change my attitude. So what if she does? That's my business. But I hope she changes her mind. I don't know why I even bothered writing this letter. What do you care? I got enough to deal with without this [expletive deleted]. Forget it.

Sincerely,
Don Pullit

Dear Don Pullit,

Whoa! Are you using barbed wire to floss your teeth? From what you say, you have an even temper: always grouchy. If you're walking around with the same hostility that's in your letter, it's only a matter of time before your ticker stops. Here are a few suggestions for changing your attitude.

In order to change, you must determine your motive for making that change, whether it's some internal reward, like living a happier life, or an external reward, like being a better role model for your children or improving your chances for a healthy retirement. This clarity about motive will act as the sprinkler system that keeps your fire from getting out of control.

Your next step is to find out what your pin is and what pulls it. How do you know when to blow up? Initially your answer may be "I don't know." But give it a chance. Examine some instances when you blew up. Examine multiple situations to find the common thread in what sets you off. Then decide what it is that you want to happen the next time that pin gets pulled. How do you want to respond? Mentally rehearse that until it feels natural and believable to you.

If you are an occasional Grenade, you might consider learning to express your feelings sooner, in little ventings, rather than waiting for things to reach a critical mass. Spend some time over the next few weeks developing your ability to express yourself appropriately as soon as the sparks first fly.

6. What If *You* Are the Yes Person?

Dear Doctors,

Hello. My name is Ida, and though you probably won't remember me, I really liked your seminar a lot. I felt that you were very thoughtful and considerate. I told all my friends about what nice people you are. If there is anything that I can do to help you out, all you have to do is ask, and I will try my best to do as much as I possibly can under the circumstances.

I'm certain you're very busy and don't have the time to write back to me, but that's okay. I understand. You probably want to spend that time with your families and other people who are more important.

And that's fine with me. I don't mind. I'm just happy to have had the chance to know you a little bit, and, by the way, is this letter okay? Have I been rambling? I better stop because I know how busy you must be.

Warmly,
Ida Gree

Dear Ida,

Thanks for your thoughtful letter. It was a pleasure to hear from you. You seem like a very nice person, so here's some nice advice.

Your challenge, and opportunity, is to say what you think independently of what you think others might think about what you say. And that's not as difficult as you might think. Begin by realizing that in your desire to please people, you often don't. If you make an offer that you can't keep or a promise that you can't deliver, the displeasure of those disappointed people is inevitable. You may not have believed it when they told you, but practically everyone really does prefer you to be honest and straightforward and to keep the commitments that you make.

For example, do you ever tell a salesperson that you'll be back, when you know that you won't? That salesperson, whose feelings you may not want to hurt, winds up with false hope and wastes valuable time pursuing your business. The nicest thing you could do is tell the truth that you're not interested in the product or service. The people who love you want you to be happy too, but they can't really contribute to your happiness unless you are honest about what you want and what you can do. And if you always put yourself last, withholding your thoughts and feelings from others, you deprive those people of the chance to really get to know you, with the result that there can be no real intimacy.

We recommend that you strengthen your ability to keep commitments by developing your task management skills. Learn how to set a goal and make a plan of action; how to prioritize activities to maximize time; how to delegate so you aren't doing it all yourself; and how to keep track of your time so that you can make accurate time estimates and prevent your time from getting lost in interruptions and unexpected crises.

Also, practice being assertive in small ways. If your food is not done correctly at a restaurant, send it back. If someone usurps your place in line, tell him or her that you were there first. Take every opportunity to be assertive. At business meetings, make it your goal to be the first, or one of the first, to speak up.

Since your strength is a genuine caring about people, you can serve them best by meeting them where they are. And remember yourself, because you count too.

7. What If *You* Are the Maybe Person?

Dear Rick and Rick, Dr. Brinkman and Dr. Kirschner, Sirs,

I'm not certain if this is my question, but when you asked how many procrastinators were in the group, did you actually want us to raise our hands? Because I wasn't certain, and before I could figure it out, you had already moved on. I never did get my hand up, but I think that I am. Well, at least sometimes. Well, it's not that I can't make up my mind. Uh, Okay, yes it is. Anyway, I just thought I'd tell you that there was at least one more procrastinator in the group than there was, or were, hands raised. Unless someone raised his or her hand who isn't really a procrastinator. Does that happen?

Sincerely,
Lotta Doubts

Dear Lotta,

The fact is, none of the real procrastinators ever did get their hands up. And all those other people who did get their hands up were kidding.

We have a lot of, no, actually just a little advice for you. Keep reminding yourself of these simple rules of thumb: (1) There's no such thing as a perfect decision. Every decision has some inherent costs that can't be predicted. (2) Any decision left unmade will ultimately make itself. (3) When in doubt, decide now. Eighty percent of the decisions you face can be made in the moment that you become aware of them, and they will not benefit from further information. Only 15 percent of the decisions you face will benefit from more info, and 5 percent of the decisions you face truly don't need to be made at all.

If you are concerned that your decision might hurt people, be honest with them about your concerns in making the decision. Expressing concern and being sensitive to the feelings of others is a terrific skill, as long as it doesn't lock you in counterproductive behavior.

We also recommend that you start noticing all the decisions that you do make well. For example, you decided to write and followed through. You decide to get up in the morning, to eat when you're hungry, to go to bed when you're sleepy. You decide on outfits and books to read. In fact, a whole range of choices present themselves to you daily. Notice where you're succeeding, tell yourself you can do it, and find a decision-making system you can work with. Then stay with it consistently, and you'll find that making up your mind gets easier all the time.

8. What If *You* Are the Nothing Person?

Dear ?,

I don't know. Nothing comes to mind.

Sincerely,
Dusty Blank

Dear Dusty,

If you have a tendency to be the quiet type of person, conflicting feelings in any situation can push you into nothingness. Stuffing your feelings and withdrawing from conflict only perpetuate the conflict inside of you and create distance between you and others. Distance leads to isolation, which is the opposite of intimacy.

Expressing your emotions responsibly instead of stuffing your feelings is better for your health and your happiness. You won't have to be the silent victim of pointless conversations if you are willing to speak up and move them in another direction. When feeling conflicting feelings, if you don't feel safe telling the people involved in the conflict, find someone you feel safe talking to, and start talking. Sometimes, just talking about what you feel gives you enough perspective to resolve the conflict.

What if you become a Nothing Person to avoid another person's emotional explosions, withdrawing into a shell as a survival tactic? Using the Grenade strategy outlined earlier in this book will be far more effective, with less wear and tear on both you and the Grenade. There is a very good chance that if you communicated more with the emotional people in your life, you could avoid most of the explosive outbursts, since silence is one of the best ways to pull the pin on a Grenade.

When you are in a group of people, try speaking up. On occasion, you may even want to try dominating the conversation a bit. It may seem strange at first, but you will get used to it. Tell the truth about your feelings more often to the people you care about. Tell people what upsets you in a nonblaming way, by using this form:

"When you [Describe what it is they are doing that is difficult for you to deal with], I feel [Describe the effect their behavior has on you]. In the future, I would like you to [Now ask for what you want]."

For example: "When your voice gets loud like this, I feel like you're shouting at me rather than talking with me. In the future, I'd appreciate it if you would talk to me in a more conversational tone." In this way you can responsibly express yourself and give people the opportunity to get to know you and strengthen the relationship.

9. What If *You* Are the No Person?

Sirs,

The purpose of writing this letter is twofold. First, I disagree with your remarks about negativity. Negativity can be a very positive thing if it prevents people from making foolish mistakes and costly errors. Second, I wish to question your premise that people can set realistic goals and achieve them. In my life, the greater preponderance of people I have known have failed to achieve their goals, while the rare few, usually through privilege, succeed.

There's no point in answering this letter, as you will not change my mind. Unlike the other people who attend your programs, I have no use for pop psychology and simple formulas for success. Bitter experience has taught me to lie low, and I won't be tricked by you into standing up and sticking my neck out only to be shot down.

Yours in disbelief,
Will Gripe

Dear Will,

In every person's life, a little rain must fall. All people go through tough times for which they feel ill prepared. Everyone has been disappointed, and everyone has experienced things he or she would have preferred to live without. Negativity is an essential part of the human experience. Now, we don't mean to sound discouraging, but when you're in a negative mindset, your perceptions of things and people are likely to be inaccurate.

If you really want to know what it's like to be around you, carry a tape recorder around with you and leave it on. Of course, having a tape recorder on may change your negativity level dramatically. As time progresses (or passes away), notice how many times you could have been negative and weren't because of the tape recorder. Then, when you listen to the tape, figure that you're about twice as negative as you sound on the tape.

By the way, what do you want your life to stand for? When you look back on what you did with what was given to you, what will be the achievement of your lifetime? "I devoted my life to stealing people's energy and motivation." That's not a proud legacy; it's a shroud legacy! Look around you, at the planes, televisions, automobiles, all the inventions and achievements of humanity. All of those blessings were brought to fruition by people who were willing to believe in the possible rather than the impossible, and sometimes they did so against impossible odds. They chose to be part of the solution instead of part of the problem. Sometimes, in the face of obstacles and dangers even you can scarcely imagine, people found within themselves the will to win. So can you, but only if you decide to look for it.

We suggest that you do a *change history exercise* on the bitter moments of your life. Make a list of the biggest or most painful disappointments. Ask yourself what you know now that, had you known it then, would have made your life turn out differently. Access resources, and go back to those memories in a more powerful way. Learn the lessons they have to teach you, and let go of the disappointment. All things must pass, and if you let them, this can happen before you've passed away with them. We recommend that you read, and reread, Chapter 9, "How to Change Your Attitude." Use all the skills you find there until you get good at them. You may want to find some professional help: a counselor or therapist who can help you to clean up the past and get current with events. On the one hand, life is too short to spend it feeling bad about the past, and on the other hand, you have the rest of your life to make up for lost time.

In your relationships with others, be wary of criticizing. Feedback helps people improve their performance, and as such, is a positive thing. Criticism rarely improves, and generally destroys, whatever it is aimed at. When people offer suggestions or share their ideas and accomplishments with you, practice noticing and talking about what you like before offering your feedback on how to improve it. Gather information to understand more, especially the criteria. You may be on to something important, and pointing out specific valid flaws is an important part of the problem-solving process. But sweeping negative generalities tend to throw the baby out with the bathwater, so force yourself to be specific, and keep things in perspective.

Finally, let people know that you want to be constructive. If they have known you for a while, then you will have to give them time before they believe you really have changed.

All the best (or none of the worst).

10. What If *You* Are the Whiner?

Dear Kirschner and Brinkman,

Oh, no. This program is too complicated. There's too much to learn, and it goes by too quickly to remember it. Not only that but if everybody learned this, it probably wouldn't work. And even if it did, it wouldn't be very enjoyable because everyone would know what you were doing. Also, there are other books and tapes and seminars that claim to tell you how to deal with difficult people, but they don't all agree with you. Then there's the problem of misunderstanding what you've told us and doing it wrong, which would be awful. You have no idea what a difficult situation you've created with your program.

Sincerely,
Mona Lott

Dear Mona,

Like the No Person, you have become focused on what is wrong with everything, rather than what can be done about something. You probably can find fault with yourself too. You have four choices if you want your future to turn out differently than your past:

1. *Switch to a problem-solving mode.* Going on and on about what you don't want is like driving a car backward to avoid hitting something you see in front of you. Instead, ask yourself, "What do I want? Where do I want to take this? What can I aim for?" Remember that you can't take aim without a target! Write down some specific goals.

2. *Take a second, and perhaps more realistic, look at the world around you.* Break down the huge generalizations that you've formed about

everything into little specifics that you can actually see, hear, and feel as well as do something about. People who are doers rather than Whiners waste very little time reacting to things. Instead, they use their energy to move closer to the results they believe possible.

3. *Notice and appreciate what is working in your life and what you accomplish.* On your path you may have passed many milestones without noticing them. That robs you of the satisfaction and energy that comes naturally with accomplishment. Post some notes to yourself in prominent places that say, "Remember to Appreciate."

4. *You could do all of these things as alternatives to feeling helpless, whining, and subsequently driving the people around you crazy.* We believe that would be much more satisfying. So the next time you start to complain, stop! Make a commitment to do something, anything, rather than whining about it. Then you, and everyone around you, will be done with it once and for all. Thanks for writing, and if you change your mind, let us know!

11. What If *You* Are the Judge?

Dear Idiot Doctors,

As hard as it is for me to believe this of myself, here I am writing to you for some of your juvenile and moronic advice. Why do I do this? Perhaps it is only so I can experience firsthand the immaturity that is the hallmark of advice generally given by self-help and business book authors such as yourselves. Frankly, I am frequently perplexed at how you can justify offering such simplistic advice to people about the very complex and difficult problems they face in their dealings with each other. If anyone is guilty of reductionism for convenience sake, surely it would be you two. And I for one find that when people fail to measure up, it typically precedes their downfall, as they make pitiful excuses to explain away their incompetence. But that's neither here nor there. Essentially, I'd like to hear your meager response to just one question: How do I get off my high horse so that I can talk with instead of over the idiots who surround me?

Yours disrespectfully,
U. R. Guilty

Dear U. R.,

We appreciate your wanting to do the right thing, and we know it isn't going to be easy. It might help to know that when you think of

people as idiots, your behavior follows after. So the first step in step-
ping down is to put down the put-downs in the way you're thinking,
so that instead of getting nothing but a bad reaction, you can get a
good one. While that's not going to change the entirety of your
problem, it is the best answer to your question. Beyond that, it gets
more complex. You're going to have to pass sentence on yourself,
and that sentence must include a more realistic and useful understanding of what makes people do what they do. That's the hard
part. Expect the jury to stay out for a while as you learn this new
behavior of thinking clearly and insightfully about others. But as
you replace your opinions with insights, those times when your
judgments are necessary for better results, they will ring true
instead of false, and they will help you do right by people you care
about instead of adding insult to their injuries and forcing them
through lengthy appeals.

12. What If *You* Are the Meddler?

Dear Drs. K and B,

I understand that you may be incorporating questions into a chapter
about "What if I'm the difficult person?" With that in mind, I'm going
to ask you something. But before I ask you the question that I'd like
you to answer, I'm going to make a few suggestions on how to
approach answering it.

First, you should consider your words and phrases. Short words are
easier to understand than complex ones. Also, remember to punctuate
properly. Bad punctuation might make it hard for people to understand your meaning. And you might benefit from improving the quality of your examples throughout the book. In fact, if I were writing
your book, I would reorganize it by putting this "difficult me" chapter
first, since most the people complaining about problem people are the
problem people that people are complaining about.

In fact, just send me the manuscript and your contact at McGraw-Hill.
I know you'll thank me later.

Oh, and my question is this: Why do people resent it when all I'm
doing is asking a few helpful questions?

Please reply ASAP,
Bette Way

Dear Ms. Way,

First, thank you for the many suggestions and offers of help. It's obvious that you care about us. The problem you've been running into with people is that when you ask those few helpful questions, people feel like you are trying to take over their lives. So perhaps the best way you can help us and yourself is by letting people know that you don't want to interfere and that you will respect their choices. Then, learn to ask the most important question of all: "I am curious though. May I ask you some questions about that?" If the answer comes back no, it means it's too soon, and it's the first chance you'll get to prove what for them is your newfound respect. Of course, it's up to you. Your life, your choice, your results. Oh, and we're choosing to leave this chapter where it is, and we appreciate your respecting that choice.

13. What If *You* Are the Martyr?

Dear Sirs,

I don't expect you to answer this, even though you should. But then, I'm sure you're too busy to find a moment for a stranger like me, and that's just fine. So what if I need help and nobody cares or is available? So what if I go out of my way to take care of everybody else every single moment of every single day only to find that these same ungrateful people whom I sacrificed everything for seem to have forgotten me completely or can't find a moment for me when I need their help? So what? I'm used to it. Nobody appreciates how hard I've worked and all I've done for them. So what? I'd just like to know how people can take so much and give back so little. But don't worry, if I can't figure this out on my own, as usual, I can always just stick my head in the oven, right? I don't think you appreciate just how hard it is for me to do so much for so little in return, and I'd like to know just what I'm supposed to do to get people to care about me as much as I care about them.

Sadly,
Didit Foryu

Dear Didit,

For someone who has known the struggles you've known, you did an amazing job of cutting right to the key question. Way to go! And that question is, how do you get people to care about you? The answer may surprise you. You get others to care more for you by freeing them from strings of obligation. In other words, let go of needing something back when you give, so that you can give freely. Mean it when you tell people to go ahead and do what they want to do. Really mean it. And when everything in you wants to feel sorry for yourself, look around, because there are so many people with so many needs that need people like you to care. There's something about consistently serving the needs of others that invokes loyalty, true admiration, and even love. As Albert Schweitzer, the famous humanitarian, told his class of students, "I do not know what your future holds. But I do know this. The only ones among you who will really be happy are those who have sought and found how to care." It means a lot to us that you cared enough to ask.

PART 4

Communication in a Digital Age

We Reveal the Limitations and Pitfalls of Phone Communication and E-mail and Show You How to Turn the Limitations into Advantages with a Pound of Prevention.

24

Communication and the Challenge of Technology

Face-to-face communication has always been challenging enough. Now, thanks to the convenience of modern technology, it is possible for even good relationships to turn sour and for your problems with people to go from bad to worse with unprecedented speed! In Chapters 4 through 6, we discussed the importance of looking and sounding like you're on common ground with someone under the basic assumption that "people don't cooperate with other people who seem to be against them." Face-to-face communication offers numerous ways to send and receive signals that indicate this common ground. However, phone and e-mail communications block some of these signals, and they emphasize others, offering some important advantages and disadvantages.

In this part of the book, we will reveal the nature of the problem and offer strategies to reduce conflict and improve communication by phone and e-mail.

The "Numbers of Meaning"

Back in 1967, Dr. Albert Mehrabian, a professor at UCLA, conducted a study on the relative importance of verbal and nonverbal messages when people communicate their feelings and attitudes.° He observed that most people send mixed messages much of the time, and he wanted to gain understanding into how it is possible to make sense out of the messages.

Mehrabian devised a study that involved filming people who were communicating about their feelings. He then produced three different versions of the same interaction in that film and presented these versions to a group of people. They viewed a copy of the film with no soundtrack. Then they listened to a soundtrack that had been run through a synthesizer that made the words incomprehensible but left the tone, volume, and speed intact. Then they read a written transcript containing the actual words spoken by the people in the film.

He found that most of the people in the study group thought they were experiencing three different interactions: a business meeting, people angry with each other, and friends talking. They were quite surprised to discover that all three versions were from the same inter-action. Based on their responses he reached the following conclusions:

- 55 percent of the meaning people make in any communication about feelings and attitudes is based on what they see.

- 38 percent of the meaning is based on how it sounds (tone, volume, and speed).

- 7 percent of the meaning is based on the actual words that are spoken.

This is what we affectionately refer to as "the 55, the 38, and the 7," or if you prefer, the "Numbers of Meaning." We believe these Numbers of Meaning are important for understanding communication in general.

Now, in many ways, these percentages should come as no surprise. After all, common axioms such as "Seeing is believing" and "Actions speak louder than words" point to the stronger influence of the 55 per-cent, the visual component, of communication. Television directors seem to be aware of this too! Perhaps you've seen episodes of the origi-nal Candid Camera television series. Host Allen Funt created amusing

---

° Albert Mehrabian, *Silent Messages: Implicit Communication of Emotions and Attitudes*, 2nd ed., Wadsworth Publishing, Belmont, CA, 1980.

scenarios of mixed messages, and then he filmed unsuspecting people dealing with them. In one show, he filled a doctor's waiting room with actors and actresses reading magazines waiting for the doctor, but they were dressed only in their underwear. Real patients walked in the room, had a moment of shock, and then got undressed and picked up magazines to read while waiting for the doctor! This just goes to show (pun intended) that the visual element of our interactions with others is profoundly compelling, which is why some parents must resort to the futile admonition, "Do what I say, not what I do."

The way people sound when they talk to you, 38 percent of the communication, usually reflects their emotional state and sends an ego message. It is a personal message about you, and it plays a significant role in how you make sense of mixed messages.

As mentioned in Chapter 7, people take your tone of voice personally. The tech support person on the phone may be giving you excellent advice, but his voice seems to say, "You moron!" You may be giving a friend reasonable directions to your party, but your rushed tone makes it sound like you're saying, "Could you at least try to catch up? I've got more important people to talk to and things to do than talking with you!"

And while the actual words we use may constitute only 7 percent of the meaning of a particular communication, we all know that just one small word can serve as a trigger, or "buzzword," that sets entire chains of reaction in motion!

We once had a patient who told us about the neighborhood kids who tormented her when she was a little girl. They gave her the nickname "Moose," and they were relentless in repeating it. Thirty years later, she was at a cocktail party with fellow professionals. The word moose came up during a casual conversation, and her whole experience of the party changed in the blink of an eye. Her feelings about the person who used the word became negative, and all she could think of was getting away. While this reaction made no sense to her consciously, unconsciously it had brought up a whole realm of insecure feelings. For this reason, many adults are reluctant to share their childhood nicknames with others.

The greatest value of knowing about the 55, the 38, and the 7 is in helping you to remember the order of priority by which people make sense of each other and how it is possible that mixed messages produce misunderstanding.

Anytime there's a difference between what you see, what you hear, and what is actually said, there's a potential for people problems. Even in face-to-face communication, a common mixed message occurs when there's a difference between what is said and how it sounds. If, in an argument, a husband declares his love for his wife by screaming, "I love you! Don't you get that???" she probably won't. Yet if we examine the words by themselves, "I—love—you—don't—you—get—that," they seem all right. Add an angry tone and loud volume, however, and the behavior just doesn't match. And when there is a mismatch, people tend to respond to the higher number.

Tone of voice tends to reveal a person's emotional state, even when the person is trying to keep it hidden. Suppose you're having an intense emotional response to something you're seeing or hearing. You may want the interaction to be a positive one, and your good intentions may attempt to keep your feelings pushed down, shoved aside, and out of the way. The problem is, while your conscious mind is busy selecting the words you'll use to express yourself (the 7 percent), your suppressed emotions tend to leak out through your tone of voice. Unfortunately for you, the receiver of your communication may ignore your carefully chosen words and respond only to your voice tone. Why? Because whenever there's a mixed message, people tend to respond to the higher number in the 55, 38, and 7.

Something Lost, Something Gained

When you're talking on the phone or communicating in writing, you lose access to the subtle visual clues that would help you to account for what you're hearing. You can't see how the other person looks, and she can't see you. Some people know they're being listened to when you look them in the eyes or nod your head while they're talking. But those signals don't transmit over the phone line. As a result, you could be nodding your head, and for all the other person knows, you've gone for a cup of coffee! In written communications, you lose 55 percent and 38 percent and only the words remain. It is quite natural to hallucinate freely how the other person sounds, and even to react to that hallucination as fact.

In communication, just as in life, when something is lost, something may be gained. In this case, phone and written communications have some profound advantages that outweigh the seeming disadvantages. If you are aware of and utilize those advantages, you can expand your communication success.

25

The Eight Ounces of Prevention in Phone Communication

When you talk on the phone, you're cut off from the visual clues (the 55 percent) that would help you to make sense what you're hearing.

On the phone, communication comes across in how a person sounds, the 38 percent, and what they say, the 7 percent. What happens to the 55 percent? When the visual elements of face-to-face interaction are removed, people often make up their own mental images. Let's say you're on the phone with someone you've never met. The voice you hear may remind you of someone else or some other time in your personal history. Or you may associate the tone, speed, and volume with a certain kind of person, based, of course, on your own experience. So you create an image in your mind's eye that makes sense out of what you're hearing, and then you respond to what you see in that mental image.

Have you ever had the experience of meeting someone face-to-face that you'd previously talked to only on the phone and the person looked completely different from what you expected? That's because you believed the image in your mind to be real until you were faced with reality! Now suppose that you had negative feelings associated with the image you made up in the privacy of your own mind. Do you suppose this could influence the way you make sense of the words you hear? Do you suppose that the way you hear the words might influence your reactions? Of course, and quite often, that's exactly what happens.

Here are eight ounces of prevention that can turn the phone to your advantage.

1. Shape Perceptions

A phone conversation comes down to small moments in time that shape perception. All phone conversations are a string of such moments, from how you greet people when you or they answer the phone, how you respond when they tell you something, their response to your response, what you say and how you sound when you put them on hold and vice versa. And in those moments, either you're adding to or subtracting from the ease of the relationship, simplifying the next moment or growing the complexity of what's required of you. And the funny thing is, these moments have little to do with truth and everything to do with perception!

You can think you're doing everything right while everything is going wrong because there is no visual feedback in a phone conversation. You can believe you're saying and doing all the wrong things only to find that the person you're talking to is grateful for your time. For this reason, it is important for you to assume that you do not know how you're going to be perceived. Then, do everything you can to actively shape the perception of the person on the other end of the line. For example: Taking notes while listening to what someone is saying to you over the phone is a great way of keeping track of what you're hearing. But since that person can't see that you're writing, he or she may become concerned at the sounds of silence on your end of the line, unless you mention that you're going to take some notes. You could be smiling at something the other person is saying, but unless you verbalize that fact, the person may never know. You could be concerned about the problem being described to you, but unless you mention your concern, the other person is free to assume you don't care.

It's ironic how little it takes to have successful phone interactions, even with people behaving badly, considering how big a problem can become if you fail to do those little things that make the big difference. The heart and soul of all human relationship comes down to the simple fact that little counts big! And little things add up—both the good and the bad. For example, people only need two or three examples of something to form a generalization. And once people form such generalizations, they will automatically and unconsciously seek aspects of their experience that fulfill the generalizations.

Have you ever told someone on the phone your name, and then a little later the person asked for your name? Have you ever given someone your phone number over the phone, and a short while later the person asks for your phone number? What generalization did you make about that person's listening skills? Once a negative opinion is formed, anything that can be judged as a negative will be judged as a negative in the light of that opinion!

Generalizations can work *for* or *against* you. And it often boils down to these little moments that shape perceptions, moments where the little things count big.

2. Use Your Body for Tone Control

Your ability to control your emotional reactions and the sound of your voice is one of the biggest advantages of talking on the phone. Your tone of voice is wired to your body, and what you do with your body has an effect on your tone. This is probably why some of the most successful telemarketing people keep mirrors on their desks, along with signs reminding them to "smile."

You can use this to your advantage. When you find yourself getting a little too intense in a phone conversation, lean back, put your feet up, and get in a relaxed posture. That relaxation is likely to have a noticeable effect on your tone of voice. When you need to sound more assertive or commanding, you can get up, take a position of stability and strength by spreading your legs a shoulder length apart, and then add some flexibility by bending slightly at the knee. When you want to sound casual, you can lean against your desk.

The phone actually allows you to have more mastery over your emotional reactions than you might have in face-to-face communication. Hank, a tech support rep for a high-tech company, told us how he deals with upset customers if he finds himself starting to take their verbal abuse personally. Thanks to the headset he wears, he's able to get up out of his chair and move around. So he does yoga stretches while working with aggressive clients. This helps him to relax because he just can't take things personally when he's in a yoga posture! Admittedly, if you were face-to-face with difficult people and you started doing yoga, you probably would confuse the heck out of them. Such behavior might seem insane at worst and inappropriate at best in most circumstances. The phone, thankfully, creates a shield of privacy that allows for offbeat and highly effective behavioral strategies that can change your emotional state to something more productive.

Marci, who works for a government agency, was required to do a radio interview over the phone. She was nervous about being on the radio to begin with since she had never done a radio interview before. Making matters worse, the person who would be conducting the interview was known to be hostile to this particular governmental agency.

Marci had heard about a speaking technique that professional presenters sometimes use to combat nervousness: they visualize the audience dressed only in their underwear. She decided to apply it in reverse. She did the interview from her home, completely naked. And no matter how hard the interviewer tried to provoke her, she wouldn't take the bait because all the while she was smiling over this very private joke, and that came through her tone.

Unfortunately for Marci, everyone at the office was so impressed with her performance that they voted to have her do all future interviews.

3. Breathe for Your Life

Breathing intentionally is a great way to control your emotional reactions without having to suppress them into a grievance that might surface and sabotage your efforts at a later moment. As you pay attention to your breathing, inspiring yourself when you inhale and releasing tension as you exhale, the person on the other end will hear only your occasional backtracking and clarifying.

You can breathe much more deeply when on the phone than you might be comfortable with in person since such behavior in person might draw attention and elicit a negative reaction. You may want to hit the mute button to take a few breaths. If you don't have a mute button, move the receiver away from your mouth, and take some nice deep breaths while the other person is talking. Breathing advantage to the phone!

4. Chart a Course

It's also easier to take notes while talking on the phone than it is while dealing face-to-face with an aggressive person. If you're being targeted with an angry diatribe, you can write down keywords or phrases that the person says and use those phrases to backtrack effectively. You can even write down keywords to remind you of what you want to say in response when it's your turn to talk. Such notes become a helpful map that you can use to implement the behavioral strategies we provided in Part 3 of this book, or you can just use them to return some semblance of rationality to the interaction.

You can also use note taking as a way of venting your emotional response to someone behaving badly on the other end of the line. Draw a silly picture of how you think the person looks. Put horns on the face, add a mustache, scribble all over the picture, and then X the face out entirely. When it comes to handling your feelings with people out of control, maybe you did learn everything you needed to know in kindergarten!

5. Know When to Hold 'Em and When to Fold 'Em

While the *hold* button can be your ally, it also poses the danger of making things worse. That's because *wait* is on the other side of *hold*! Most people have a whole life going on outside of their relationship with you, and every moment spent on *hold* is a moment stolen from some potentially more productive activity. And what makes the *wait* unbearable? Not knowing when it's going to end. Two minutes can seem like an hour to people who have pressing agendas and don't know when you'll be back. In general, before putting people on hold, ask their permission, and tell them how long they'll likely have to wait. If they don't like the choice, give them options.

If someone is behaving like a Tank, then putting that person on hold will likely escalate the problem. Remember, the Tank is moving forward fast, and anything that takes time or seems irrelevant may be deemed a provocation. If you are going to put a Tank on hold, first state the purpose of doing so and how it serves the interests of the Tank. This is what we call in Chapter 8, "Get What You Project and Expect," a *statement of intent*: "In order to solve your problem fast, I need to talk to someone else. It will take only a minute, two minutes at most. May I put you on *hold*, or would you prefer that I call you back?"

The statement of intent is this: "In order to solve your problem fast, ..." This blends with the Tank's desire for action. By providing a time frame, that is, "It will take only a minute, two minutes at most," you give the Tank some sense of control over the wait. After all, you can be certain that the Tank doesn't have all day. But make sure the time frame you give is realistic. Do not tell the Tank "this will take only a minute" and then take four minutes, because by the time you get back, your Tank will be ready to launch a full-scale assault. Asking for permission and waiting for an answer also blends with the Tank's desire for control, as does offering the option to call him or her back. It's a safe assumption that the Tank has places to go, things to do, and people to see.

With a Grenade, on the other hand, *hold* gives you a tremendous advantage. The fourth step in the Grenade strategy is "Take a break." Because Grenades do not like losing it, your use of the *hold* button gives them some private time to compose. If you have ever had to deal with a Grenade on the phone and you passed the call along to someone else, it is likely that the next person found a more normal person on the other end of the line. Or you can always make up an excuse for ending the call and let the Grenade know you'll call back in a few minutes. When you call back, you will find yourself dealing with a somewhat calmer, more rational person.

If you ever find yourself in the situation of taking the call of a person who's been left on *hold* for a long time, prepare to blend by acknowledging the long wait and by apologizing for the inconvenience. "I know you were *holding* a long time. I really apologize for the inconvenience. What did you want to talk about?" By quickly blending and then focusing forward, it is highly likely that the person will stop brooding and brewing about what has passed and focus instead on the reason for the call.

6. Send Listening Signals!

Many of the signals that people recognize as listening behaviors—eye contact, head nodding, note taking, and meaningful looks—are seen more than heard. Since you can't send those signals over the phone, you must be certain to give verbal signals of listening instead.

Instead of meaningful looks, do more meaningful grunting:

"Hmmm."
"Ugh."
"Oh no."
"Wow."
"You're kidding! Then what happened?"

You say parts of words and parts of phrases because you want people to know you are right there with them, but you also want to stay out of their way.

Backtracking, as we discussed in Chapter 5, is always important. But the power of backtracking is multiplied when on the phone. Remember that when you backtrack, you not only let people know that you have listened to them but you also buy some time to think about what you want to ask or say next and how you want to steer the conversation.

When you take notes and backtrack, you let the people you're talking to on the phone know that you're still on the line. That's better than the sound of silence, which might mistakenly give the impression that you're not listening.

7. Sound Prepared, Even When You're Not

It sometimes happens that people provide you with personal information in a phone conversation. When they do, make note of it for future reference since these personal details allow you to build a relationship. Then, before making a call, or while taking a call, you can look up the details and use them as points of reference that tell the callers you value talking to them.

Note: Beware of multitasking. Don't go off and surf the net or play a game while talking to people, unless you want to give them the distinct impression that you're *not* listening!

8. You Can Close Your Eyes

The eighth advantage of talking on the phone: you can close your eyes to concentrate, not to catch up on sleep (unless you have a tape recording of you grunting occasionally!). When you close your eyes, you remove visual distractions, and this may actually help you focus on what you're hearing. This might be useful to you when the precision of your communication is important or when difficult details are being discussed or when past experience tells you that you're going to be tested on what you've heard.

There's a method to making the most out of listening with your eyes closed. First, begin with the assumption that you know nothing. Picture a blank slate in your mind's eye. Then allow the other person's words to provide the details in your thinking. If something is missing, you can always backtrack and ask a clarification question to fill in the blanks.

While you can't do this for long periods in face-to-face communication, closing your eyes while you listen is a naturally good choice over the phone.

When it comes to ounces of prevention, the phone is an advantage waiting to be taken for implementing the strategies given in Part 3. Using these ounces of prevention, you may be able to avoid the pounds of cure for dealing with the 10 (+ 3) Most Unwanted.

Quick Summary

When You Are Communicating on the Phone

THE EIGHT OUNCES OF PHONE PREVENTION

1. Shape perceptions.
2. Use your body for tone control.
3. Breathe for your life.
4. Chart a course.
5. Know when to hold 'em, and when to fold 'em.
6. Send listening signals!
7. Sound prepared, even when you're not.
8. You can close your eyes.

26
The Eight Ounces of Prevention in E-mail Communication

We'll say it again: in interpersonal communication, when something is lost, something else is gained. In the case of e-mail, you lose the nonverbal *and* auditory set of signals that add color, depth. and dimension to the words that are communicated. That's a lot to lose! Without the 55 percent and the 38 percent, the remaining 7 percent becomes 100 percent of the interaction. Adding to the loss is an artificial gain of 38 percent hallucinations, based on how you think the other person sounds!

But here's what you gain from using electronic communication tools, including e-mail, texts, and social media: the element of time. Written communication, no matter how urgent, generally does not demand the same kind of immediate interactive response that face-to-face or phone-to-phone communication requires. Even if you only take a few minutes before hitting Reply, you gain at least that much time to relax, to clarify, and then to transmit a reasonable and well-thought-out message.

In the "old days," depending on how far back you go, writing to another person meant sitting down with paper and quill, then paper and pen, then paper and typewriter, then paper, printer, and computer. After composing your letter, you might reread it, correct it, and then rewrite it again, knowing that once it was gone, it would be gone. If you were satisfied with what you had written, you put it in an envelope, dropped it into a mailbox, and waited for it to be picked up and delivered. And having taken all that time, you still might have to run to the mailbox to pull it out before the postal carrier arrived! The lengthy process of producing a written document gave people the advantage of plenty of time to think things through. So much time accrued to correspondents that, sometimes along the way, they might decide there was no point in sending a reply!

The information age changed all that. Where written correspondence, by its nature, was a thoughtful and time-consuming process, you can now copy, paste, quote, respond, and skip printing and go straight to Send in mere minutes. Where once your message might not be delivered and read for days, weeks, or months, the acceleration of communication in the information age first changed that to days and then a day (overnight delivery!) and now in no time at all as e-mail is delivered almost instantly. As the amount of electronic communication has mushroomed, the amount of misunderstanding has exploded right along with it. Time is only on your side if you intentionally make the choice to take advantage of it.

The problems caused by the speed of electronic communications are compounded daily by the sheer quantity of it. The astonishing volume of e-mail messages pouring into people's inboxes has many people feeling overwhelmed, and it is likely that the more e-mail you receive, the less time you're apt to take for a thoughtful reading and reply to a particular message. If you respond to 50 to 80 messages a day, you're far more likely to cut to the chase and leave out the social pleasantries of nonelectronic interaction from a less frenzied time. Instead of beginning a conversation with "Hi, how are you doing? What's new? blah, blah, blah …," now it's "Re: Your message. Do this. Do that. And here's where to go."

The friendly or frustrated nuances of voice and facial expression are gone, so the readers of e-mail don't see the writers' emotions. Nevertheless, it is common for someone reading a message to hallucinate freely about the writer's emotions. And this is influenced in turn by the reader's hormonal and blood sugar levels at the time of reading. Often, any reference to a previous message is missing. As a result, hastily written words make the wrong point; well-intended humor written with a gleam in the eye is misunderstood as a snipe or smirk; a casual reference with multiple meanings is taken the wrong way. All too often, the lack of context and cues becomes the focal point for conflict; sentences lacking perspective produce a tunnel vision reaction that rolls through time.

Yet another contributing factor to electronic messaging conflict: people compose their messages in front of a computer screen, where their thoughts become words in isolation. Without the ameliorating influence of immediate feedback from others, the distance between correspondents can remove the social inhibition that might otherwise cause a person to think twice before speaking. Perhaps you recall Mark Twain's caution: "Better to say nothing and be thought a fool than to open your mouth and prove it beyond a doubt." Sadly, the words composed in isolation get sent when they should have remained the private thoughts of the sender. E-mail allows for more blatant and raw expressions of one's actual thoughts.

So between the lack of visual and auditory clues, the pressing volume of messages, the missing niceties of polite society, the lack of humanity in staring at a screen, and the acting on impulse instead of taking the time for a considered response, these electronic misunderstandings have become a miscommunication epidemic.

Use the Advantage of Time

While it's true that e-mail comes in on someone else's timetable, it is up to you when to read and respond to it! We've heard so many stories of e-mail replies sent in haste that produced nasty side effects and awful results. Like firing a shot that launches a thousand ships, when you push the Send button, the damage has already be done. So our first piece of advice is simple: never reply quickly or impulsively to any e-mail that even seems to have emotional content, and never initiate an e-mail interaction with messages containing strong emotional content.

An emotional e-mail deserves the advantage of time, and you must take that advantage. After all, the emotion you perceive may be your own. Your state of mind or feelings about the topic could cause you to misunderstand the intensity or meaning of what you've read. It takes less time to write a reasoned reply than it does to deal with the consequences of a message that is sent hastily.

When you take back the advantage of time, you can use it to deal with your emotional response to what you're reading. Time lets you safely vent your reaction with a spouse (if home is where you go when you're tired of being nice to people) or a friend (who has the emotional stamina to tolerate your rant). Meanwhile, you can consider and reconsider what you ultimately want from the interaction. Time lets you compose a first draft and get back to it in the light of the next day to take it the next step. Time lets you open up this book to the appropriate chapter, find the best strategy, and then craft your reply so to utilize it.

Better still, by taking the time, you give the difficult people some time too. Yesterday, those people may have acted like Tanks, trying to blast you out of the way. By waiting to reply, you've given them a day to move out of the danger zone, to shift their blood sugar, and to attend to other things that were eating at them and fueling their attack. By taking some time to reply, you're more likely to communicate effectively, and the people to whom you send your messages are more likely to be able to hear them as you intend them. Advantage yours!

There are going to be times when the strategies offered earlier in this book for dealing with difficult behavior in person will apply to your written communications as well. Perhaps you've had that unsettling experience after a face-to-face interaction of realizing the perfect thing that you wish you had said. Unfortunately for you, it was too little, too late. Person to person, its easy to feel like you're "under the gun" with a Tank, at a loss for words with a Sniper, feeling foolish with a Know-It-All, and furious at a Maybe Person. But in electronic correspondence, you gain the advantages of clarity and self-control when you take back the advantage of time.

Perhaps more important, when using e-mail, if you want to avoid the misunderstandings that bring out the worst in yourself and others in the first place, get time back on your side and make clarity your highest priority.

The Eight Ounces of Prevention

As always, an ounce of prevention is worth a pound of reaction. So take the time to apply these ounces of prevention to your electronic correspondence.

1. Vent It, but Don't Send It

When you get an inflammatory message demanding a reply, sometimes you feel compelled to say something, and you just can't bear to wait. If everything in you wants to get mad and get even, go ahead and do it. Just don't send it.

Venting emotions in heated rhetoric can be incredibly therapeutic, liberating even, but it's dangerous when you share the heat. Action begets reaction, and if they have to deal with your reaction, you can be fairly certain that you'll have to deal with theirs. In the terminology used to describe difficult behavior on the Internet, you may frequently come across the term *flame*, as in *flame wars*.

Flame wars often erupt when someone sends something to someone that is intentionally or unintentionally aggravating and/or insulting. If it is done intentionally, it's a *flame*. But the road to hell is often paved with good intentions, so an innocent message may also provoke a heated reply. It isn't uncommon for someone on the receiving end of a perceived flame to reply in kind. That's how flame wars get started. Someone sends a flame, which provokes a flame, which provokes a flame, until the landscape is ablaze with juvenile and thoughtless sentiments. When hard words are spoken, they often prove harder to take back.

Our advice? No matter how strong the urge to turn up the heat, hold your fire. If you're sure that the sender needs to feel the heat, save the message as a draft, and revisit it until it says exactly what you need it to say, but make sure you wait at least a day. Another important safety tip: If you are going to vent, don't do it in your e-mail software program. Do it in a separate text document. We constantly hear horror stories of people who vented and accidentally hit Send instead of Save.

From the very beginning of this book, we've asked you to ask yourself what you want in your dealings with people. In the case of e-mail, take the time to reconsider what you want and what you need. Do you need a good flame war? Do you really need to spend time dreading the next message? Do you need the anxiety of wondering what damage you've caused? We don't think so! Save yourself a world of trouble. Vent it, but don't send it!

2. Read It One More Time

If you think a message you are composing has the potential to cause or increase conflict, then no matter how much time you've spent composing it, it's in your interest to read it again, to make sure you've removed all the potential hot-button words and phrases that could create conflict and misunderstanding. Every message deserves at least one more reading before you hit the Send button. Think of your message as a draft, not a finished product, and you can improve on it as you read it again.

3. Read It at Another Time

Better still, read the maddening e-mail you received again at another time of day before deciding you're finished with your reply. As your blood sugar rises and falls throughout the day, the same words may sound different to you. You may even notice words and phrases that escaped your notice the first time around. Perhaps rather than responding to what you think the sender means, it would be worth composing a message that asks clarifying questions. Make every effort to be certain that you've understood what you read and why it was said, before composing your response to it.

4. Get a Second Opinion

If a message hits you the wrong way, it may be wise to offer it to someone else to read, so you can find out what other possible meanings you may have missed. You may be surprised at the different interpretations others derive from the very same words. And it wouldn't hurt to have other people read your reply, either! Ask them to give you feedback about how you might respond before composing your response, or at least get a second opinion on what you've written before making the final decision to send.

5. Begin with Intention, End with Direction

In Chapter 7, "Speak to Be Understood," we talked about the importance of stating your positive intent at the beginning of what you have to say. Electronic messages are a powerful medium in this regard because your intent remains visible to add context to the rest of your message. Begin your message with a clear *statement of your intent*, so that your recipients will know why you're writing and what you hope to achieve before they get very far into what you have to say. Then end your message with a *statement of direction*. Tell your recipients what you want from them as a result of having read what you wrote.

If your intent is to provide your recipients with information that requires no response, a simple "FYI" (for your information) at the beginning of the e-mail message lets the recipients know you are informing them of information and you do not need a response from them:

"FYI, I am writing to give you a brief history of what I've been doing on this project because I think it will be of benefit to you in understanding my requests for help at our upcoming meeting."

Now your recipients know that they don't need to reply to each point as they read them, but rather, they can take in the information and be ready to consider requests for their help at the meeting.

By wrapping your message with a strong beginning and end, you provide an informed perspective that makes your words as meaningful as you intended them:

Daniel was part of a group wanting to improve a website. He found an Internet site that he particularly liked, and he thought it made an excellent example. He sent a message to his associates that said, "Check out this website. I think it's great in many ways. Tell me what you think about it." Without his recipients' knowing what specifically Daniel thought was so "great" or taking the time to clarify, in their attempts to do as he asked, his recipients were left to apply their own criteria for a "great" website.

Margaret looked at the site from the perspective of web design, and she immediately began questioning the wisdom of Daniel's involvement in the project. "This is his idea of a great site?" she thought to herself. "It violates many of the most basic precepts of intelligent web design! I'm not sure Daniel should be allowed anywhere near this project." Lucas, on the other hand, looked at the content of the site, and he was so put off by it that he almost resigned from the team then and there. And Harriet, who looked at it from the perspective of navigation and ease of use, was moved to send an e-mail immediately to Daniel, suggesting that if he thought this was a great site, he had demonstrated a profound lack of discernment that had not only raised serious doubts about his involvement in the project but would also, she was certain, lead to greater difficulties on the project down the road. A flurry of e-mails followed, and things got worse. Finally, the group was able to resolve the problem in a conference call, once Daniel had the opportunity to make it clear what specifically he liked about the site and what he wanted them to see.

But the problem could easily have been prevented. If, instead of a general direction, he had told them his intention in making a request, and if he had then told them what specifically he wanted them to evaluate about the site, and if he had ended with directions about how to respond with their evaluations, the chances for these misunderstandings would have been avoided completely: "Dear Colleagues: I would like you to review the following website from a marketing perspective. Ignore design and content, but look instead at how they present opportunities for their visitors to interact with the site and how they make it possible to purchase their products in each and every section. Then get back to me, and tell me if you see anything that we might be able to implement on our own site in order to boost interactivity and product sales."

Daniel's colleagues could have responded differently to his initial request too. They could have used e-mail to "listen to understand," they could have clarified Daniel's intentions in wanting them to evaluate the site, and they could have asked for direction in how to respond to it. The overall lesson here is simple: begin with your intentions and end with directions, so you can avoid the complications.

6. Quote Early, Quote Often

When you respond generally to an electronic message, without referencing specific words or phrases, readers can apply your words to anything else in either their message or yours. The problem with general responses is that they can produce very different responses than the ones you intend. In Chapter 5 of this book, we discussed the importance of *backtracking*, that is, using a person's own words, in face-to-face communication. Backtracking is a powerful way of providing context for questions or statements. It has great value in phone conversations too, turning long strings of words into meaningful ideas that relate to other meaningful ideas. But backtracking is actually easier to do in electronic correspondence than in any other form of communication since you can actually let the other person's words speak for themselves. A method for doing this has already been developed by the pioneers of Internet and e-mail communication: to backtrack, you simply use the karat right sign > in front of the words someone else wrote. This symbol is now generally recognized as a symbol for quoting what your correspondent said, and it helps him or her know to what you are responding.

Quotes serve other purposes in electronic messages. You can use quotes to question the meaning of a word, phrase, or sentence. For example,

When you say,
> Let's see if you can get this one right.
I cannot tell if you are being sarcastic or just kidding around. Which is it?

You can also use quotes to offer choices. Let's say you wrote:

> Let's see if you can get this one right.

If your intention was to be sarcastic, then my response is this:

Really? Then here's an idea., Let's play horse. I'll be the head, and you just be yourself.

If, on the other hand, you were just kidding around with me, then my response to you is this:

LOL, yeah, I'll do my best to not screw it up.;)

7. Make Better Sense with Emoticons (Smileys)

Which brings us to another valuable communication opportunity of e-mail. Since the early days of e-mail, a set of cybersymbols called *emoticons* has emerged into common usage on the Internet. Nicknamed "smileys," you can use these little symbols to indicate your emotional state when replying to or sending an e-mail. This adds contextual information to your words, and it decreases the likelihood or your being misunderstood.

Emoticon	Meaning
;-)	Wink; denotes you are kidding
:-)	Smile; denotes happiness
:-(	Frown; denotes unhappiness

In our previous example, the sender could have used an emoticon to make clear the intention behind the words:

> Let's see if you can get this one right.;-)

The recipient of the message would know at a glance that these were friendly words rather than fighting words.

Because not everyone using e-mail knows the shorthand of emoticons, it is useful to get everyone you correspond with up to speed, so the symbols become a shared form of language rather than a private joke. In the text-based cyberworld, we believe that adding at least some emotion to what you say by using these smileys makes for more fun and less conflict. Here are some of the most popular ones:

:-o	Surprised
:-@	Screaming

:-I	Indifferent
:-e	Disappointed
>-/	Mad
:-D	Laughing
:-$	Put your money where your mouth is
:-P	Sticking out tongue

As with spoken language, there is generally more than one way to say something with smileys. For example:

Full Version		*Abbreviated Version*
:-)	Happy	:)
:-(	Sad, frown	:(
;-)	Winky	;)
:-O	Yelling; shocked	:O

The range of emotions that you can express with smileys is astonishing. And you can add a few common abbreviations to provide even more direction, feeling, and meaning:

Symbol	*Meaning*
BFN	Bye for now
BTW	By the way
<G> or <Grin>	Grin
HTH	Hope this helps
IMO	In my opinion
IMHO	In my humble opinion
EOM	End of message
NNTR	No need to reply
LOL	Laughing out loud
OTOH	On the other hand
ROTFL	Rolling on the floor laughing
YMMV	Your mileage may vary
RTFM	Read the freaking manual
TTFN	TaTa for now (goodbye)

And of course …

RSI   Repetitive strain injury, what you get from typing too many e-mails!

8. Use Jokes Carefully—Jokester Beware ...

Funny, isn't it, how different people are when it comes to what's funny? We don't mean to say that you should never try to be funny in your electronic correspondence. Go ahead and try! After all, humor can help people regain their perspective in difficult situations. But remember that a little kidding goes a long way, and then it works only if the other person gets the joke. Some forms of humor, like puns and other wordplay, are effective without the 55 and 38 percent. Other humor depends completely on a voice tone or facial expression. And when it comes to humor, one person's trash is another person's treasure. Unless you know for sure what makes certain people laugh, you should probably avoid being humorous. Sending them communication that they will perceive to be trash is a recipe for disaster!

To gain insight into how humor works through the written word, we suggest you read almost anything ever written by Dave Barry. Of course, there's no accounting for taste. If you know for a fact that someone else shares your taste in humor, then you can share a joke with a friend or kid around with a colleague at your discretion. But when in doubt, leave the humor out!

Take the Time, Save Your Time

By applying these eight ounces of prevention, you can save the time that you otherwise would have to waste on negative reactions and misunderstandings. You don't have to read our book *Life by Design* (available at www.thericks.com) to recognize that you have more important things to do than fight it out with ones and zeroes on the Internet. There's no doubt that taking back the advantage of time will save you time AND energy in your dealings with others that can better be used elsewhere.

Quick Summary

When You Are Communicating Via E-mail

THE EIGHT OUNCES OF E-MAIL PREVENTION

1. Vent it, but don't send it.

2. Read it one more time.

3. Read it at another time.

4. Get a second opinion.

5. Begin with intention, end with direction.

6. Quote early, quote often.

7. Make better sense with emoticons (smileys).

8. Use jokes carefully—jokester beware …

Afterword

How to Take the Big Step of Applying the Little Steps in This Book

And so we arrive at the end of this book and at the beginning of your future dealings with people you can't stand. We hope that, as a result of what you've learned, you'll be able to tolerate your difficult people better and successfully bring out the best in people at their worst. For that to happen, you'll now have to take the big step of applying the little steps in this book.

Here are a few simple action steps you can take immediately:

1. Make it your goal to become an effective communicator, and take all available opportunities to learn and try these techniques. Whether

you're watching a movie or attending a meeting, you'll find examples of people using or failing to use the skills and strategies in this book, if only you remember to look for it.

2. Team up with communication partners—people who are as eager to learn as you are. That's what we did! Share resources, like this book, with your partners so you'll have a common language in your discussions. Meet once a week to discuss what you have observed, learned, and tried during the preceding week. More than any other action you can take, regular meetings with communication partners can remind you to pay attention, while keeping you focused on developing and improving your skill.

Which brings us to the final action step:

3. Count your blessings. If you have the luxury to read this book, you're already better off than perhaps 80 percent of the earth's population, in ways that you may sometimes take for granted. You probably have a roof over your head, sufficient food, people whom you care about, and some that care about you. Life is difficult, and there's enough hardship as it is without filling yourself with negativity and wasting your life-force on worry and stress. If you remember to count your blessings today, maybe even right now, and every day, you'll have the strength and focus to enjoy the challenges presented by difficult people.

The communication strategies outlined in this book were not intended to be a quick fix for relationship problems. The longer it takes for a problem to develop, the more time and energy you must invest in turning things around. As you begin to apply these attitudes and strategies, chances are that you will have some easy successes and some unsuccessful efforts, that you'll win a few and lose a few. More important than winning or losing is having more choices, opportunities, and alternatives to suffering. You can now empower yourself to be the cause of what happens next, rather than the victim of what others have done. Though you cannot change anyone else, your flexibility and knowledge can assist people to change themselves. Commitment and perseverance will inevitably lead you to success in dealing with difficult people.

Difficult people are a part of every person's life, and apparently they've been with us since the beginning of history, when the Lord said, "Let there be light," and difficult people first came into the world. They've been here ever since, waging war and engaging in interpersonal conflict, blaming, placating, distracting, and withdrawing. Yet each of us can do something to reduce the misunderstanding and eliminate the conflict that has plagued the earth. In fact, the future of humanity may depend on each of us learning how to stand each other in spite of our differences, and in that sense there is no better time for bringing out the best in people at their worst than right now. Our children see their future in our efforts. They ask us to set a good example, do the right thing, and run a good race. So the next time you're dealing with someone you can't stand, remember this: Life is not a test. It is an actual emergency. Good luck.

About the Authors

Dr. Rick Kirschner and Dr. Rick Brinkman are world-renowned professional speakers and authors. They began their careers as holistic physicians whose specialty was working with the mental and emotional aspects of healing and wellness.

They are the coauthors of the bestselling audio and video program *How to Deal with Difficult People*, as well as six other audio and video training programs. Their book *Dealing with People You Can't Stand* is an international bestseller with translations in 20 languages. They have also coauthored the books *Life by Design: Making Wise Choices in a Mixed Up World*, *Love Thy Customer*, and *Dealing with Relatives*.

They now present their entertaining keynote speeches and training programs worldwide. Their client portfolio includes the astronauts at NASA, AT&T, Hewlett-Packard, Texaco, the Inc. 500 Conference, the Young Presidents Organization, the U.S. Army, and hundreds of other corporations, government agencies, and professional associations.

For information about keynotes and seminars, visit their websites:

Rick Kirschner: www.theartofchange.com

Rick Brinkman: www.rickbrinkman.com

An Invitation from the Authors

If you would like to request our availability for a speaking engagement, find out more about audio and video programs based on this book or about our other books and recorded programs, or even tell us your success stories, then visit our websites or contact us by e-mail:

The Ricks	www.DealingWithPeople.com
Dr. Rick Kirschner	drkinfo@theartofchange.com
	www.TheArtOfChange.com
Dr. Rick Brinkman	dr.rick@rickbrinkman.com
	www.rickbrinkman.com